Through the Wall

Through the Wall

Anna Bligh

HarperCollins*Publishers*

HarperCollins*Publishers*

First published in Australia in 2015
by HarperCollins*Publishers* Australia Pty Limited
ABN 36 009 913 517
harpercollins.com.au

Copyright © Anna Bligh 2015

HarperCollins*Publishers*
Level 13, 201 Elizabeth Street, Sydney NSW 2000, Australia
Unit D1, 63 Apollo Drive, Rosedale, Auckland 0632, New Zealand
A 53, Sector 57, Noida, UP, India
1 London Bridge Street, London, SE1 9GF, United Kingdom
2 Bloor Street East, 20th floor, Toronto, Ontario M4W 1A8, Canada
195 Broadway, New York NY 10007, USA

National Library of Australia Cataloguing-in-Publication data:

Bligh, Anna, 1960– author.
  Through the wall: reflections on leadership, love and survival / Anna Bligh.
  ISBN 978 0 7322 9953 8 (hardback)
  ISBN 978 1 4607 0342 7 (ebook)
  Bligh, Anna, 1960–
  Politicians – Queensland – Biography.
  Premiers – Queensland – Biography.
  Cancer – Patients – Queensland – Biography.
  Queensland – Biography.
994.3092

Front cover image Steven Baccon @ Reload Agency
Cover design by Hazel Lam, HarperCollins Design Studio
Typeset in Bembo Std by Kirby Jones
Printed and bound in Australia by Griffin Press
The papers used by HarperCollins in the manufacture of this book are a natural, recyclable product made from wood grown in sustainable plantation forests. The fibre source and manufacturing processes meet recognised international environmental standards, and carry certification.

To Greg, Joe and Oliver, for every, every thing

Contents

Preface

The Australian ideal is essentially egalitarian. We hold dear the view that our country is a land of opportunity, unfettered by the rigid traditions and hidebound class system of our European origins. Here, with a good heart and hard work, anybody can make their dreams come true. My story is cut from this template. A girl from the Gold Coast, from a family of modest means, becomes the first woman to be elected premier of an Australian state despite her background, her circumstances, her gender, her political leanings and sometimes even her own inclination. A Labor premier of the long-time conservative state of Queensland at that.

In the nooks and crannies of that winding path have been some big, shifting moments of upheaval. In what follows, I've tried to capture some of what it's like to become a leader, especially as a woman; to lead through times of peril and times of change; the lived experience of shaping history; and facing the unthinkable and the unknowable. These are my personal reflections on the moments when I broke through walls, when drive and ambition pushed me beyond what had been expected of me. I hope these reflections might be useful to those of you who stand in front of similar walls and those of you who haven't yet noticed there are walls to be breached, but might be open to persuasion.

As a lifelong reader, I know that a book demands a good story. And a good story has something to say. Whether I achieve that is for you to judge, but the parts of my story that I set down here are some of those big public moments I've lived and the private experience of that public life. It's impossible to tell those stories without setting down a little of the path I trod to get there and you will find some of that here too. However, you are not embarking on a comprehensive biography of my life – there are so many experiences that form and shape us and I do not pretend that you will find all mine here.

We all have our vanities. Among mine is the hope that as a former politician I can write a memoir that will escape the usual clichés and standard forms these things tend to take. For one thing, I have no interest in writing a back-stabbing, tell-all critique of my colleagues in public life. While I have plenty of stories that would shock, distress and amuse, I'm a 'dance with the one that brung ya' kind of girl. So those readers who've come looking for gossip and intrigue can return this book to its shelf. As for those of you who have confided in me, conspired with me or betrayed me: you can relax.

Of course, to write a book about oneself is a vanity of titanic proportions and I have been deeply conscious of this as I set out what follows. Anaïs Nin said of writing that 'We write to taste life twice, in the moment and in retrospection,' and there's a bit of that here too. It's a chance to relive in ink and on paper, to taste again the big moments, the extraordinary and the inglorious, to savour the size of it all and in doing so to inspire just one among you to want it like I wanted it, to believe you can do it, to chase it and burn for it, to make it count.

Flying Into Lightning

Heavy cloud dogs the small plane, and dark rain blurs visibility. The eight of us on board – my staff and two pilots along with a few journalists – are returning home on 9 January 2011 after visiting flood-stricken towns in central Queensland. Some read, some doze. We are hot, sticky and exhausted. It has been a long day, viewing homes destroyed by flooding, talking with people overwhelmed by disaster, all in the sweltering heat of the tropics in summer.

Queensland is a vast state, more than twice the size of Texas. Two-thirds of it is now underwater. Floods have washed across an area larger than France and Germany combined, leaving ruin and devastation in their wake. Intersected by the Tropic of Capricorn, Queensland is no stranger to unpredictable weather. Floods are a fact of life in many regions and towns. But the scale of this unfolding disaster is beyond anything previously experienced.

For more than two weeks, relentless rain has left town after town engulfed by floodwaters. Local economies have ground to a halt as crops are destroyed, mines are closed and shops are shut. As roads are washed away, bridges close and rail lines buckle and twist, towns and regions are left isolated and vulnerable. As families evacuate their ruined homes, and precious possessions are washed away, lives are changed forever.

Everyone is battle-weary and ready for these floods to end, for the rain to stop and for the miserable job of clean-up and recovery to begin. The latest river to flood, the mighty Fitzroy, which threads its way through the busy regional centre of Rockhampton, reached its peak two days earlier. There is a sense among all of us on board the plane that these terrible weeks of rain and mud and loss are nearing their end.

Inside the cabin, my mind is on my next duty as premier of this state in crisis. On landing, I will have a brief opportunity to get out of my grimy flood clothes and clean myself up before I head to the set of a national telethon to raise money for those who have lost so much to these floodwaters. As I gather my thoughts, we hear a tremendous bang on the roof of the plane, as if a large fridge has descended on us from a great height. The plane makes a sudden, terrifying drop through the air, forcing each of us to leap involuntarily in our seats. I hear screams as a flash of light rips down the centre aisle and escapes through the closed windows. Sick to my stomach, I look out to see the wing tip on my side of the plane fried to a black stub. The smell of something electrical burning fills my nostrils.

One minute, our tired party was quietly preparing for the telethon that will end a long day. The next, we are alert, our hearts pounding, checking with each other if we all saw what we think we saw. The pilots soon confirm that we have just been struck by lightning, although technically, lightning does not so much strike a plane as a plane flies through the lightning flash. The plane is fine; we are fine. We have just flown into lightning and survived. Our relief slips into humour as we back-slap each other and make jokes. We cover our momentary terror with laughter, letting the fear slip out of us. Soon we will descend into Brisbane. Our plane will land safely, but it will be out of action for several weeks as every electrical circuit is dismantled, checked and reassembled.

None of us aboard the plane that night see it as an omen. But looking back, for me, that was the moment when things began to go seriously awry. When the already disastrous situation of the Queensland floods started to turn into something of an altogether different magnitude; when something difficult, but known and understood, began to shift into a phenomenon that none of us had ever experienced. As that lightning struck our plane, we couldn't have known it would be later that very night when an event that we thought was nearing its end would tilt on its axis and come close to overwhelming us.

*

A telethon is a curious invention of television. Several hours of peak viewing time are set aside for a live event to raise money for a particular cause or charity. Tonight's event brings together celebrities, performers, political figures, sports stars and those who've been affected personally by the extensive flooding. The event is backed up by a bank of telephones, staffed throughout the show by the celebrities and sports stars, which enable viewers to ring in and make a donation.

I take my turn on the phones and am overcome by the generous outpouring from across the country. I speak with an eighty-year-old pensioner from Perth who apologises for only being able to give ten dollars. I speak with children who are donating their Christmas money or pocket money. Everyone who takes calls tells similar stories, and it lifts our hearts to feel all this goodwill.

As I criss-crossed the state, I met so many of the people who will receive these donations. In evacuation centres, in ruined homes and streets, I listened to their stories, held them as they cried and saw firsthand the size of the task ahead of them. The money being sent from every corner of the country will help to rebuild these lives. But more than that, I know that many of those who have lived through these floods will watch the telethon and take great strength from it. As they hear about the generosity of strangers, as they watch the response from every part of Australia, I know that many will feel a little less alone, a little more able to face the hurdles ahead. In a myriad of small ways, their lives will never be the same.

During the telethon a massive rain cell hits Brisbane, playing havoc with the live three-hour broadcast. This is further complicated by a series of failures in the phone banks that sees callers waiting in long queues and dropping out. Perhaps Mother Nature is not quite done with us yet. Despite these technical challenges, the telethon is a great success, securing a huge national audience and raising millions of dollars. There is almost a party atmosphere on the set, charged with a sense of relief and optimism that the floods seem to be nearing an end.

As I rush to my waiting car after that long day, the rain is coming down in sheets. It has poured down all evening and seems to be getting heavier. The weight of the water makes driving almost impossible. With a sense of foreboding, I check the weather map on my phone while my driver navigates the slippery streets. For weeks, while vast areas of Queensland have been underwater, our capital city and the heavily populated areas in the south-east corner of the state have been spared. Now there is a large heavy-rain system over Brisbane and the surrounding region. Despite the telethon, we are clearly not yet out of trouble.

When my head finally hits the pillow, torrential rain is thundering on the tin roof above me. I wonder what will come next. I cannot know it as I drift into sleep, but within twenty-four hours I will be contemplating one of Australia's most frightening natural disasters and one of the most challenging moments of my premiership. This moment will redefine me. It will cause everyone who knows me, whether they are close friends or total strangers, to change the way they see me. This moment will also change the way I see myself. It will demand from me more strength and courage. And as I dig inside myself to find them, I will learn, as I have learned before, that strength and courage are not finite attributes of which we have only our own small allotted share. In using them, I find that they proliferate, that the more I reach for them the more they multiply. What others will see as leadership, I will feel as a deep and conscious summoning of the grit and mettle I need to exercise it. Like flying into lightning, this looming moment will be a powerful lesson in facing fear and pushing right through it.

ONE

Going Through the Wall

In the 2011 film *Moneyball*, Brad Pitt plays Billy Beane, the manager of the Oakland A's Major League baseball team. The movie tracks Billy's attempts to revolutionise the game using computer-generated data and analysis to select and buy players. His efforts are thwarted and mocked by the baseball establishment, but his team has a record-breaking streak of twenty winning games. It's great fun to watch the little guy, the enthusiastic agent of change, being blocked by the dinosaurs of the game, taking on the big guys and winning.

Given the unpopularity of his methods, Billy is surprised when John Henry, the wealthy owner of the Boston Red Sox, tries to recruit him. John looks him in the eye and tells him: 'I know you are taking it in the teeth … but the first guy through the wall, he always gets bloody. Always.'

I was watching the film at home on the couch with my sons in 2012 when I first heard the line. Immediately, I recognised my own experience. Yes, I thought, that's right. *I went through the wall and I got bloody.* It's such a powerful analogy for any pioneering effort, about being the first to break through. The first one through the wall always gets bloody – *always*.

I got bloody as I challenged the status quo.

I got bruised by the sexism of the doubters and resisters.

I got pummelled by the double standards applied to women in public life.

I got roughed up by the relentless media criticism, harsh cartoons and constant public scrutiny.

I got battered when I lost the state election.

But none of this is the point. The point is there's now a hole in the wall. I want others to see it, I want them to feel excited and emboldened by it and I want them to jump through it themselves.

Being the first to go through a wall means pushing into the unseen and the unknowable. When you get through it, you will have no map to navigate the new territory. You will be cutting a path where one did not exist. The navigational effort is often exhausting, frustrating and infuriating. But at every step, it is an effort worth making.

No one makes it through the wall without help. As you make the first jump, you need a team of supporters pushing you through. I had plenty of help. That help came from both men and women who recognised something in me, supported and promoted me, encouraged me to aim higher and hardened my resolve every time my self-belief faltered. But in the end, you go through the wall on your own.

The wall I ploughed headlong into was the wall that holds women back from leadership in every sphere; political leadership no exception. On the other side of it is power. The power to make a difference, the power to get things done, the power to shape our world, the power to make things fairer and better for everyone.

So what is this wall? I have always imagined it as one built of sturdy red bricks, a good six or seven deep, and I felt every scratch and tear and bruise as I wrenched the bricks out of the way, sometimes one by one, sometimes in a heavy clump. It is a barrier built of many layers, a wall that rests on the strong foundations of centuries of history where women never, or rarely, assumed positions of public power. It is built from the solid bricks of prejudice. Its base is the age-old belief that women are biologically unsuited to being in charge. That we lack the strength and mental toughness to make the hard decisions, to inspire others and carry them with us. There are many who still hold firm to this belief: some voicing it in public, others only daring to in private. It manifests itself in resentment, a hostile sense that a woman in the number-one job goes against the natural order of things and has crossed the line, got too far above her legitimate role in life. It's a wall built too of doubters, those who don't question a woman's right to give it a go and will sometimes even cheer her on as she climbs the ladder, but who are worried that when push comes to shove she might not be up to it. It's a niggling doubt that the experiment is a risky one. A genuine curiosity also forms part of the wall. Women in positions of power are still a novelty in Australian politics, and we are all interested to see how the idea plays out in practice. It is a wall fortified by the weight of political history, gender stereotypes, political party structures and personal and political caution. And just as in *Moneyball*, there is a fair smattering of good old human resistance to change. These building materials are constantly swirling like gravel and concrete in a mixer, solidifying to form powerful social barriers. The barriers are both external and internal.

As a politician, I had a very healthy ego, but I too had fears, doubts, cautiousness and curiosity, and was conscious always that I was an experiment. After all, when I entered parliament in 1995, barely ten per cent of the members were women. Nevertheless, it was the highest percentage of women in the Queensland parliament since it first sat in 1860. Despite most Queensland women (excluding Indigenous women) earning the right to stand for election to state parliament in 1915, ten years after they gained the right to vote, women have been elected to the Queensland parliament only rarely. This progress is mirrored in parliaments around the country. A hundred years on from women securing the right to stand for election, a total of seventy-one of them have been elected to the Queensland parliament. In the seventy-five years between 1915 and 1989, only ten women entered Queensland's parliament. With the election of the Goss Labor government in December 1989, this changed dramatically, with the election of a further six. So recent is the phenomenon that only two of the seventy-one women who have ever held a seat in the parliament have died. Queensland's Parliament House, constructed in the 1860s, was built with no female toilets in the areas reserved for parliamentary members. While this was remedied some time ago, it speaks volumes about who was expected to be walking those corridors of power.

The slow pace of change has not just been restricted to the halls of government. When I became deputy premier of Queensland in mid 2005, I also took on the roles of Minister for Infrastructure and Minister for Finance. Among my new responsibilities was the task of building a good relationship between the government and the corporate sector. The premier, Peter Beattie, and I embarked on a round of boardroom lunches with local captains of industry, senior players in each of Queensland's key industry sectors. We had just left a lunch with construction industry CEOs, having met with mining and finance sector leaders the previous week, when Peter shared a light-bulb moment.

'I know that this will probably sound stupid to you,' he said, 'but when I used to do those lunches with your predecessor, I never noticed that they were all men. I just never saw it; it was invisible. But now that you're there, it stands out like dog's balls, doesn't it?'

'Welcome to my world,' I said with a laugh as we walked across the verandah of the parliament building.

It was a sharp observation on Peter's part. He went on to explain that he had spent some time during the lunch wondering what that might be like for me, and how he might feel about always being the odd one out if the tables were turned. But by the time Peter noticed, I was largely inured to it. After ten years of working in a parliament where women remained a very small minority, I had long become used to finding myself the only woman in the room, a situation that grew more frequent as I gained more senior positions. Sometimes it mattered more than at others, but it was difficult to ever be unaware of it. As Treasurer, I had led an annual global roadshow to bond markets in major financial centres. It was commonplace on these missions for me to address large audiences of financial analysts, almost exclusively male, promoting Queensland government bonds. Despite the fact that women have graduated from finance and commerce degrees in roughly equal numbers to their male counterparts for more than two decades in most of the countries I visited, they were rare visitors to these events. While I got a good hearing in these rooms, it was always an odd and isolating experience.

So when I became Queensland's first woman premier in 2007 and then the first Australian woman to lead her party to a successful state election victory in 2009, it was a crash-through experience. It came with the added responsibility of representing my gender, of being a flag-bearer for women, of proving not only that I, personally, could do the job and do it well, but in so doing prove that women in general are capable of meeting the challenge. When you are the first woman to do a job there is a deep fear that your failures and shortcomings will not only reflect on you but will reinforce the prejudiced views of those who doubt that women are up to it. For me, this need to be a champion for my gender was an ever-present responsibility, heaped onto the many others that come with positions of power.

So too the responsibility to be a role model. All leaders are role models, and their behaviour and character are rightly expected to be exemplary, in order to inspire and lead others. But when you are among the first women to hold the reins of political power, you are watched particularly keenly. And women, even those who don't support your side of politics, want you to acquit yourself well, to not let the team down. The weight of this expectation sits always on your shoulders and sometimes it can be a heavy load. More often than not, though, I felt it as an encouragement, spurring me on.

I've always been bloody-minded about walls. Rather than being discouraged by them, I've felt an urge to break them down or jump right over them. Far from being discouraged by the doubters and the naysayers, I have been spurred on by a fierce desire to prove the bastards wrong.

Being the first also means imagining and becoming something that you've never seen. It requires constant inventing and reinventing. The questions of whether women can be effective leaders, whether we are 'suited' to leadership and, if so, whether our leadership style differs from that of male leaders are constant. Sometimes the questions are voiced; other times they lurk as a covert presence. In the first days of my premiership, one of the most frequent questions journalists asked was 'How do you think it will be different as a woman?' I told them the truth, that I had no idea, as, after all, I'd never done it as a man. The curiosity and questions are understandable and inevitable. I share them. But the effect of them is that you are never free of your gender. With every question comes a reminder that you are doing something that few before you have attempted, and that everyone is watching to see what you'll make of it.

I am now often asked to reflect on whether women make for different leaders. In my view, the jury is still out and is likely to be out for a long time. How can any judgement be made on such a small sample? It's an egg that is still being hatched. There are little more than a handful of us who have done it, and all of us have held the office of leader in just the last twenty-five years. For those of us who have done it, there was no vast canon on which to draw as we navigated our way through it. The same is true for all those who watched us do it. As the electorate assessed and evaluated us, they had no yardstick by which to measure us.

We were and are pioneers, and it is an effort, exhausting and exhilarating in equal parts. It's the kind of pioneering work that is done with a machete, daily chopping away at the gnarly vines and heavy dense undergrowth of difference and sexism and resistance. It's the kind of effort required when everything you accomplish in one day, every bit of new path you've cut away, sometimes has to be cleared again the next day and the day after that.

Every leader, male or female, in every sphere of activity – in politics, business, the military, the community, academia and beyond – has to be able to command authority. Authority springs from the unique chemistry between the power you hold and your personal characteristics. It is founded on the status of the position you hold. Founded too on your ideas, your intellect, your values, your experience and your ability. It is equally founded on your presence, the way you carry yourself, the way you articulate an idea, the way you dress, the tone and timbre of your voice. For women in political leadership, every part of this is fraught with constant self-assessment and decision-making. In the context of so few examples, it is a daily act of invention. Let's take just voice as an example. Political leaders need to command the parliament, especially during parliamentary question time. This is done with a mixture of argument, ideas and wit. It also takes a particular voice. Your voice has to rise above the howls from the opposition, but do so without sounding like you are screeching. It needs to have gravitas and resonance. I have a woman's voice. When I listen in my mind's ear for the authoritative voices of great women orators, they are hard to find. I can hear Winston Churchill, Paul Keating and John F Kennedy, but they don't sound like me. Every time I launched a political attack on the opposition during question time, a small monitor in my head would check my voice as I raised it to bring home a point. Did I sound authoritative and commanding or did I sound shrill? 'Shrill', of course, is a derogatory term used to describe the raised voices of women. In politics, there are important things to be angry about, ideas and issues against which voices must be raised, and I raised mine often as male leaders have before me. But 'shrill' is not a word that embodies leadership. It implies a slightly hysterical tone and every woman leader is wary of it.

As I went through the wall of political leadership, I knew that there were many other walls being assailed by women. Politics is not the only field in which women are crashing through fortresses that have stood untouched for centuries. There are many who know what it feels like to be the first, and many more who know what it feels like to be in the vanguard, chipping away at another piece of the wall. It is a remarkable moment in history to be a woman. Together, we are all living through the largest sustained movement in human history of women out of the private domestic sphere into the public sphere of work and influence. It is a profound, tectonic shift in gender relations and it is changing everything. It is changing whole economies. As women enter the paid workforce in unprecedented numbers, their productivity is lifting the gross domestic product (GDP) of nations around the world. In Australia's case, a 2009 Goldman Sachs report (*Australia's Hidden Resource*) estimated that this growing shift has increased the nation's GDP by twenty-two per cent since 1974. In a 2006 article ('A Guide to Womenomics', 12 April 2006), *The Economist* estimated that the increase in the employment of women in developed countries over the previous ten years had added more to global economic growth than the rise of China. It is changing markets, creating demand for whole new sectors of economic activity, such as childcare, aged care and a range of domestic services. It is changing workplaces as parents seek more flexible work practices, new forms of leave and different ways of working. It is changing the size and shape of families. It is changing the way that men and women see themselves and relate to each other. And every day, we are all of us navigating these changes, bit by bit, inch by inch.

For many of us, we are not only navigating the change, we are inventing it and reinventing it. The shifts are profound and historians looking back from the vantage point of a century or more will see them with a force and a clarity that eludes us as we live through them. The shifts pervade our lives in small but constant ways. When a father negotiates the childcare drop-off arrangements for his toddler over breakfast, he is likely to be having a conversation he never heard his father have. When a woman negotiates a graduated return to work after maternity leave, she is doing something that was almost impossible for her mother and unimaginable for her grandmother. In this context, it is little wonder that we sometimes feel exhausted by change and even less of a wonder that we very often don't get it right.

*

Going through a wall requires strength and courage, and I have often wondered about the source of mine. When I speak with women about leadership, they often say they doubt they have what it takes to step up to the big job. They question whether they have the life experience, the mettle, to rise to its demands. So how do we become strong? Where does courage come from? How does life set down the layers of experience that toughen us and keep us steady in the hardest moments?

For all leaders, it is most often their experiences *outside* their job and its responsibilities that have forged their character and built their ability to lead. Male leaders will often point to their time on a sporting field and the leadership lessons it taught them. They are right to do so. Sporting clashes forge grit and determination, they teach hard lessons in winning and losing, success and failure, team-building and inspiration. For years, I have watched my sons learn lessons on soccer fields that could never be learned in the comfort of home and family. But it is also the more personal experiences in life that forge us, and it is these that have taught me most about my strength and helped me understand what I can do when hard things need doing.

When I think of fear, of times that threatened to overwhelm me, of moments when I knew I had to find something stronger in myself, it is rarely the big public moments that make me catch my breath. It is the most private of times, the intensely personal experiences, that can still rattle my bones. It is the terror of parenthood, the perilous emotional navigations of relationships and family and friendships that challenge us all. The lives of women are no less full of them than those of men, and we should ascribe far more value to these experiences than we do.

Ask me about fear and I am immediately transported back to a hospital emergency room in 1988, holding my very ill five-month-old son. I can see the doctor's mouth moving, I can hear the words she is saying and I can understand their meaning, but I know she can't be talking to me, she can't be talking about my baby: 'Lumbar puncture … spinal fluid … meningitis … inflammation of the brain … deafness, blindness … life-threatening …'

These words are too hard and harsh for a baby boy still so small, so very little. These words are huge and monstrous. I feel cold, empty and frightened. I feel clammy and am fighting the rise of nausea in my throat. I feel all my early confidence as a new mother seeping out of me.

I am in a cold, sterile white room, smelling the bleached, antiseptic cleanness of it, listening to a young doctor talk quietly, seriously, urgently. But I am also not there. I am somewhere behind the walls, watching myself hold this sick, limp child, watching myself listening and disbelieving. Terror has somehow taken me out of myself. How often had I heard or read of people who experience a shocking event – a car accident, the sudden death of a loved one, an assault – as something that is somehow happening to someone else at the same time as it is happening to them? And in this moment I know what that feels like. It feels cold and deeply frightening.

Taking myself out of myself like this gives me a quiet, still moment to fight back the panic. I want to fall down on my knees but that would risk dropping my tiny son on the floor. I want to feel the comfort of big, fat, hot, wet tears on my face but then I wouldn't hear what the doctor is saying. I want to scream at the doctor to shut up and stop uttering these terrible words, but that would likely mean they would sedate me and take my baby away. And so I very consciously start telling myself what to do. I tell my mouth to clench my teeth to stop myself from trembling. I make my brain tell my arms to remain still, to keep holding this baby boy tight no matter what the doctor says. I send the message to my thighs and knees and calves to stay strong and hold me up.

And it works. I stay standing, I keep my baby boy in my arms. I hear and understand what the doctor says and I make the decisions that have to be made, letting the doctors do the unthinkable things that have to be done to save my son's life. When my body obeyed I was astounded. The urge to crumble had been so strong and overwhelming that I couldn't imagine having the strength to resist it.

There are so many moments that make and keep making us who we are, but there are some that we somehow know are changing us – pushing, shoving and reshaping us – while they are happening. This was one of those moments for me. As I spent the following days and nights watching and waiting and nursing that sick boy back to wellness, I could feel a new confidence being hard-wired into me, an almost conscious forging of bone on bone. I learned a lot about myself and about what I can do when something difficult needs to be accepted and endured with fortitude, determination and even optimism. I learned what it feels like to have one of life's lessons laid like a foundation stone inside me.

I still look back on these long days in 1988 as the moment when I really became a grown up – not when I graduated, not when I chose a life partner, not when I signed my first mortgage, not even when I gave birth, but this moment when I fully understood, in the most visceral way, that real responsibility feels like such a heavy weight in your heart and that the biggest decisions demand all you have and then some more.

When I think about getting strong, I also remember being weak. I can close my eyes and arrive in the school playground where I am nine years old. My brothers and sisters and I have just transferred to this new school because our family has moved house and it's our second day here. My eight-year-old brother in Year Three has made a mistake – he has played on the swings reserved for Years One and Two. It's an easy mistake to make when nothing is familiar, but now he is in big trouble. When he is called up in front of the whole school assembly, he walks bravely out, not knowing why, and he is made to put out his hand and is caned repeatedly. I feel sick with horror, ashamed that I did nothing to stop it, angry that I couldn't rescue him.

I only have to give this memory the lightest prod to feel again the sting of tears as I relive the moment, to feel again the terrible injustice, the almost gratuitous cruelty, the public humiliation of it. The awful sense of helpless participation in it and the guilty, shameful powerlessness that swept over me as we were all made to watch is almost as intense now as it was that day. It's one of those days to which I wish I could return and change its course or even expunge it from our shared history; that I could somehow undo it.

I doubt that I knew this experience was changing me as it unfolded, but I think it remains so alive in my memory because it was such a raw early experience of weakness and I knew I hated it. I knew I didn't want to feel it, that I wanted to be the opposite of it. I wanted to be what I wished I had been on that day, the one who spoke up, the one who said no, the superhero who put on a cape, flew in and carried my brother to safety. It's a different kind of building block from the strength that comes from facing and overcoming fear, but I think that knowing the humiliation of weakness is a powerful motivator. Understanding what I don't want to feel, understanding that regret can be corrosive, has often driven me to do the brave thing.

It is deeply personal and private experiences like these, lived long before I entered parliament, that built my strength and drove my confidence in public life. When I found the courage to live through these moments, I found the valuable tools that have strengthened my hand when I've had to tackle the demands of the public realm. Because there's no doubt that public life demands courage. Courage of your convictions, courage to stand against the tide, to take a risk and be the first one out on a limb. We all know this. Even if we don't think about it very often, we do understand that being out the front takes a lot of guts. But when you're actually standing there, when you're the one standing in front of that noisy crowd or announcing that risky policy, you really do have to summon courage, to call on all those foundation stones that life has laid, layer upon layer, deep inside you. It's no accident that we so often talk about 'summoning courage', as if that courage is in storage somewhere and has to be commanded to appear. For me, as I crashed through the wall, it always felt as if my courage lived down deep inside me and had to be consciously called and physically elevated onto centre stage to keep me still and focused as I shoved the bricks out of the way.

TWO

Learning to Surf

As the eldest of four children, I have been to some extent out the front, calling the shots all my life. I don't believe my mother consciously set out to build leadership qualities in me. But like many first-born children, I learned that achieving goals and taking responsibility brought rewards.

The four of us arrived quickly, my youngest brother making his entrance just five weeks shy of my fourth birthday. It made for a busy household, with two babies in nappies and a mother who could always use an extra pair of hands. I loved being the helper at her side, doing small jobs for her that to me seemed so grown up. It also gave me a sense of authority over my sister and two brothers. I claimed the right to decide which games we would play, to declare who would be 'it' for tiggy, to appoint the characters in our make-believe worlds. Whenever we played school, I always grabbed the role of teacher.

I still remember the shiver of pleasure I felt carrying a cup of tea to Mum the first time. We were living at Burleigh Heads, so I would have been five or six years old. She allowed me to boil the kettle, to pour the steaming water into the teapot and to carry the cup and saucer all the way across the kitchen to the chair where she was feeding the baby. So unimaginably grown up; not a child's tea set, but the real thing! I remember beaming with pride and her eyes shining with love as I made my way across the room, holding the brimming cup so tensely it shook. It seemed the very height of adult sophistication. Reflecting on this moment now, I can't imagine I would have allowed my own children to have had anything to do with boiling water at such a young age, but I know how much I loved that moment. A moment like that makes you want many more just like it.

We had moved to Burleigh Heads, one in a strip of seaside suburbs that hugs the Gold Coast for forty kilometres, in 1965. My mother's family owned a wonderful old fibro house right on the esplanade. From the deep verandahs that wrapped around it, we looked out over sand dunes to the endless glassy blue of the Pacific Ocean. Here my mother, her seven sisters and one brother had spent every summer of their childhood. It was a house built for holidays and hot summers. Rows of double bunks filled the back room and flyscreens stood guard against mosquitos. Its backyard had an enormous and splendidly gnarled old banksia tree that we spent hours in and under. It was under this tree that my mother read us chapters of May Gibbs's *Snugglepot and Cuddlepie*. However, when we reached the chapters about the wicked Banksia Men, with their bushy bodies and frightening eyes, we could no longer read under the tree, and I could never go near it at night. The house, like the garden, was open and sprawling, with faded deckchairs and salt-covered windows. It carried the smell of the ocean and the heat of lazy summer days. It was proudly called Stella Maris, star of the sea, and I loved living there.

I was only a little over five years old when we arrived and have only small snatches of memories of our lives before Stella Maris. I can see the small wrinkled face of my youngest brother, John, as the three of us siblings leaned from the back seat of the car to gaze at him for the first time, held in my mother's arms on the way home from hospital. I remember the awful shock of falling into a freezing pond at a nearby park with heavy winter clothes on, and I can see the dark blood-red of the coloured concrete that surrounded the house we rented in Stockton, near Newcastle, before coming to Burleigh Heads. I can hear my mother's voice teaching my brother Stephen and me the words to 'Rudolph the Red-Nosed Reindeer' as she was making beds, the sheets billowing from her arms as we sang the words.

But it was only years later that I understood we had moved to Stella Maris because it provided a safe haven for my mother when she upped and fled her unhappy marriage. With no money or job, and with four small children in tow, there was no other place for her to go. I don't know what triggered my mother's flight to her parents' old beach place, or even how she made her way there. It must have been an incredible journey for Mum — almost 700 kilometres in a car — with four small children, the youngest still in nappies. She was twenty-nine years old and essentially on her own. I cannot remember the journey, but it would return us to Queensland and shape our childhoods. The separation did not last long, and my father soon joined us at the beach. Whatever the circumstances, we'd landed on the Gold Coast, a magical place to be a child, the place where I would grow and learn and do all my schooling.

*

In 1966, I set off with Stephen to Infant Saviour Catholic Primary School at Burleigh Heads. I wore a crisp white shirt and a dark brown box-pleat tunic. Despite being eleven months apart in age, Stephen and I started school at the same time, in a sort of job-lot arrangement that my mother came to with the local Franciscan nuns. These things were easier to arrange back then, and it certainly helped take some pressure off at home.

I took my eager desire to please from home through the school gates, and it served me well. As their name suggests, the Franciscan nuns base their traditions on the teachings of St Francis of Assisi, a gentle saint renowned for his love of the poor, and in their keeping I grew to love school and learning. Discipline was strict but fair and our nuns maintained good order. Their elaborate dark brown habits were topped off with constricting white wimples, which held back all their hair, covered their foreheads, chins and necks and revealed only a small part of their faces, rendering even the softest nun officious and stern. My first school photo shows Sister Mary Antonia with a class of forty-six five-year-olds, so she needed some authority on her side to keep the peace and teach us to read and write.

The cultural landscape of my early childhood was profoundly Catholic. Daily, weekly and annual religious traditions and conventions shaped and marked our lives as children. I said my bedside prayers every night and attended mass every Sunday in my best clothes. For one seemingly endless hour each week, I watched a distant priest in a flowing, ornate gown droning in unfamiliar Latin, his back to his congregation. It was a strange and mysterious ritual, and one that made me and every other child restless and itchy with boredom. We always observed Lent, and on Ash Wednesday we sported a black thumbprint on our foreheads. Words such as *genuflect* and *confessional, rosary* and *benediction* were part of our lexicon. We solemnly honoured the holy days of obligation and never ate meat on a Friday. A portrait of the Sacred Heart hung in our hallway. Attending midnight mass was a family Christmas tradition, and we celebrated the sacraments of baptism, confession, holy communion and confirmation as major rites of passage.

But the Catholicism of my early life was built on more than ritual and tradition. These outward displays of religion were the expression of our beliefs. These beliefs were carved more deeply into us every time we observed these traditions. The Catholic Church that nurtured my early life was one that taught the importance of helping others less fortunate than myself. It taught me about equality and social justice and, importantly, that I had a responsibility to help build a better world, a world without poverty, war, hunger and violence. Every year, Lent began with us taking home a cardboard moneybox. Each week, we put our pocket money into this box to send off to Catholic missions around the world. With every cent that went into the box, we learned that helping others was our duty and part of God's plan for us, that the sacrifice of our own needs and pleasures for the benefit of others was a virtue, that Australians held a lucky place in a world full of violence and starvation. We were told that the teachings of Christ were to be lived, were values to guide our lives. Our responsibility to do something about the misery of others was forged in us as we grew. These teachings remain a deep part of who I am and how I've tried to live my life. It was these values that drew me, and many others, to politics and the Australian Labor Party. But it was these same values that ultimately drew me away from the church.

Until I started school, most of my religious thoughts had been of a sweet and friendly baby Jesus, of a guardian angel that protected me and of the beautiful and blessed Virgin Mary who looked over me. The violence of religious belief and the brutal contest of ideas, debated and fought over for centuries, were completely unknown to me. That changed one day close to Easter in Year One, when our first school term was coming to an end. The nuns brought us all into the school hall to watch a movie about the Passion of Christ. It seemed to feature every explicit detail of His torture and crucifixion in full and gruesome technicolour, and I stood up and began screaming hysterically. I had seen the Stations of the Cross in church, but they had not prepared me for the reality playing out across that screen. Though one of the nuns took me from the room, I could not be quietened. When my embarrassed mother was summoned to the school, she found me still sobbing with fear. I have detested violent movies ever since.

As I grew older and learned more about the lives of the saints, I became more accustomed to the violence that so often accompanies strong beliefs. The heroic tales of men and women who had died for their faith held a ghoulish fascination for me. As other children might collect cards of sports stars or superheroes, my friends and I collected holy cards. The cards could be bought at church, were often given out in class for good behaviour or exceptional schoolwork and could be swapped with other girls. They depicted our religious heroes and heroines in beatific poses, often in gardens with the powerful light of heaven pouring down on them from the clouds. Their stories were written on the back of each card. Some were martyrs, perhaps shunned for their faith by their families or their rulers. Most died bravely, the women usually guarding their virtue and purity. Their deaths were often brutal and barbaric: they were eaten by lions, burned alive, boiled in oil and the like. Just as that early movie of the Passion of Christ had hardly seemed like suitable viewing, these stories now seem to me horrifying for young minds. But these tales held us in their gruesome grip and stood alongside the best children's stories, those tinged with the fear of baby-stealing monsters and demons, evil stepmothers and girl-eating big bad wolves. The heroines of these religious stories always struck me as impossibly brave, standing their ground for their faith, refusing to bow to the wicked wishes of their parents or their rulers and suffering terribly for their beliefs. These stories filled my thoughts with the ideal of a noble life, lived with a head held high, devout against all odds. Like *Star Wars* and *Harry Potter*, these stories had the irresistible pull of great triumphs of good over evil. They imprinted in me the value of individual courage and audacity.

*

When my grandparents sold the old Burleigh Heads holiday house, my family moved to a series of rented houses in nearby Palm Beach. Stella Maris joined the many other Gold Coast family holiday homes that were demolished in the 1960s to make way for the glitzy strip of high-rise oceanfront apartments that now draws millions of visitors each year from Australia and around the world.

Queensland has much of the frontier state mentality about it, a derring-do spirit of adventure and bravado that breeds larger-than-life public characters. Few parts of Queensland have captured this as perfectly as the Gold Coast of the 1960s and '70s, when a seaside town exploded like a firecracker into a city of brash, bright lights.

As with most children, my early life and that of my siblings revolved around our backyard, our neighbourhood, our school and the places where we met up with friends – the local park and the beach. Sun, sand and surf were our constant companions. For much of my childhood, I was oblivious to the fact that we lived in a place that for others was full of glamour and romance, a place of parties, excitement and honeymoons. As we surfed and played and peeled sunburnt skin off our shoulders, all around us the Gold Coast was transforming itself.

One man who came to symbolise this transformation was the man who would be the Gold Coast's mayor for much of the time I was growing up. Sir Bruce Small was wiry, energetic and flamboyant, an entrepreneur who had spent his life building a successful bicycle company. As a young man, Small bought a modest bicycle shop in Melbourne and built it into a national company that produced the iconic Malvern Star bicycle. After retiring from the business, Small moved to the Gold Coast and turned his hand to property development, buying a large tract of flood-prone mangroves directly behind Surfers Paradise. He drained the land, forming it into a series of islands and canal developments. Starting a trend that continues to this day on the Gold Coast, Small gave these developments names such as Isle of Capri and Sorrento, which to our parochial ears had the allure of sophisticated European playgrounds of the rich and famous, the kind of places we imagined that Audrey Hepburn or Princess Grace of Monaco might holiday. This branding worked for Small and it worked for the Gold Coast.

These developments, and others like them, soon attracted investment by wealthy retirees from the more prosperous southern states. They came looking for sunshine in their twilight years and brought their commercial expertise and retirement nest eggs with them. It was an extraordinary time, a property boom unprecedented anywhere in the country. Everywhere we turned, the old was giving way to the new. The first high-rise holiday apartments began to appear on the skyline: the Iluka building was the first to be built on the beach at Surfers Paradise and it seemed as high as the sun. We watched the Pink Poodle Motel, with its famous pink neon sign, take shape. When this iconic motel opened its doors in 1967, Small decided to turn his energies to politics and run for mayor of the city, at the age of seventy-two.

Bruce Small's mayoral campaign is my first memory of politics. He ran on the simple but memorable slogan 'Think Big, Vote Small'. It's the kind of slogan that a child notices and remembers; it was easy, clever and a bit funny. We would hear him on radio and imitate him as he spruiked his corny slogan, and we weren't surprised when he won. In his first year as mayor, Gold Coast beaches were struck by a cyclone, which put a serious dent in the holiday haven's reputation for fun. Bruce Small hit upon the idea of a national tour of Australia to promote his city. He then went one better and decided to take a team of Gold Coast 'Meter Maids' along with him.

To the uninitiated, it's hard to describe the Meter Maid phenomenon, but it's a quintessential Gold Coast story. Still active today, Meter Maids carry the flame of my hometown's gaudy, ostentatious and hungry heart. They were conceived by the Surfers Paradise Progress Association in 1965. The association was furious when the local council installed parking meters in the main street of Surfers Paradise, believing the move would be bad for business. Determined that tourists should not take home a parking ticket as a holiday souvenir, the association funded a campaign enlisting attractive young women to patrol the streets and top up the meters with sixpence pieces whenever they were close to expiring, allowing cars to park for as long as they liked. Their acts of kindness were confirmed by courtesy cards left under windscreen wipers. These 'maids' were mostly aspiring models and wore skimpy gold lamé bikinis, long white boots and sparkling diamante tiaras. Blue sashes across their bodies proclaimed them to be Meter Maids, as if we might have mistaken them for visiting royalty. Technically, they were breaking the law, as meter-feeding was illegal. However, they were immediately so popular that the council decided to turn a blind eye to their activities, and a Gold Coast icon was born.

As a solution to a parking-meter problem, the Meter Maids were an audacious and brash idea that was slightly outside the letter of the law and, like the Gold Coast, gloriously, unrepentantly tacky. And it worked. As Small made his way around Australia, the accompanying Meter Maids helped to put the Gold Coast on the national map. Bruce's tour was so successful that he took similar trips to New Zealand, Hong Kong, Japan and Singapore in subsequent years, laying the foundation for the city to become an international tourist destination. His colourful antics became legendary. He entered dance marathons and rode a penny-farthing bicycle in street parades. Knighted for his services to the Gold Coast in 1974, Sir Bruce Small was one local politician who was hard to miss.

As a child, I took all this colour and extravagance in my schoolgirl stride. It was just a backdrop to my life at home and at school, so didn't seem out of the ordinary. But it was nevertheless a flamboyant backdrop, marking the time when my hometown became a city, a city that still beguiles and seduces everyone from the lovers and the holidaymakers to the chancers, the property developers and the shysters looking for a quick buck.

*

At home, my parents struggled in a rarely happy marriage, which is an emotional minefield for children. My mother was my father's second wife. His first wife had died, leaving him with five children in their late teens and early twenties. When he married my mother in 1959, he was more than twenty years older than she. He was worldly and charming and, from her accounts, swept her off her feet. But her new husband's easy charm was not enough to mask his terrible drinking problem for long.

Despite all the work and research done on alcoholism and addiction, I don't profess to understand why it afflicts some people so terribly and leaves others alone. From experience, I know that it can be a confusing and frightening affliction to live with. My father genuinely struggled to conquer his addiction. He spent all the years we lived with him in a constant but losing battle with it. It was not until long after he and my mother divorced that he won his personal battle with the bottle.

When I was growing up, he was either drinking a lot or on the wagon, a reformed man. As a reformed man, he was a devoted father, energetically making up for the months that had been lost to the bottle. He would wake us early, and we'd head to the beach for a quick surf before school. All the way there, he would teach us old-time songs and tell us silly riddles. It was on these early-morning trips that my father taught me about the ocean, its perils and its pleasures. He taught me how to recognise a deadly rip and how to catch a wave. More than four decades on, I can still hear him talking me through it as I am picked up by the swell of a wave, his voice telling me to wait for the exact moment I feel the sand under my toes drag backwards and then to propel myself forward, hands outstretched, to push as the water picks me up and takes me with it to the shoreline. This memory is a gift, like a postcard from someone I don't really know. On sober weekends, my father would make my mother breakfast in bed and take us all out for dinner to the local RSL club. When Mum made spaghetti bolognese, a new and exotic addition to most Anglo-Australian dinner tables in the 1960s, he would declare it to be delicious. There would be Sunday beachside barbecues, games of football with the boys and plans for family holidays. He would seek the support of Alcoholics Anonymous and place his framed copy of their gentle prayer on his dresser. It was always a good sign when we could see its words: 'God give me the courage to change the things I can, the strength to accept the things I cannot and the wisdom to know the difference.'

And then something would happen. We would never see the trigger coming, just feel a small change in the air and know that the beach trips were over. A surly, belligerent mood would overtake my father and everything would sour. It would almost always start with a sly campaign against my mother. 'Where has she been? Who did you see her with?' he would demand as he tried to enlist us in his escalating battle. Complaints about her food or her housework, cruel jibes about what she was wearing or how she'd done her hair, would follow. Then he would set crazy new rules, such as demanding she put the kettle on at the moment his car hit the edge of the driveway, with just enough water in it so that it would boil in time for her to have a steaming cup of tea ready on the table when he walked in the front door. If she failed, he would turn on his heels and disappear for hours. Coldly and silently, he would turn the spaghetti bolognese upside down on the dinner table and call it inedible as it seeped across the tablecloth.

It was only years later that I came to see a pattern in my father's behaviour. When he was drinking heavily and regularly, we saw very little of him. He wouldn't come home after work, or if he did it was to briefly change clothes before heading out, returning long after we were asleep. My father was what is now called a high-functioning alcoholic. He managed to hold down jobs most of the time when he was drinking, although he must have quickly worn out his welcome as he often changed jobs. For the months when he had given into alcohol, he was a largely absent figure in our lives. But his absence was not a benign one. He would promise to come to events that mattered, such as our school concerts, sporting matches or birthday parties, only to fail us over and over again. The constant yearning hunger of addiction drove out everything else. Addicts are untethered by the rules of normal life. The overpowering pull of the addiction demands a double life, in which lying to yourself and those around you comes as easily as breathing. It's a life in which you say you will do one thing already knowing you will do another, you are never where you said you would be and no one can ever rely on you.

Gambling and drinking were twin demons in my father's life. Money problems were always the sparks that ignited conflict between my parents. My mother could never rely on having money in the bank to keep our household going. She took on small jobs to ensure she had some income that my father was unable to touch. She sold World Book encyclopaedias door to door during the hours we were at school, always putting aside a little to ensure we could receive Christmas presents. This too became a source of friction in their marriage. My father was shaped in the generation before the roles of men and women began to change. Despite his own financial fecklessness, he felt humiliated as a male breadwinner when she took these jobs. 'No wife of mine will work,' he would thunder at her in vain. In these moments, I was often grateful to escape to the relative peace of school.

*

My first year at Infant Saviour School, 1966, was a momentous and tumultuous time for the Catholic Church across the world. In December 1965, the Second Vatican Council had concluded three years of deliberations. Pope John XXIII had initiated the council in an effort to modernise the church. In his words, it was 'time to open the windows and let in the fresh air'. As a little girl, I was unaware of the ecclesiastical pomp of Vatican II and oblivious to its transforming decisions. But I too felt the fresh breeze of change. Now there was a mass celebrated in English that I could understand. Now the priest faced us to make sure we could hear his words, see him perform the sacred rituals of the mass and feel included in the liturgy. With Vatican II bringing a greater role for the laity in the church, I now attended masses during which my mother and the family members of school friends read from the Bible. My brothers were altar boys and I envied their involvement in the service. I would go on to do readings myself at school masses and to play guitar at the folk masses that emerged in the early 1970s.

I did not celebrate all the changes. For example, Vatican II removed the requirement for women to cover their heads as an act of piety as the church moved to become more welcoming and informal. I had loved my white lace mantilla, the lacy veil reserved for Sunday best, and now I could no longer wear it. A similar informality allowed our nuns to cast aside their dark habits and the heavy wimples that till then had completely hidden their heads, hair and necks. I remember the shock of arriving at school in Year Three to find the sisters in calf-length, short-sleeved white habits and short simple veils. We had only ever known them to float above the ground in their long gowns, and it came as a surprise for us to find they had legs. But it was even more shocking for us to realise that these nuns had hair: for some it was wavy, for some straight; some dark, some grey and some even red. Their wimples had so tightly constrained even a stray wisp that we had thought them all bald under those strange headpieces. In the sweltering heat of Gold Coast summers, I doubt that the sisters shared my regrets at leaving their old veils behind. Remembering the shock of this modern turn of events in the playgrounds of Australian Catholic schools of the 1960s, I'm struck by the fact that it's not that long ago that I and hundreds of thousands of other Australian women were routinely covering our heads as a pious act of religious worship. We would do well to remember this today when we are perplexed by women of other religions and cultures who do the same. A deep attachment to devout religious observance and a strict adherence to its symbols, superstitions and traditions are really not that foreign to us.

*

At the beginning of Year Four I moved schools. Guardian Angels was run by the Sisters of Mercy, an Irish religious order founded in 1831 by Catherine McAuley, who had built a school for poor girls and a shelter for homeless women in Dublin in 1827. Many of those who founded and built the order in Australia came from extreme poverty. Their harsh young lives were made harder by being sent to a remote continent where many of them would never see their families or their own country again. They had the comfort and solace of their faith, and they would need it.

The Sisters of Mercy are inspired by McAuley's mission to help those suffering injustice, poverty, illness or a lack of education. They've had a deep commitment to the education of girls and young women since the founding of their first school, and I am a grateful beneficiary of this commitment.

When I arrived at Guardian Angels, I was literate and numerate, but the product of the relatively gentle Franciscan system, which had never put us under too much pressure. It was a rude shock to find these new sisters appalled by my sloppy handwriting and poor handiwork. It was an even ruder shock to find that they were determined to correct it, with a ruler across my knuckles as often as they felt necessary. I quickly learned the virtues of clean pages, straight lines and tidy work.

The Sisters of Mercy believed in the pursuit of excellence and expected the girls in their care to aspire, achieve and do well. They were great promoters of Catholic education in the years when state aid for Catholic schools was a deeply contested public debate. We were expected to participate in all manner of educational competitions and be the proof of Catholic schools' value. Our sewing samplers, copybooks, anthologies and science and geography charts were sent off to the 'Ekka', Queensland's Royal Exhibition Show, every year. We were encouraged to enter essay competitions and art exhibitions. These examples of our handiwork and scholarship would be most of the year in preparation and the highest possible standard of work was expected.

From the day I arrived at Guardian Angels, I felt the urge to excel. I spent hours practising my handwriting and pulling out my embroidery until I got it right. But I learned a good deal more than this. I learned to strive and achieve. I learned to compete. I learned of the rewards that come from pushing yourself and doing your best. I learned of the thrill that comes from winning as I earned my share of prizes, and I learned how to cope with the disappointment of losing as I missed out on others.

Despite the changes of Vatican II, the numbers attending Sunday mass began to dwindle throughout the 1960s. When I was in Year Five, the sisters hit on a cunning idea to tackle the problem. All children in Year Four and above were required every Monday morning to write an essay on the subject of that Sunday's sermon. Each week a prize would be awarded to the best essay and each weekly winner would go into an end-of-term draw to win a silver watch. In one of the early weeks of term, my essay won. I can no longer remember the topic of the sermon or what my essay had to say about it, but I remember my prize with absolute clarity. I had won a small plastic statue of the Virgin Mary that glowed in the dark. Glow-in-the-dark materials are now commonplace, but in 1969 we had never seen anything like it, and friends came around to my house just to see her glow. I loved my luminescent Virgin.

At the end of term, my name was drawn out of the hat and I walked up through the school assembly to receive my watch. I'm not sure that any of this increased my religious devotion, but winning did teach me the value of effort. Experiences like this one made me embrace competition, do my best and seek out challenges. This urge to excel, to keep at something until it's as good as I can make it, to be out the front whenever I could, stayed with me long beyond the convent gates. It propelled me into adult life at full tilt and spurred my move into public life.

*

My father's failings were disappointing, and his absences were sad times when we wished he would come back to us, but they were rarely frightening. It was the in-between times that were the most dangerous for us. The perilous, slippery weeks when he felt himself falling from grace, when his months of abstinence were marred by a single beer that he feared would soon become two, when the reformed man could feel himself giving in to the tidal pull of his craving.

I can see now that the tests he set for my mother were designed for failure. He was creating reasons to justify his return to drinking. In his mind, her failings and our shortcomings would drive any man to drink, so who could blame him for seeking the solace of alcohol? In this in-between zone, we were all at risk. As he craved a reason to escape his responsibilities and us, to drift back into the comfort of late-night hotels, any or all of us could become the target of his misery. Like many fathers in those years, he often disciplined my brothers with a strap, though his violence was otherwise not physical. But he had an aptitude for cruelty and applied it without mercy. Growing disappointment with himself drove his cruelty at these times. He could feel himself slipping and loathed himself for it. This loathing grew a malignant meanness in him. He would taunt and humiliate us until we broke into tears, make us do and redo jobs until we argued or sobbed. His attacks would find our vulnerabilities with military precision. They were alarmingly unpredictable and unprovoked. They were often designed to pitch us against each other, to take one's talents to humiliate another. At these times, he would take my love of helping out and use it to demonstrate my mother's failings. If he found me proudly getting the dinner on while my mother was doing something else, he would start to praise my efforts only to quickly turn this into sneers about my mother. He would pretend to pity me for having a lazy, negligent mother, using words from another era like *sloven* and *slattern* to convey his contempt for her.

When I was about seven or eight, he coined the name 'Little Mother' for me. It was not a term of endearment or admiration. It would appear only when he was on the nasty, vicious slope back to drinking, and it was used to shame and degrade my mother. Having attended Catholic boarding schools and trained as a nurse in the 1950s, my mother is an exceptional example of her generation's ability to run a household and keep it clean. My father's criticisms had no basis in fact, but he knew the pride she took in her housework and the pain these attacks would cause her. I would freeze with the shame of collusion as he berated her by using me as a yardstick. 'So, Little Mother has to fold the washing again. Poor little thing, the real mother has left you all alone, picking up after her and her filthy mess,' he would sneer. I was distressed by these taunts, confused about whether I was making things better or worse when I helped out. He would applaud the sporting success of my youngest brother and then use it to humiliate my other brother for his academic talents, throwing balls at him he couldn't catch while calling him terrible names.

When he was in these moods, it was not possible for us to accept his praise, which of course we all craved, without joining in his psychological warfare against the others. His attacks soon meant we lived in fear of him, cowering out of his sight as quickly as we could lest his vicious gaze land on us. His temper was always on a short fuse and its unpredictability was a source of terror. When he was desperate to find a way out of the house and itching with the need to drink, we could feel the steely chill in the air, and dinnertime was a fearful, silent warzone. Emotional landmines lay everywhere and the slightest movement could trigger an explosion. If one of my brothers put too much salt on his meal, my father would detonate, leaping up from his chair and, in one swift move, smashing his plate against the wall and storming out of the house. We would be left silent in his wake, tears streaming down my mother's cheeks, food dripping down the wall that we would then quietly clean up. It was a landscape of relentless psychological violence.

My mother did her best to shield us, always putting herself in the path of danger when she could. When she could read his mood, she would ensure we were in our rooms, out of his way. As his anger grew, she would bear the brunt of it, enduring his abuse, silently waiting him out until he left the house and we could safely come out of our rooms. But for us, this was little relief. Bearing witness to his unsparing attacks on her was harrowing. Cringing together in our bedrooms as we listened to him humiliate her was unbearable. I would pray and sometimes count, pleading that he would be gone by the time I got to a hundred or two hundred. In the dangerous shadow world between his drinking and not drinking, my mother could do nothing right. While each incident in itself might seem a minor trial, it was the constant nature of my father's attacks that made life at our place so emotionally perilous. Experiences like these went on daily, sometimes for hours, eroding and shifting our foundations without warning, without cause. As a family, we were fearful and utterly miserable.

*

Adding to the difficult times at home was the common assumption when I was growing up that girls would marry soon after school, have babies quickly thereafter and spend little, if any, time in the paid workforce. The education of girls was not highly valued. The 1960s saw entrenched ideas about the role of women and girls being challenged around the western world. But the new ideas took a while to reach us on the Gold Coast. My father, so much older than my mother, brought the ideas of his generation to this question. He would loudly assert that too much education was wasted on girls and that he saw no reason for me to finish high school. He would deride my mother for filling my head with foolish ideas. But my mother understood that she was trapped in an unhappy marriage by financial dependency, and she wanted something better for me. She would often tell me that I had to be able to make my own way in the world and that I should study hard to guard against becoming trapped like her. Independence was a glittering prize that she wanted for all her children, and she knew that it would be a harder struggle for her daughters.

Mum would find times when the two of us were alone to urge me to be ambitious and aspire to further education. I remember being in the car with her when she turned to me and said, 'Don't be like me.' That seemed crazy, because I wanted to be just like her.

'If you can't get a job, you're trapped,' she would say. 'So stay at school, study so you can go to university and you'll be free to do what you want in life.'

In my neighbourhood, nobody went to university. For the Gold Coast of the 1970s, going to university meant leaving home, leaving the beach and heading to Brisbane. All I knew of it was that the youngest and my favourite of my mother's seven sisters, Patti, had started university, but I had no idea of what it was or what happened there. My father believed it to be no place for a woman, this place that bred hippies and radicals and dangerous subversives. I knew that my mother's words would be regarded as heresy by my father, her encouragements could never be uttered at home or in his company. Her urgings were all the more persuasive for being delivered as a clandestine pact, a secret agreement that bound us together. Studying hard and becoming something more was a way to secure her happiness, and I wanted this more than anything. Perversely, my father's constant disparagement of the education of girls was an incentive for me. Proving him wrong became another powerful driving force for me to study and do well.

At school, the Sisters of Mercy reinforced Mum's aspirations. At a time when little was expected of girls, these fierce, strong women pushed us to achieve. For them, it was our religious obligation to use the talents that God had given us. Reaching our potential was a way of honouring Him and we had a duty to make the most of ourselves. The sisters who taught me were deeply conservative, particularly on the subjects of boys and morals. The hems of our uniforms were measured to confirm their regulation length and girls found talking to boys at bus stops were in big trouble. But in their own way, the sisters were also subversive. They encouraged us to stand up for ourselves, to believe in our own value and to do something substantial and meaningful with our lives. Between my mother and the nuns, I learned to have hopes and dreams. By the end of primary school, my admiration for the nuns in my life led me to believe I had a vocation and would become a nun, devoting my life to God.

*

My father fought, and was injured, in Borneo during World War II. Along with many other men of his generation, he spoke little of this experience and I've come to wonder what part it played in his drinking. Now in my fifties myself, I wonder too about the pressures of raising another four young children, having already raised five in his first family. Ultimately, the endless cycles of his drinking were impossible to fathom and impossible to live with.

With the introduction of the Supporting Mother's Benefit for single mothers in 1973, Gough Whitlam and his government gave my mother the means to leave this unhappy marriage and strike out on her own. I was entering high school when she took this step. It would change our lives, and it would not have been possible without this simple change in public policy. She would go on to work in a number of jobs as we navigated our teenage years, but she always knew she had this benefit to fall back on if needed. With this confidence, she could take on raising the four of us on her own. It was my first experience of the direct impact a government can have on the lives of real people. I was not privy to the discussions my parents had about ending their marriage, but it ended with more of a whimper than a bang. It was negotiated during one of my father's dry spells, when he was thinking clearly. Their marriage was miserable, and he did not stand in the way of ending it. As the legalities were sorted through over the next two years, he often made it as difficult as he could for my mother, but the actual leaving was civilised and reasonable. They both talked to us and explained what was happening, and then he simply walked out of our home for the last time.

My father's permanent exit felt like the lifting of a dark cloud of fear and unhappiness. Immediately, everything became easier and brighter. We could invite friends to our house without fear of shame or embarrassment, and our home opened up to the sound of my mother's laughing friends for the first time. We could be silly, messy, loud or funny without any fear. In my memory, we seemed to come out of ourselves all at once. It must have happened more gradually, but I remember it like the sudden opening of a door. The government benefit was barely a living income, but its introduction had liberated us. It was a powerful lesson in a government's making a difference.

My shift to the Star of the Sea Convent High School coincided with my mother's return to the full-time workforce. Before marrying, she had studied nursing, but a serious back injury forced her to withdraw before completing her qualification. As we entered our teens, she returned to hospital work as a nurse's aide at Pindara, a new private hospital near our home. Mum chose mostly night and afternoon shifts as they enabled her to be at home in the morning to get us off to school, do some housework and generally manage the household. During these years, my siblings and I all took on more responsibilities. Our household could function only if everyone took on some of the load. When Mum was rostered on afternoon shifts, we all pitched in preparing dinner, clearing up and leaving something for her for when she came home after ten o'clock. We were supposed to be in bed by then but often waited up to see her, to hear the stories of her day and tell her something of ours. She would always come home elated if a baby had been born on her shift and would recount the details, the new baby's vital statistics and name.

My mother gave all of herself to us through the years of our childhood. She poured herself into us, working to fill the hole left in our lives by our angry, absent father, loving us with the force of two parents. We had our share of ups and downs. But my mother has a happiness in her that my father could never extinguish, and she filled our lives with affection. It is not possible to live your formative years in the psychological battleground of a father's angry addictions and emerge unscathed, and we all bear the scars of it. But it is a testament to the strength of my mother's unquenchable love that we have become adults who know how to love other people and between us have raised eight gorgeous and much-loved children.

My mother had always found joy in her faith. She had been an active member of the church community: cleaning the sacristy, providing flowers for the church and meals for the priests, teaching the catechism in the local public schools, leading women's prayer groups and ensuring her children were raised to share her faith. She was devout in her beliefs and strong in her convictions. When the unhappiness of her marriage was no longer tolerable and the effect of it on her children too great, she took the courageous step to leave her husband and looked to her faith and the church to support her.

Instead, she found harsh judgement. Divorce ran counter to the teachings of the church, and she was prohibited from taking communion. She was shunned by some who had shared her parish activities and lectured by the priest about her decision to leave my father. When my parents separated, I was thirteen years old and, like all teenagers, beginning to question everything. The once inviolable place of the church in my life, its authority, its comfort and its inherent goodness became the object of my withering questions. I found the answers wanting. I felt a hot sense of protective outrage on my mother's behalf. Knowing the courage it had taken for her to leave my father, I deemed the church's treatment of her a great injustice. She had given so much to the church and asked for so little in return. The flames of my indignation burned white-hot when priests and nuns repeatedly pleaded that she apply to the Pope for an annulment of her marriage. She would be an outcast for admitting the misery of her marriage and acting to protect her children, but embraced if she accepted an expedient theological contrivance that denied her marriage had ever existed. This seemed to me a gross hypocrisy. To this day, Mum snorts at the idea of annulment. 'How can I say I wasn't married to the man I lived with for fourteen years and had four children with? What would that make me? It's preposterous!' And so began our schism with all that had shaped and influenced us to that point.

I left behind my small sheltered convent and entered a whole new world at Miami State High School. A universe of more than two thousand students, where questions of religion and faith burdened few and where half those in the playground were boys. I soon realised that becoming a nun was no longer my vocation.

These were happy years, but full of hard work for each member of our family. As the eldest, much of this responsibility fell to me, and throughout my teens I really did become 'Little Mother'. On my fiftieth birthday, my brother John, the youngest sibling and the one who felt my parents' divorce the hardest, surprised me by writing a poem, which he called 'My Second Mum'. He wrote lines including 'You mixed the life of a teenager / And that of a mum' and 'You would cook, wash and clean / Without a whinge or a whine / While most of your friends / Were out having a good time'. He wrote 'There would be no one prouder / To call you my second mum'. As I read this birthday gift, tears rushed to my eyes. There is something still so raw and intimate in these lines, all these decades later. I had thought those years were long in our past, but I felt again the emotional tenderness of them, realising they were not so far from the surface after all.

*

Although Mum worked hard and took on night and weekend shifts that attracted higher wage rates, money was always tight. I started a part-time job at a local fish and chip shop, and my brother Stephen soon joined me there. Like most young people, I was excited by the more adult responsibilities I was given at work. I grew in confidence as I was allotted new tasks and duties like ordering stock and managing the cash register, and I relished the sense of independence and freedom that came with earning my own money. The work was hot, hard and tiring, and I couldn't get enough of it. This enjoyment of work reinforced my mother's exhortations to study hard, and I also did well at high school. I was by no means the most gifted student, but I loved learning and the pleasure of doing well.

In the 1970s, Miami State High School was one of the largest schools in Queensland. I was fortunate to be there under the leadership of Bill Callinan, a widely respected visionary principal who had high aspirations for his school. It was bursting at the seams as it filled with the children of the Gold Coast's booming population, but Mr Callinan set high standards and enforced them. Miami State was overcrowded, but he expected the grounds to be clean, uniforms to be worn with pride, the school song to be sung with gusto and high academic, sporting and artistic standards to be reached. He united the school community around his dream to build a large hall and performance centre and worked tirelessly to raise funds until his dream became a reality. His hall was the first of its kind on the Gold Coast. It put the school on the wider community's radar, because so many people had made some small contribution to it and thousands more went to concerts and events there. It was here that I sat in school assemblies, went to school dances and performed in school plays such as *Joseph and the Amazing Technicolour Dreamcoat*.

It was also in this hall that I got my first taste of electoral victory. After securing student and teacher support in elections for house captain and prefect, I was presented with my badges on the stage. I hadn't sought the school captain position and had been unsure whether I would even be voted house captain. I had never put myself forward for a position like it and really had little idea of what to expect. I don't remember planning it or thinking about it very much, but again I had that urge to be out the front, to be one of the chosen ones, to strive and give it a go.

Being house captain earned me a place on the school council, a forum where student leaders joined the senior teachers and parent representatives to plan for the school and develop ideas for its future. Here was my first experience of decision-making, the chance to have a say in how things would be done. I remember the pleasure of it, the satisfaction and enjoyment of being listened to and feeling a little important. The position of prefect brought with it some small power over younger students such as being able to tell them to pick up their rubbish or rectify a uniform infringement. Of course, we all felt a little smug and giddy with our success. Thankfully, our teachers talked with us explicitly about the responsibility that comes with leadership and the need for our power to be used wisely and sparingly, tempering our adolescent hubris.

*

My time as an elected official was cut short around Easter of my final year, when my mother decided to send me to Nowra, on the south coast of New South Wales, to complete my studies in the care of her sister Nonie. I had formed a relationship with an older boy who had left high school completely. It had all the intensity that teenagers bring to matters of the heart, but we were from two different worlds with very different aspirations. He didn't want me studying on weekends or being involved in school activities. He had a job, was earning money and wanted to go out late, have fun and enjoy himself. I had tried to end the relationship without success. He would wait for me at the school gate, follow my bus home from school and call me at all hours of the night. After all her encouragement and hard work, Mum now worried that the emotional pull of first love was too much for me, that my schoolwork was suffering and I was at risk of failing or, worse, leaving school without finishing. She could feel that all she wanted for me was suddenly at risk of slipping away. And so off to Nowra I was sent. We laugh about it now, but it was very painful at the time. Mum's decision made me both resentful and relieved. She had been right in her assessment that I was out of my depth, but I was desolate about leaving my friends and family.

Nowra is a quiet coastal town on the Shoalhaven River about one hundred and sixty kilometres south of Sydney. It's a popular holiday and fishing spot. Nowra High School was welcoming, and I was once again studying hard and making new friends, many of whom, like me, wanted to do well and head to university. My time in Nowra gave me the chance to start learning the skills of living away from my family. Nonie, her husband, Henry, and their young daughter, Bernadette, made space for me in their lives. My time with them was warm and loving, but it also helped me to grow up and be away from my mother.

Living on the south coast of New South Wales also gave me my first understanding of how others viewed my hometown. Suddenly, I saw the Gold Coast through the envious eyes of the

Nowra High School students, who found it simply astonishing that someone could actually come from this exotic place they had all dreamed of visiting. 'What's it really like?' they asked constantly, as they might have interrogated a Californian exchange student from Hollywood.

And Nowra gave me my first taste of the way the rest of Australia viewed Queensland. As alluring as they found the beaches and the sunshine, they regarded our long-term conservative government, led by former peanut farmer Joh Bjelke-Petersen, as an object of humour, if not ridicule. As a teenager, I had paid little attention to politics but knew that we had a colourful and unusual premier. Now I came to understand that because of him, Queenslanders were the butt of national jokes. I saw the antics of our government through the eyes of people who were not inured to it, and I saw that the government of New South Wales behaved quite differently. Almost without fail, when I met new people they would tell me how lucky I was to grow up on the Gold Coast and then follow with an easy joke about Queensland politics. People would often imitate Joh's distinctive speaking style and repeat his nonsensical declarations. My time in Nowra was largely spent with my head in books, with a part-time job at Pizza Hut and at a whirl of parties. But it was also my first big step out of the nest and into the wider world. The girl who headed home at the end of that year, with the results she needed to enrol at the University of Queensland, was more independent, more confident and asking more questions than the girl who had left.

When I think now about that girl about to head off to university and launch into life as a young adult, I know she is at once self-assured and self-doubting, that she carries with her the protection of her mother's fierce and shining love and the scars left by her father's anger and absence. I know that the legacy of her Catholicism carves her worldview and softens her heart to the weak and the needy. I know that the hurdles she has jumped to get here make her strong and gritty and ready to put her hand up when something needs doing. I know that the people who believed in her – her mother, her siblings, her teachers, her nuns – have made her hungry to do well. I know she loves the Queensland that has shaped her but is beginning to see that not all is right about her home state. She has no thoughts of being a leader, but she does want to achieve something and make her life matter.

THREE

A Bigger World

The Channel 7 interviewer sports long sideburns and hilariously wide lapels on his grey suit. The twenty-year-old woman wears short cropped hair, baggy jeans and a loose-fitting chambray shirt, the young feminist uniform of the late 1970s and early 1980s on the University of Queensland campus.

'Adolf Hitler had a way of dealing with books he didn't like: he had them burned,' says the TV presenter to camera, 'and now the student union is getting into the censorship game too.' The interview is about the decision of the student union in 1980 to ban the sale of *Playboy* and *Penthouse* magazines from the union's bookshop. For the journalist, this story is about ridiculing the decision, painting the young woman and her organisation as censors who want to gag freedom of speech.

The interviewee explains carefully, with an almost weary patience, that these magazines contain images that are 'degrading and humiliating to women', which 'treat women as just bodies'. She fervently insists that making money out of that would 'put the student union on a par with the publishers of these magazines, making a profit from the degradation of women'. She explains that it is not a campus-wide ban or censorship;

rather, a principled decision not to make a profit from selling pornography in the union's own bookshop. She confirms that the union has also written to the publishers explaining its stand.

It's the young woman's first television appearance and her first political interview. She is grappling with big ideas, trying to understand politics and how to reshape her world. She is not yet a member of the Australian Labor Party. She has no inkling that this interview will be the first of thousands nor that she will one day lead the state.

I had forgotten that this footage existed until one of the senior journalists in the press gallery came across it in the station's archives and gave it to my staff not long after I became premier. It's remarkable that it has survived in such perfect condition. In this footage, I am younger than almost all of my staff, and we all had a good laugh watching it.

In contrast to the interviewer's almost playful enjoyment of the story, this baby-faced version of me is deeply thoughtful and clearly passionate about the issue. No playfulness here, but clear eyes straight to camera, backed by a solid belief that the clarity of her arguments will persuade this interviewer and his audience. At times, when she briefly looks away to gather her thoughts, I can see her brain working, reaching for the right words, stretching for the most compelling logic. She is articulate, remarkably calm and admirably unfazed by the interviewer's questions.

As I watch, I try to remember being her. I know she is me, but I simply do not remember ever looking or being so young and fresh. Maybe as we struggle out of our teens, we are so busy searching for the adult in ourselves that we can't see the youth?

I do remember that, for her, all this serious business of new ideas was pleasurable, that taking on these causes and planning ways to get others thinking about them was as enjoyable for her as any party or rock concert. I wonder about all the paths that brought her to this earnest interview, to her hunger to change things. I also wonder if she would recognise me now if the experience could be reversed. Would I live up to her expectations? Would she find me worthy of her?

The story ends with the interviewer's jovial suggestion that the *Australian Women's Weekly* should also be banned, because its title is sexist and should be changed to the *Australian Person's Weekly*. For him, this has been just a bit of a laugh, a chance to talk about sex on TV, which in 1980 is still risqué.

From a thirty-plus-year vantage point, my first instinct is to tell the younger me to go out and have more fun, to party more and play harder, to enjoy more and worry less; to tell her that she doesn't have to be this serious when she's so young, that these carefree days will evaporate while she's not watching. But I envy her certainty and even her naiveté. I'm intrigued by the strength of her belief and her steady demeanour, knowing these characteristics will lead her to every new path she takes. I'm also struck by the fact that I like her. If she was one of my sons' friends, I'd enjoy getting to know her.

Of course, I also reflect on that decision to ban *Playboy* and *Penthouse*. You can hear, in this interview, my earnest belief that this tactic would have a good effect, that it would make people think about what these magazines, and pornography more generally, were doing to our views about women and women's views about themselves. Clearly, the ban got people talking. It got me on television talking about pornography and the degradation of women, so it was not without some of its desired effect. It is equally true that after many long, hard-learning years of making public policy, I know that bans involving human behaviour rarely work. They need to be considered with great caution lest they, perversely, make the offending behaviour even more desirable. I doubt that the ban and associated furore would have harmed *Playboy* or *Penthouse* sales in the local area. More likely, sales would have increased. Without doubt, banning smoking in a range of public places, as well as banning cigarette advertising, has helped make smoking undesirable and contributed to the continued decline in smoking over the last two decades. But I suspect it's equally true that to ban completely the sale and distribution of cigarettes would enhance their appeal, especially among young people; we would see a resurgence of interest in smoking – not to mention the emergence of a lucrative black market.

Looking back, it's easy to judge the student union's effort as clumsy, amateur and naive, as some silly sandpit politics. But I have no regret or embarrassment about having raised these issues, to have worried about them, to have tried to stop the march of pornography. I regret only that our efforts weren't more successful.

Today I am confronted by the reality that in the intervening thirty years pornography has become a bigger and bigger part of our world. At my gym, I'm assaulted by a barrage of music videos that makes the *Playboy* centrefolds of the 1980s look like greeting cards. If you wanted bondage or sadomasochism in 1980, you had to go to specialist magazines, which definitely were banned in Queensland. Now you just have to look up from your rowing machine to find a woman being bound, gagged or dragged in leather, in chains, as part of a music video. My friends who are the parents of young girls despair at the relentless sexualisation of their daughters. I have my own concerns about what these images are telling boys, like my sons, about the girls in their lives.

So when I see the young woman on the screen saying the plain truth about these magazines, knowing that it will be unpopular, knowing that the interviewer is making fun of her, knowing that she's probably on the losing side of this argument, I want to cheer her on, to tell her that thirty years on the world still needs more like her, and to keep giving it everything she's got. I remember as I watch her that when the request for this interview came none of the other young women wanted to do it, that it was this young woman, this early me, who put up her hand and took it on. As I watch her now, I realise that she has begun to pull away from the others and that she has no qualms about being out the front and leading on this issue. Here she is beginning her first assault on the wall, demanding a better and different place for young women like her in the future.

*

The chance for me to study at university arrived courtesy of another Whitlam government initiative: the abolition of university fees. This decision was designed to open the doors of tertiary education to all who had the intellectual ability, regardless of the financial circumstances of their family. As the child of a single mother, with another three siblings still finishing school, it certainly did that for me. I worked throughout my university years to supplement my income and make ends meet. But without the abolition of these fees, I could never have dreamed that university would be within my grasp. It was a momentous decision by a bold and brave government. While fees have since been reintroduced, they have never again been the upfront financial barrier to entry they once were.

I arrived at the University of Queensland to begin a Bachelor of Arts in 1978. Without a firm sense of where I wanted to head beyond university, I chose a general degree in which I could explore new paths. I loved reading and enrolled in English literature. I was also interested in social work. By enrolling in the required first-year subjects for that degree, I could switch from Arts at the end of the year if I wanted to pursue it further. In the end, I graduated with an Arts degree with majors in English, psychology and sociology.

These days, arts degrees are too often spurned for a perceived lack of career options. But it was the greatest intellectual experience of my life. It tested and challenged my still-forming mind and put a powerful set of tools for thinking into my hands. And most wonderfully of all, it set alight a lifelong love of books, of stories and language and poetry. Wherever my life has taken me, a book has been my most loyal and constant companion, words and language my inspiration and comfort. When I accepted an honorary doctorate from the University of Queensland in 2010, it was this world of literature and learning that I acknowledged as the university's most enduring gift to me.

It seems unlikely now, but during my first months on campus, I was achingly homesick and lonely. I had arrived in Brisbane excited to be starting my university studies, but without friends or family in the city. There were only three other students from Miami State High who headed to the University of Queensland that year. I knew none of them well. None lived at my college, and all of them were studying medicine or science. On a campus of more than 20,000 students, they were needles in a haystack.

Despite having lived away from home in Nowra for much of the previous year, I felt quite alone and was very grateful for the camaraderie I experienced at Women's College, a residential college for female students located on the University of Queensland campus. It was set up in 1914 by bold and pioneering women who saw the need for a safe and nurturing place for women students as they began to enrol at university in the early years of the twentieth century. Here, I met girls from all over Queensland, most of them from much further afield than myself. College gave me ready friends, many of them girls with a long history of boarding school who knew how to endure months of absence from home and old friends. I quickly became part of college life and made friends with whom I could study, walk to lectures and explore the campus and the wider city.

College was like any other institution in its rules and routines. Dinner started at 5.30 pm sharp every evening, and at first I was stunned to see girls lining up at the dining room doors soon after 5 pm. To my surprise, it wasn't long before the other first-years and I joined them as our stomachs adapted to early meals. College doors were locked at midnight and our rooms were protected by security bars. We soon found that it was difficult, but possible, to squeeze through these bars if absolutely necessary. But it was such a tight fit that we avoided missing curfew whenever possible lest we become stuck between the bars. On more than one occasion, one or other of us had to wake our neighbours to help pull us through the bars from the inside. There were plenty of girls attending the same classes as me, and we studied together in our rooms, swapped lecture notes and shared textbooks. For all of us, college was a further step away from the restrictions of our families and a step closer to adult independence. We talked late into the night and we swapped dresses, make-up, life stories and confidences. We danced and sang to Carly Simon's 'You're So Vain' and Fleetwood Mac's *Rumours* as we dressed for parties, laughing at lyrics that are now forever etched in my memory.

But in those early months, I was often drawn back to the Gold Coast, to the beach and the surf and my old friends. In Brisbane, my first city, I was reinventing myself, casting off some of my small-town-girl identity. In that first year, the effort of it would send me back to the easy comforts of home. Almost every weekend, I returned to my mother's home cooking and the lively fun and affection of my brothers and sister. I returned to my friends from high school, our Saturday night parties and underage adventures to the Paradise Room disco of the Surfers Paradise Hotel. But more than this, I returned to fit easily into the Gold Coast. Here, my shorts and homemade sundresses, like my surf-culture language, were right at home. Here, the boys with their matted salt-bleached hair and the girls with beads, surf mats and Indian sandals were as familiar to me as my own fingertips. But month by month, week by week, I sought it less.

My life gradually began to pull away from the beach, and the old familiar ways became less so as my school friends got jobs, moved out of home and began to change their lives too.

A friend of my mum had a son, Richard, who was older than me and also a student at the University of Queensland. Richard had an old car he drove back and forth to Southport most weekends. When I say Richard had an old car, it is better described as a vehicle that should not have been on the road. The entire floor of the passenger side had rusted away, requiring me to travel the whole hour and a half to Brisbane with my feet on the dashboard. Even so, I hitched a ride with him as often as I could. Richard and I hadn't known each other well before I headed off to university, but I got to know him better when he began dating one of my college friends. Our car trips cemented a friendship.

*

It was with Richard that I first headed off to a political demonstration in October 1978. It was a protest against the state government's prohibition on the right to assemble and the right to march. This protest had been brewing for some time and was set to be the biggest show in town. It loomed as an act of mass civil disobedience, with many ordinarily law-abiding citizens expected to break the laws to bring attention to their draconian nature.

Some background is important here. The conservative Country (later National) Party government that led Queensland had been elected in 1957, three years before I was born, and in

1978 had now been in power for two decades. Sir Johannes 'Joh' Bjelke-Petersen was the premier and the most controversial Australian politician of his time. His government preserved its power by way of a gerrymander, an electoral system that assigned a higher value to rural votes than those cast by city-based citizens. This gerrymander meant that despite consistently securing fewer votes than either of the Liberal or Labor parties, Joh's National Party stayed in power. Ironically, it was an earlier Queensland Labor government that had first introduced a gerrymandered electoral system, but the Queensland Nationals under Joh took it to a previously unknown extreme. A government that is shored up by a system of electoral malapportionment is a government that soon comes to believe it cannot lose power. And that makes it dangerous.

Bjelke-Petersen ruled Queensland with an iron fist. He was stubborn, obdurate and pugilistic. He was a strong and aggressive leader with deeply held religious beliefs and entrenched conservative convictions. He had a flair for capturing media attention and a personal style that was easily mocked, often misusing words and mixing metaphors. He was an object of ridicule and was called names including 'hillbilly dictator' and 'Bible-bashing bastard'. As his government's decisions sparked dissent and protest, Joh cracked down on the public with a heavy law-and-order response. He banned political demonstrations and protests and gave the police unprecedented powers to overwhelm dissent. Nationally, Queensland became known as the 'police state' in recognition of its unhealthy focus on law and order, and was often referred to as the 'deep North' in a direct reference to the political backwaters of America's 'deep South'. Joh was oblivious to all criticism. He held power with a corrupt electoral system and didn't need to worry too much about responding to his critics. Indeed, he became adept at avoiding answering questions. When press conferences became difficult and he found himself facing awkward questions about the government's poor handling of an issue or yet another government scandal, he would famously decree 'Don't you worry about that!' and the press conference would be over.

Neither Richard nor I were political activists. We thought the government an embarrassment and these laws unnecessary and undemocratic, but neither of us was strongly motivated by political principle. We were curious, and like many others we headed into the city to watch the spectacle of it.

When we arrived in King George Square in the heart of the city, the police were out in extreme force, amassed in line after line of uniformed might. They were equipped with batons and riot gear and had clearly been told to use whatever force was necessary to push the crowd back. This was not a crowd of professional agitators. This was not a crowd that was armed or dangerous. Here were grandparents and lawyers, nuns and clergy, mums and dads, office workers and tradesmen.

Before this day, I'd seen individuals scream and yell at each other. I'd seen boys at school have a fistfight. But until this moment I had never seen a large-scale clash of the powerful and the powerless. Up close, it was terrifying. Police used their batons and shields relentlessly. They arrested hundreds of people, literally dragging them into police paddy wagons. As waves of people tried to walk from the city square onto the streets, they were pushed back with brutal force and fell to the ground with torn clothes and bloodied faces. I did not march but huddled scared on the steps and watched in disbelief. I don't know what I had expected, but nothing had prepared me for the violence and repression I saw from the Queensland Police Force that day. It was an abuse of power on a grand scale that frightened and horrified me.

I left with the conviction that what I had seen was deeply wrong. The unnecessary use of police brutality had shocked me into understanding that something deeply troubling and undemocratic was happening in my community. It was clear that despite the pronouncements of Premier Joh to the contrary, there was in fact a great deal to worry about in my home state. With their overzealous efforts to quell the anti-government protestors that day, the Queensland police had inadvertently recruited another foot soldier to the opposition cause.

When you are young, you are a world unto yourself. Absorbed by the adventure of becoming your own person, you can find it easy to not see what's going on around you. But as I began to take more notice of politics, I became increasingly incensed by what I saw. Allegations of cronyism and corrupt land dealings were rife, the abuse of executive power was commonplace, sex education in schools was banned, evidence of police corruption mounted as prostitution, liquor licensing and gambling laws were openly flouted, a 'Special Branch' of the Queensland Police Force was created to maintain secret files on government opponents and Queensland slid from scandal to scandal. I began to understand more fully why the rest of Australia regarded my home state as a backwater, a place run by roughshod political cowboys and something of a national joke.

*

As I made my way into my second year as a university student, the government decided to change the law regulating abortion in Queensland. The criminal code already prohibited medical termination of pregnancy, but the Supreme Court had ruled that in certain medical circumstances these procedures were legal. The court ruling effectively viewed abortion as a decision relating to the health of the mother and a decision to be resolved by a woman and her doctor. It allowed abortions to be performed but left doctors and health professionals in a precarious legal position. Nevertheless, it was a law that was consistent with most other Australian jurisdictions and represented a manageable truce between the passionate opposing forces on the issue.

In 1979, Ed Casey, the leader of the Labor Party in Queensland and a devout Catholic, tabled a petition in state parliament demanding the closure of a clinic where abortions were known to be performed. Not to be outflanked on the right by the Labor Party on this issue, Bjelke-Petersen had new abortion laws drafted. These new draft laws were the most draconian possible, prohibiting abortion in any circumstance, including when the pregnancy resulted from rape or incest, and providing for the criminal prosecution of doctors who so much as referred a woman to an abortion clinic.

The draft laws caused an outcry, with the medical profession and the broader community uniting against them. One of Bjelke-Petersen's own government members, Liberal MP Rosemary Kyburz, described the laws as 'the most frightening piece of fascist legislation I have ever seen in my life' (*Courier-Mail*,

17 April 1980, p 3). She set about organising opposition to the legislation within the government itself.

These draft laws galvanised me, along with thousands of other young women, into action. I well knew the teachings of the Catholic Church on abortion, and I knew just how fervently many people opposed this issue. I had once felt this fervent opposition myself. But as I got older, the messiness of real life complicated the issue for me. Like many others, I knew young women who had found themselves pregnant as teenagers and had made the agonising decision to terminate the pregnancy. I felt passionately that no good could come from criminalising and jailing these young women, their boyfriends or their doctors. I started turning up to meetings on campus to organise action against the draft laws. I had chosen the most contentious of all issues on which to cut my political teeth.

There are few issues that divide people as strongly as abortion and few which cut across other allegiances as it can. The draft laws not only divided the government, they divided the Labor Party along religious lines and divided many families and friends too. As I slipped quietly into those first political meetings, I also found division about how opposition to the laws should be organised, how radical it should be and whether it should involve street marches, which were themselves illegal in Queensland. The arguments were vociferous, fiery and intriguing, and I was spellbound by the fervour of it all.

As powerfully as the proposed changes to abortion law divided people, they also unified people, bringing together the most disparate of activists, from the zealots to the clear-minded, experienced activists to the new recruits. Among them were grandparents, librarians, academics, students, trade unionists and politicians from all parties. These men and women all coalesced around the right of women to control their fertility and stood together to oppose the attempts by our deeply conservative government to expunge this right.

For the first time, I was part of something much bigger than myself and felt the power of it. I was stirred and lifted by every meeting I attended. I found myself putting up my hand as the arguments were resolved and the tasks delegated, relishing the chance to make signs, put up posters and hand out leaflets.

I was alive with a burning sense of injustice and full of the kind of fierce conviction that is peculiar to the young. It fired me with an almost evangelical sense of higher purpose. I met others who shared my passion, who asked the same questions. These angry, smart, articulate people quickly became my new friends. Gone was the fearful teenager hanging back from the fray. This time I was in the crowd as we marched together against the government, as we rallied outside Parliament House and as we kept a vigil in front of the police watch house for those who had been arrested. Exhilaration and fear fuelled me in equal parts as we chanted slogans and did our best to evade the police. No doubt there was some youthful daredevil spirit to my activity, but something more drove me. I felt my life grow bigger as I fought alongside others for something important, something that mattered. I was proud to be making a stand.

Attracting the attention of government and changing its mind takes a lot of hard work. Large protests are part of that effort, demonstrating the strength of feeling in the community. But they are not enough. Letters and petitions were organised, groups of prominent women sought meetings with members of parliament, doctors' groups held media conferences and political parties felt the heat internally as their own members began to complain at local meetings. It was a concerted effort, bringing the pressure of people power to bear on the government.

After a campaign lasting almost a year, the government lost the vote on the legislation when nineteen government members crossed the floor to vote against it. It was a remarkable result and one of the rare moments in his two decades as premier when Bjelke-Petersen had not prevailed. I felt a real sense of power when we won the battle. Through the combined forces of purpose, passion and protest, we had broken through a once-impenetrable wall. With this campaign, I became a political activist, determined to oppose a government I believed to be corrupt, backward and undemocratic.

*

After the campaign against the abortion laws, I became immersed in the activities of the women's rights office of the student union. The women's movement was making its mark around the world, and here I began to actively explore feminism. I read and learned and challenged myself. I joined campaigns to oppose sexual harassment on campus, to provide better lighting to make it safer for women after night lectures, to inform young women about contraception and toxic shock syndrome and, yes, to limit the sale of pornography on campus. I met strong, smart women, both academics and students, who questioned and rejected the limited stereotypes of who they could be and chafed against the constraints on their lives as women. They were inspiring and confronting, and they challenged me to see myself differently. We talked and debated and argued. Friendships formed and friendships failed, but we encouraged each other to take up opportunities, to put ourselves forward and take a chance.

The women's rights office was part of the university student union, and through it I learned how I could play a part in the broader activities of the union. I met people such as Anne Warner, an experienced and passionate political activist who would go on to become a member of the Queensland parliament, a member of the first Labor government in more than thirty years, and the first woman in a Queensland Labor cabinet in the party's history. When I met Anne, she was part of the leadership team of the student union executive. Older than most of us by at least ten years, she was married, had three children and had been involved in politics in England prior to migrating to Australia with her family. She stood out as influential and charismatic. We became firm friends and I learned much from watching and listening to her as she became a formidable force in Queensland politics. Anne loved nothing more than analysing a problem and plotting a campaign. She was an active member of the Labor Party and a seasoned campaigner in the ongoing battle against the excesses of the Bjelke-Petersen government. She was an adult with real-life experiences, but completely different from our parents. Anne taught me the value of building alliances as I watched her work with a cross-section of people both on and off campus. Along with others, she built a coalition of people and organisations that would work to secure real change in Queensland and, importantly, within the Labor Party. While she had all the courage needed for the fight, never fearful of being arrested or taking on a new campaign, it was Anne who most often counselled the younger hotheads among us, including myself, on when to pull back or make a tactical retreat.

With Anne's encouragement, I joined the student union council and, a year later, its executive. I met students involved in broader groups both on and off campus, students involved in political parties and social movements to protect the environment or enhance civil liberties. I learned the basics of debate and the responsibilities that come with these elected roles. In the 1980s, student unions were alive with political debate and activity. However, unlike today, they also provided student services such as subsidised cafeterias, bookshops, sporting clubs and health clinics. They provided representation for students in appeals against academic or disciplinary decisions and a student voice on the governing bodies of the university, including faculty committees. On the student union executive, we spent as much time trying to keep the meals in the union cafeteria affordable and the equipment in our sports clubs serviceable as we did on ideological debates and tactical disagreements. I loved being right in the thick of it.

In 1982, my friends on the executive encouraged me to lead a team and run for the position of president of the University of Queensland student union. Having recently graduated, I had enrolled in a couple of additional subjects while I began the search for a job. I had one foot on campus and one foot in the world beyond. As I wrote job applications and looked for full-time employment, I had begun to see myself outside the confines of campus life. But the prospect of actually running the organisation that had been so much a part of my life in those important final years of university was tempting.

The elected candidate would take up the position the following year, 1983. This would be a state election year and the student union would be a strong focus of activity. Up to that point, I had been one of a team of students all playing our part. Now that team was asking me to be their captain. They saw something in me that I hadn't seen in myself, something that gave them confidence in seeking me out to lead the team. I was flattered, of course, but I felt too the itch of excitement about taking it on. The prospect of electoral politics proved irresistible.

My opponent was Fleur Kingham, and it was the first time two women had contested the race. The winner would be the first woman president in the history of the student union, a possibility which had added to my excitement about taking on the challenge. Fleur and I were both progressive, left-of-centre candidates. Members of both our teams would later end up active members of the Labor Party and in my cabinet as premier. Fleur and I kept each other busy, giving speeches, writing pamphlets and visiting lecture theatres around the campus. I ran the Education Action Team and Fleur led the Student Interest Team. Our teams slogged it out daily, making full use of every corny play on the acronyms EAT and SIT.

Fleur won the election decisively. She was a formidable opponent who has gone on to a distinguished legal career and is now a judge of the District and Children's Courts of Queensland.

Losing that election was a hard and painful experience. I was very young and the loss felt so raw and public. I felt burnt, naked and exposed by it. The brutal, winner-takes-all truth of politics came home to me with shocking force. But it was a big life experience and soon delivered some other powerful lessons. In a matter of weeks I realised that the loss was behind me, that the people I loved still loved me, that I had survived intact and was respected for having had a go. There's nothing good about losing – it's always an awful experience – but knowing what it feels like is a great motivator, and knowing you can survive it is a valuable lesson. It's not possible to get on the field and play to win unless you have a healthy fear of losing. But if that fear is crippling, you can't take the risks necessary to play a winning game. Facing this loss helped me to put that fear of failure in its place, and I've come to realise that it was a valuable early foundation in building the kind of resilience I would need to push through some much more daunting walls later in my life.

*

As much as our opposition to the Bjelke-Petersen government united my university friends, the Labor Party was not the obvious vehicle for many of us to channel that opposition into. The Queensland branch of the ALP was in a parlous state by the late 1970s. It had remained stubbornly untouched by much of the modernisation that had spurred the Whitlam government to victory in 1972. It was intransigently male, blue-collar and determined to keep its doors closed to younger members, students, women and those who wanted to seriously take on the conservatives. It lacked electoral appeal and seemed punch-drunk from endless losing battles with a corrupt and cocksure government. There was little about it to attract fiery and impatient young women like myself.

But change was brewing within its ranks. A broad group of Labor Party members had started to meet and call for reform. Among them was Peter Beattie, who would later become premier and in whose cabinet I would serve. But there also were many of the people I had met through my university activities. People like Anne Warner, Cath Rafferty, Di Fingleton, Tim Quinn, Alice Cavanagh, Hamish Linacre, Norma and Lindsay Jones, Senator George Georges and Bill Hayden, who was then leader of the federal Labor opposition. The federal Labor Party had felt the Queensland branch as lead in its saddlebags during every federal election. The reform group was fuelled by the belief that if the Bjelke-Petersen government were to ever be defeated, it would require a new and different Labor Party.

I was neither part of this group nor a member of the Labor Party at the time. But I was intrigued by the internal battle and I shared the reform group's aspirations for a viable and electable alternative to the conservative rule of Bjelke-Petersen. In 1981, their work culminated with the ALP federal executive's intervention into the Queensland branch. The federal executive effectively took charge of the branch and its finances, using its powers to appoint new senior party officers and change the rules of the Queensland branch to alter its operations and open it up to new people and new ideas. Federal intervention changed everything. It changed the leadership of the Queensland Labor Party, it changed the rules and it changed the culture. Suddenly, it seemed like an organisation that might really make a difference. People from all walks of life began to swell its ranks.

*

Having graduated from the University of Queensland, I was thriving as a childcare worker at Women's House, a refuge for women escaping domestic violence. Women's refuges had emerged across Australia as the women's movement gave voice to issues that had previously been hidden behind the doors of the family home. These refuges gave women safe shelter for themselves and their children, while they regrouped and began the long slow process of changing their lives. They played an important part in giving women the choice to leave violent relationships, but they were not glamorous or easy places to live. With five or six women accommodated at any one time, there could be up to twenty children, ranging from babies to teenagers, living at the refuge. These women and their children usually escaped their homes quickly, bringing little with them and leaving behind what little security they had. Their lives were uprooted overnight, separating them from friends, neighbours, local schools, churches and services.

My job was to help women enrol their children in the local school, find new school uniforms, obtain medical care for the children when needed and, importantly, run activities and excursions to keep the kids busy and everybody else sane. Women's House was run by a deeply committed group of women who were not only providing a service, but also challenging the status quo. Our refuge, by its very existence, asserted a woman's right to leave a violent relationship. We lobbied for changes to the law and changes to police practice, we collected data and talked loudly and openly about the extent of the problem. We were breaking the silence that protected the men who had beaten their wives with impunity for years.

At Women's House, I felt a keen sense of purpose. I loved working with the children and among passionate colleagues. I could see the difference we were making in the lives of the mothers. But I missed the broader political activity and camaraderie I had been part of on campus. As a childcare worker, I saw firsthand the consequences of the Bjelke-Petersen government's failures in social policy and social services. I was more convinced than ever that Queensland needed a new government.

In 1982 I joined the Labor Party, for the first time seeing it as a vehicle for progressive social change and as an organisation in which I would be welcome and could work with others of a like mind. It was a decision that I had grappled with for several years, unsure that the Labor Party wanted to be a force for change. Now, the decision came easily. I could see the party changing and I wanted to be a part of the new agenda. Queensland Labor now wanted to be an electoral force to be reckoned with. It had begun to actively recruit inspiring candidates cut from a different cloth to those of the past. People like Anne Warner, Wayne Goss, Dennis Murphy, Paul Braddy and David Hamill, younger, educated, progressive and hungry for change, were being sought as Labor candidates. Peter Beattie was now the party's state secretary and along with others in the party office was building a team that could take on Bjelke-Petersen and the

Nationals and win. The decision gave me a political home, a network of friends who shared my values and my passions, a place to learn and grow, a tribe. It was a decision motivated by the chance to shape the new Labor Party in Queensland. It was a decision that ultimately shaped me and my life, in every possible way.

FOUR

Boarding the Train

My early Labor Party branch meetings were full of intrigue. They had a formal and an informal agenda, and the latter was much more interesting. As our councillor concluded his report and the meeting formalities drew to a close, the intrigue began. Many of those present were banding together to help my friend Anne Warner get preselected for the local state seat in the lead-up to the 1983 election. We drew into a small circle and discussed where the support might come from, and where the opposition was likely to arise. These preselections would occur under the new rules of the party, which were designed to give a wider group of candidates a fair go. In Anne's case they worked. She won the preselection and went on to win the seat.

Anne wrested the seat from the sitting Liberal Attorney-General of Queensland, a remarkable feat given the political circumstances of Queensland in the early 1980s. Female, Anglo-Indian and left wing, Anne was everything that, according to conventional Labor Party wisdom, was electorally unappealing. Her victory against all the odds was a vindication of the changes that had swept through the Queensland Labor Party in the preceding years. It was also an inspiration for those, like me, who had watched her overcome her own hesitation to bravely put up her hand and dare to take on a public position. In Anne's decision to stand and her tenacious campaign to win, I saw leadership and ambition firsthand and up close. It required such grit and personal determination on her part, but it made everyone around her see new possibilities. Anne's journey was instructive and it would remain with me as a powerful lesson when my own mind turned to a parliamentary career some years later.

In my early twenties, however, I had no such thoughts. Instead, looking for adventure, I headed for the bright lights of Sydney in 1984. During a brief stint of work at a childcare centre at the University of Sydney, I met John Faulkner, whose children attended the centre. At that time John was the Assistant General Secretary of the New South Wales branch of the ALP, and he wasted no time in signing me up to a local branch. John would later serve as a senator and a minister in the Keating and Rudd governments.

Then, in 1985, I began work in a new support program for young families living in Redfern's high-rise housing commission apartments. It was a program funded by the New South Wales Labor government that would provide support, counselling, playgroups and home visits for some very isolated and vulnerable single parents, mostly young mums. We were starting from scratch, and my first responsibility was to find premises. In the always crowded real estate market of inner Sydney, this was no easy task. After combing the area, I eventually sought a meeting with the South West Inner Sydney Housing Co-operative, a local social housing organisation, hoping they might know of something suitable.

I met with the coordinator, Greg Withers, on 29 May 1985. It was no ordinary work meeting. Greg's workplace had a tradition of monthly staff lunches, with a different staff member charged with its preparation each month. May 1985 found Greg on cooking roster, so we met in the large kitchen of the old church on Regent Street that housed the co-op. Greg and I talked and talked as he busied himself making fresh pesto for a large meal of pasta and salad. By the end of the meeting he had asked me on a date to a Leonard Cohen concert.

At the time, Leonard Cohen seemed to be nearing the end of his music career. His powerful lyrics resonated with all the power they have always held, but he seemed almost bored to find himself singing in the Sydney Entertainment Centre. But no amount of boredom on Leonard's part could dampen what was happening between Greg and me that night as we began the awkward business of getting to know each other. We liked what we found, although Greg was appalled by my taste for pop music and I was dismayed to learn of his fervour for Frank Zappa.

Some might say that a Leonard Cohen concert is an inauspicious start to a love affair, but as it turns out the songs of this remarkable poet are one of the few places where Greg's and my musical tastes intersect. Thankfully our minds and hearts intersected on many other fronts.

Politics in Queensland had continued to deteriorate while I had been travelling and working in Sydney. I continued to maintain my close friendships there and was involved in many Sydney events to raise funds in support of political causes at home. Increasingly, I felt the pull of the north as friends and fellow Labor Party members continued to oppose the excesses of the Bjelke-Petersen government. Having sought the big city lights, I had become homesick for friends, for my family and Queensland, and in late 1986 I left Sydney for a job with the federal Education Union in Brisbane.

While we were weighing up whether Greg would move to Brisbane or I would return to Sydney, I discovered I was pregnant. It was a welcome, but unexpected and unplanned, development. I was absolutely certain that I was going ahead with my pregnancy and keeping my baby. Happily, Greg was equally certain. My pregnancy settled all our questions. Greg found a job in Brisbane and headed north.

When Greg arrived, I was five months pregnant and loving it. I was entranced by the powerful changes happening in my body and looked forward to meeting this growing child. But we had never lived together, and four short months later we were parents. It was a time of miracles and wonder as we became new parents and marvelled at the beautiful boy who had joined our lives. But it was also a time of exhaustion, quarrelling and doubts. Following a short period of separation, when all the pressures of Greg's move and new parenthood collapsed around us, we resolved the doubts. These were happy and hard times navigating early parenthood, new friends and a new way of being together in a new place.

*

Ten days after Greg moved to Brisbane, politics in Queensland lurched in a new direction. On 11 May 1987 the ABC's *Four*

Corners program aired the results of a major investigation into prostitution and police corruption in Queensland. The allegations were explosive and the government was under extreme pressure to respond. In a serendipitous twist, Joh Bjelke-Petersen was out of the country when the ABC program aired. His deputy, Bill Gunn, felt the public pressure and in his capacity as acting premier announced a Commission of Inquiry into police corruption in Queensland.

The Fitzgerald Inquiry quickly got into full swing. As I began to swell with pregnancy, the commission began documenting extensive police and political corruption. Former colleagues gave evidence against each other. The nation watched aghast as everything that had been suspected of Bjelke-Petersen and his crooked regime was proven true. Though I had spent much of my life fighting against this government, even I was appalled by the extent of the corruption and its deep systemic roots, which tapped into almost every corner of government and public life. The public heard a litany of stories about 'bagmen' overseeing a well-established system of bribes, of the abuse of political power and the use of the police service to spy on citizens.

It became clear that many within the National Party had known about the corruption, which had flourished in part thanks to a lack of parliamentary accountability and a supine media that turned a blind eye.

In late November 1987, I lay in a hospital bed, exhausted but beaming with happiness, having just given birth to our first son. News began to filter through that Bjelke-Petersen was in real trouble. His party had mutinied, demanding his resignation. In typical Joh style, he responded by demanding the resignation of five of his ministers. Each visitor who came to see our new baby brought fresh stories of disintegration in government ranks, and talk of the premier resigning gained momentum.

Joh Bjelke-Petersen had led the state for almost twenty years. It seemed impossible that it might all be really coming to an end. But within a week of the birth of our son, Bjelke-Petersen had resigned from the premiership and from the parliament.

With the departure of Joh from the political stage, Greg and I happily named our boy Joseph, confident that the abbreviation 'Joe' would never be a problem for him.

The inquiry spent almost two years uncovering systematic corruption in the police service that reached all the way to the police commissioner, Terry Lewis. It finally issued its report in July 1989, documenting a litany of crimes and the deep corruption of public administration.

Terry Lewis, along with other senior officers, was charged and jailed. Joh Bjelke-Petersen was charged with perjury, but narrowly escaped a conviction. Not so three of his ministers, who spent time in prison for misusing public funds.

As the charges and prosecutions proceeded against senior police and political figures, the momentum for a change of government gathered pace.

Greg and I spent the first years of Joseph's life working together in a renewed and enlivened Labor Party. We could all feel the strong possibility of a change of government and we lifted our activism. Joseph's first outing was to a Labor Party branch meeting. As I became more active, I took on more responsibilities, becoming branch president, joining the state council and running fundraising activities. I flipped burgers, wrote leaflets, chaired meetings and sold raffle tickets with a toddler in a backpack.

In early December 1989, just a few months after the Fitzgerald Inquiry handed down its report, the hopes of many were fulfilled with the election of a Labor government led by Wayne Goss. An intellectually powerful and energetic young lawyer, Wayne Goss became the first Labor premier of Queensland in thirty-two years.

For those, like me, who had spent so long working for change, it was almost impossible to believe. After a long, hot day, Greg and I joined other tired booth workers from the southern electorates of Brisbane at the Wellers Hill Bowls Club, grateful for a cold beer and hopeful of victory. Soon, hundreds of people were squeezing in the door, all wanting to celebrate and be a part of this extraordinary moment in history. After years of electoral defeat, many of us had steeled ourselves for another loss. But this time Wayne Goss and his team had won a decisive victory despite the gerrymandered electoral system. The Wellers Hill Bowls Club had never seen a crowd like it. A swarm of people spilled out of the doors and across the manicured greens.

After giving his victory speech at the tally room, Wayne, his wife, Roisin, and senior party officials headed straight to the bowls club to celebrate. Wayne was greeted as a hero, and was swamped by ecstatic party members and supporters. As he autographed posters and T-shirts, none of us could wipe the grins from our faces. There was quite a repair bill for the damage done to the bowling greens by so many feet, but it was a bill we were happy to pay.

At that moment we understood that a venal, hide-bound and repressive government was behind us. Before us stood the chance to modernise and transform our state, to challenge the narrowing stereotypes that had defined us and to carve out a new place for ourselves on the national stage. In every sphere of activity the agenda seemed huge and limitless and the mood was youthful and full of a joyful optimism. Everything seemed possible.

The enduring political mission of my twenties had been realised. Soon I would be turning thirty, and ahead lay the new challenge of a different kind of activism, a real opportunity to make a difference. I was soon to learn that if winning government is one long, hard battle, the task of holding it and doing something worthwhile with it is another battle entirely.

*

A change of government after thirty years is momentous. It sets off shifts in every direction, it reorients the social, economic and cultural compass. In Queensland it brought an overwhelming sense of transformation. The new premier could not have been in sharper contrast to Joh Bjelke-Petersen. Joh had been seventy-six when he left office; Wayne was thirty-eight when he assumed office. A long-distance runner, Wayne brought a youthful energy to the leadership that most Queenslanders had never seen. Well educated, intelligent and articulate, with a deep commitment to human rights, he was everything that Joh was not.

With Wayne Goss at the helm, overnight Queensland began to look and feel different. He set about implementing the recommendations of the Fitzgerald Report, establishing the architecture to prevent corruption from ever again flourishing in Queensland. New, fair electoral boundaries were set and the Criminal Justice Commission was established as a watchdog over both parliamentarians and the public sector. Wayne quickly turned to the business of bringing public administration in Queensland into line with other states, modernising the police force, introducing a merit appointment process, delivering anti-discrimination and equal opportunity laws, decriminalising homosexuality and abolishing the Special Branch. They were heady days of reform and it was impossible not to feel the liberating tempo of the new government.

In the first year of the Goss government I watched the activity from the sidelines while I worked as a trainer on a year-long project funded by Mitsubishi-BHP (as BHP was then known) with the Trade Union Training Authority (TUTA). Long since abolished, TUTA was established by the Whitlam government to ensure that workers and their unions had the basic skills and training in the industrial relations system required to negotiate with well-funded employers on wages and workplace improvements.

The job was tough and it stretched and pushed me. My work took me to every BHP coal mine in Queensland and into the heart of Queensland's largest industry. It took me underground with coalminers, into the canteens of the single men's quarters and into large meetings of dirty miners as they came off their shifts and followed their union's directive to participate in the training sessions. It kept me waiting at rail crossings while coal trains two kilometres long snaked their way across the dry country to port. It took me down long highways to the hot, small towns of central Queensland, into the homes of local union leaders and Labor Party members and supporters, and the languid front bars of country pubs. For all its challenges, that job remains one of the big lessons of my life, one that opened the eyes of a Gold Coast girl to a much bigger Queensland and laid the foundations for my understanding of regional Queensland, so crucial for a Queensland premier.

Meanwhile, the government was continuing its reform push. Like most other governments of the time, the Goss government established a Women's Policy Unit (within the Department of Premier and Cabinet) to guide and implement policy and programs to address discrimination against women.

As the TUTA contract came to an end, I applied for a position with this unit and began work there in 1991. It was my first experience working as a public servant. Learning the ropes from within the Premier's Department gave me the chance to experience government from the centre, to see and understand all the arteries as they radiated out from the heart. Talented and experienced public-sector reformers were recruited from around Australia, drawn by the challenge of reforming Queensland.

My boss was 34-year-old Kevin Rudd, who was Director-General of the Cabinet Office. Previously, Kevin had been Chief of Staff to Wayne Goss. He had left a very promising career in Australia's foreign service to take up the position, and was a capable and talented public servant who was driven by the same reforming determination as Wayne. Like so many others, Kevin had grown up in the Queensland of the Bjelke-Petersen years and relished the chance to play his part in cleaning up the state and dragging it into modern Australia. He was impatient to make a difference and drove an ambitious agenda, expecting his team to put in the long hours needed to get things done. Kevin was widely respected for his intelligence and awesome capacity for ploughing through volumes of material. He had a big reputation and was intimidating because of it.

Kevin and I first came face to face when I had to brief him about a tricky policy issue in the drafting of Queensland's first anti-discrimination legislation. Some recent cases of women being asked to leave premises because they were breastfeeding babies had highlighted the discrimination many women still experienced in connection with this most primal of activities. There was no doubt in the government's mind that it wanted the new laws to protect women in these circumstances. The question was how best to do that. Legal purists held the view that breastfeeding arises from a woman's gender and any discrimination because of it would be amply protected by the inclusion of gender as a grounds of discrimination in the draft bill. Women's groups and breastfeeding proponents, however, wanted breastfeeding expressly included as a specific ground of discrimination in the bill. Of such split hairs is the daily business of government made.

Kevin was finishing a phone call when I was called into his office. In my mind I was nervously going through the legal points and political imperatives in preparation for his likely questions when Kevin abruptly finished the call and looked straight at me. He leaned forward. 'So this argument is all about women having breasts and men not having them, is that right?' he said.

I was startled to hear my fearsome director-general put things so bluntly, but he had quickly got to the nub of the problem. I told him it was more about politics than breasts, that in my view if the government intended to protect women from discrimination when they breastfed their children then it was best to be explicit about it, even if the lawyers were right and the additional clause was superfluous. 'Better to be superfluous than leave doubt about something that people feel this strongly about,' I told him.

He agreed with me, and breastfeeding is today an explicit ground of discrimination in Queensland law. Years later, when Kevin was prime minister of Australia and I was premier of Queensland, we would laugh at the memorable first conversation of our friendship.

The years I spent working in Queensland's public sector, in the women's policy unit and later in the Enterprise Bargaining Unit of the Department of Industrial Relations, were years of enormous and accelerated learning for me. The experience gave me the chance to work with some extraordinarily talented people. Carolyn Mason was the Women's Advisor to Wayne Goss and headed up the Women's Policy Unit. She had come from a strong career in the Commonwealth public sector and was a terrific manager. Most importantly, Carolyn knew how to make things happen in government, a skill that is seriously underrated. Government is a huge and complicated behemoth and having the right navigational skills is the key to making it work. I have seen some very capable people struggle with it. People who come into government departments from the corporate world often find it hard to translate their skills.

Similarly, new ministers often flounder in the absence of navigation.

On the other hand, it is unusual for people who have middle or senior level bureaucratic experience to make the jump into politics; they are vastly different career paths and they rarely cross over. As I began to make my way up through the ranks of the public service, I would face this choice myself. Watching and learning from experts like Kevin and Carolyn proved a great building block in my early years as a minister.

*

One of those who joined Goss in his reforming efforts was my old friend from university days, Anne Warner. Anne had been elected to state parliament in 1983 and became the first woman to sit in a Labor cabinet in Queensland when the new government took office in 1989. In opposition she had been a loud and passionate voice on civil liberties, government corruption, human rights and the welfare of women and children. In government she became Minister for Family Services and Aboriginal and Torres Strait Islander Affairs and led the charge on social policy reform throughout the Goss years. Anne's two terms in the cabinet were tough ones, as they were for everyone around the cabinet table. They had come into government full of zeal and determination and with the party's and public's highest hopes pinned to them. However, the Labor Party had not been in government for thirty-two years and there were precious few in any part of the organisation who remembered being in power, let alone had any experience of it.

And government is hard. For all that politics is about lofty ideals and big visions, the daily experience of it demands grinding patience and discipline. After three decades on the sidelines, the Labor Party had precious little patience and no appetite for discipline. We wanted it all and we wanted it now.

So after six years in opposition and six years in government, Anne Warner decided to retire when the 1995 election loomed. She had been mulling over her future for a year before she made the decision, but it still took many by surprise, including me. This was despite Anne's encouraging me to think about standing for her seat whenever she did retire. A retiring member doesn't always have an influence on who will replace her, but as a respected minister Anne had influence and was ready to use it on my behalf to secure local and central support.

Faced with the sudden reality, it was I who was reluctant. Opportunity was knocking at the most inopportune time. Greg and I had had a second son, Oliver, less than eighteen months earlier. I had only been back at work full-time for six months and, for all of us, juggling two small children and two jobs felt like plenty on our plate. I didn't feel ready and I didn't feel like my family was ready. I urged those who were spurring me on to consider me for another electorate at the election after next when Oliver would be in school. But Anne urged me to make a decision. 'This train is at your station with the doors open,' she said. 'It will only stop at your station once. Voters permitting, the next person who wins this seat will stay in it for twelve years or more. This is where you live, where your son goes to school, where you have all your political support and connections.' She encouraged me to jump on the train.

Greg and I talked at length. We both believed that I had a good, secure career in the public service ahead of me if I wanted to stick with that track. But he challenged me to think about where my passion lay, reminding me that for the ten years he'd known me, politics had been my greatest enthusiasm. He reminded me also that my passion for public sector work was for delivering the agenda of this particular government, a Labor government, and that I might have a limited capacity to independently serve both sides of politics in these roles. We reasoned that if I stood and was elected, I would be a backbencher in a Goss government. I could sit quietly, learning the ropes from the inner-city electorate of South Brisbane, almost a stone's throw to Parliament House. I didn't have to face the harsh difficulties of long distances and endless days away from loved ones that confront those in rural and regional Queensland who decide to stand for parliament. The more we talked, the more possible it felt and the more manageable it seemed. And so, in late 1994, I jumped on the train and nominated for preselection as the Labor candidate for South Brisbane for the 1995 election.

I had faced the judgement of the Labor Party branch members in my electorate just six months earlier in a ballot to elect delegates to the party's state conference. I had topped the poll, so other possible contenders knew that it would be a tough contest. But South Brisbane was a rock-solid Labor seat and recent preselections in other vacant seats, with lower margins, had been fiercely contested between the right and left factions of the party. I braced for the next round in the process.

In the end, the fight didn't come. On the day nominations closed I was the only one in the contest and became the Labor candidate for South Brisbane unopposed.

*

I had campaigned for local Labor candidates for more than a decade, but as my branch members and I began to pull together the beginnings of my own election campaign it all had an air of unreality. I was going through the steps I had gone through many times before, preparing materials, leaflets and posters about the candidate and writing step-by-step campaign plans. But this time the candidate was me. I was confident that I could be a good, strong member of parliament. But as large signs with my face on them began to appear around my neighbourhood, I felt strangely confronted. The public self-promotion seemed a monstrous vanity. I had put up my hand for the job, but the application process was a constant challenge. The decision of the Labor Party to endorse me as their candidate propelled me from a private life to a public one. As a candidate, it is public life on a relatively minor scale, but public nevertheless.

In all my busy thinking about jumping on the election train I had understood that this would happen, but I had not contemplated what it would feel like. This campaign was no longer a political exercise or a wrestle of ideas, it was suddenly deeply personal. I felt an awkward and unexpected self-consciousness and with it an urge to avert my eyes from the constant images of myself. I felt too an uneasy sense of danger and an instinct to pull away from the exposure. This exposure grew over the years with every election. As the backyard signs and local leaflets turned to roadside billboards and state-wide television advertising, this unease never left me. For my children, spotting signs of me around the suburbs became a game. In that first election campaign, they were young enough to be delighted to see their mum's face along roadsides. Later, in the campaigns during their adolescence, the signs caused them excruciating embarrassment. For me there was always an anxious discomfort that I was somehow courting trouble, that drawing this kind of attention to myself would tempt a spiteful fate.

Accommodating these feelings and others like them is part of the adjustment to political life, but it's not one you learn about in candidate school. And it doesn't stop with being a candidate. The truth is that on the day you are elected something happens. You feel that you are exactly the same person you were the day before, but that is not how everyone sees you. Everyone else now sees you as someone imbued with power, someone elevated to an office above them. They will feel it was their vote that elevated you and will feel ownership rights as a result. You now occupy a public office and a large part of you – your life, your time and your self – will belong to the people who put you there. All this is as it should be, but when you first begin to be recognised, to be approached while grocery shopping, lobbied when stepping out of the public swimming pool, interrupted while out with your family, it takes some getting used to. As I became more senior within the parliamentary Labor Party, I would often speak to new members as they arrived, fresh from their first election, and tell them that getting used to being an identifiable, recognisable figure was just as important as learning the rules of the parliament.

The expectations that Greg and I had harboured about my smooth entry into political life were disrupted early in my first election campaign. Our suburb was home to the infamous Boggo Road prison, which had been effectively closed in 1992 after being plagued by riots, hunger strikes and escapes. On the first Sunday of the campaign, I woke to the front page headline that the Goss government planned to redevelop Boggo Road as a 'justice precinct' housing new court facilities, a new city watch house and a new remand facility. In other words, my neighbourhood was about to get a new jail.

The newspaper story was a revelation to me. As the local candidate, I had not been consulted on this election promise, but I knew immediately that it meant trouble. Like inner-city suburbs around the country, my local patch was changing. Young families were moving in and the tired face of the old suburb was being altered by renovators and gentrifiers. They had not bought into the area to live next door to a prison.

Within days, a local action group had formed to oppose the prison redevelopment. In the fever of an election campaign, the issue was a gift for the local Liberal Party candidate. Soon it was no longer a local issue – like any spark of trouble in an election campaign, this one became a bushfire and took on state-wide significance. Conservatives from across the city quickly swelled the ranks of the local group. The group called a hasty public meeting to protest against the government's decision and invited all candidates to attend.

I spoke with staff from the prison minister's office and

the premier's office, piecing together the facts and the policy rationale so I could defend the government's unpopular decision at the meeting. Late one evening I was surprised to receive a call from one of the premier's most senior advisors. He told me that the central strategy group had discussed the public meeting and determined that not only would no senior representative of the government attend it to defend the decision, but that I should not attend either. They believed that the embarrassment of an empty chair on the stage with my name on it was a lesser evil than television footage of the Labor candidate being jeered and heckled.

As he spoke, I felt all my feisty hackles rise. I was affronted that they were walking away from a fight they had started, and affronted that they thought I was made of the same stuff. In a moment of absolute clarity, I knew he was wrong. I felt it unconscionable to stand for election and refuse to listen to the views of my would-be constituents. I knew instinctively that in a democracy the first duty is to turn up. This duty was strengthened, not absolved, by the fact that the voters would be demanding and hurt and angry. I refused to accept the direction of the strategy group.

As the evening of the meeting drew near, the campaign against the justice precinct gathered momentum. It became clear that this would be a big public meeting, that every media outlet would be there, that my first public test as a budding politician would be broadcast by all television stations and live radio, and would feature in the major dailies. My resolve was not quite what it had been when I told the premier's advisor what I thought of his advice.

When I walked into the Dutton Park school hall I was armed with facts and arguments, but felt nervous, scared and intimidated. My job was to absorb the anger of the people I was hoping to represent. As predicted, there was plenty of jeering and heckling, along with plenty of questions. The Liberals turned up in force, with their shadow minister in tow. But it was a local show and the locals held the floor, demanding answers and venting their frustrations. After several hours, when I felt as bloodied as a punching bag, unsure whether turning up had been the best idea after all, an older man rose from the back of the hall to have the last say.

'I've been listening to this for hours and don't like much of what you've said, but I give you ten out of ten for coming and staying and for listening. Tell the truth, I didn't reckon you'd show, but you've been a bloody trooper here tonight, taking a lot of crap, showing a lot of guts, and I reckon you deserve a round of applause for that!' With his words, the hall broke into loud applause. With the applause came a lesson in political leadership that was burnt into me: show up. When there's a problem, run towards it and try to fix it; don't back away from it. Courage is something people can sense, almost like a smell, and they want and need to sense it in their leaders – it's how they find the leader in the room.

I promised the protesters that I would take their concerns to the Minister for Corrective Services, Paul Braddy. A widely respected senior member of Goss's cabinet, Paul had been one of those at the forefront of the battle to bring down Bjelke-Petersen and I had great admiration for him. But I barely knew him when I walked into his ministerial office.

He greeted me with his deep, gruff voice and a soft punch on the arm. 'I like you, girl, you've got bottle!' he boomed. I wasn't sure what 'bottle' meant but it seemed a great affirmation of the decisions I'd made in the past week. We proceeded to plot out a strategy for managing the issue and including local voices in the government's planning for the site if we were re-elected. Paul became a great ally and teacher. He has a fine legal mind and brought a wisdom to his deliberations that I watched and tried to learn from. He was cautious but brave, and later I felt his loss from the cabinet when he retired midway through Peter Beattie's premiership.

The local action group resolved to stage a nonstop protest for the duration of the election campaign. A makeshift camp was set up on a vacant block of land across the road from the prison site. Tents and large banners were erected and the protesters established a roster to keep a 24-hour vigil against the government's plans.

The protest camp became a highly visible symbol of a government in trouble and on election night many seats fell to the conservatives. I was elected as a member of the Queensland parliament representing the seat of South Brisbane, but had won my seat with a drastically reduced margin. It was 15 July 1995, the day after my thirty-fifth birthday. I would hold this seat for the next seventeen years.

The Boggo Road issue had been only one of many issues that bedevilled the government, but it had played its part in the local result and the state-wide result. Early on the morning after the election, the head of the local action group, Warwick Marler, rang my home to seek urgent discussions to get the justice precinct policy dropped. Unfortunately for Warwick, Greg answered the phone. Greg has a deep interest in politics, but little interest in the niceties its practise sometimes requires. He had been stung by the local campaign against me and surprised that some of the parents from the boys' school and people we knew had joined in and campaigned against me. For him, this local group had opposed me and that was all he needed to know to form his judgement of them. 'Why don't you just fuck off!' I heard Greg say before abruptly hanging up.

When Greg told me who had called, to his horror, I rang Warwick back. Warwick and I would go on to talk a lot over the weeks and months ahead. He wasn't my enemy or an enemy of the Labor Party. He was a local solicitor who had recently bought a house in the area with his family. His back fence directly abutted the Boggo Road perimeter and he was just a guy who didn't want a prison at his back door.

*

Wayne Goss had been seeking his third term in government, and after the ignominious defeat of the corrupt and failing National Party government only six years earlier he had been widely expected to succeed. But we had underestimated the demands of an electorate feeling the pressures of growth and change and came perilously close to losing government, hanging on with a one-seat majority. With the unexpected loss of so many seats came widespread criticism of Wayne and his leadership style. He was accused of relying on too small a group of inexperienced advisors. He was particularly criticised for failing to include any of his cabinet or parliamentary colleagues in the inner circle of his campaign strategy team. Wayne did his best to listen to his critics and vowed to be more inclusive in his approach.

He proved true to his word five months later, in December 1995, when a Liberal Party court challenge to the electoral result in the far northern Labor electorate of Mundingburra was successful, triggering a by-election. To oversee this campaign, Wayne appointed a more broadly based strategy group and included two members of his parliamentary team. One was his Minister for Local Government, Terry Mackenroth. The other, one of his newest backbenchers, was me.

While I had run my own local election campaign and been a foot soldier in countless others, I was no expert in campaign strategy at this level. Deeply conscious of my shortcomings, I headed off with some trepidation to the first meeting of the campaign strategy team. As I opened the door to the premier's office, I heard the booming voice of advertising guru John Singleton. 'This guy is rolled gold, I tell you, he's rolled gold,' he told the group, reporting his polling research on Tony Mooney, the popular Labor mayor of Townsville. On the back of this research and John's ringing endorsement that Tony was 'rolled gold' in the electorate, we endorsed Tony as our candidate for the by-election over the incumbent member, Ken Davies.

The Mundingburra electorate lies in the southern suburbs of Townsville, a major regional city on the coast of north Queensland. A mixture of old and new suburbs nestled on the banks of the Ross River, it was now the focus of national attention as the fate of the Goss government hung in the balance.

This was a high-stakes by-election and all sides and every lobby group beat a path to Townsville to contest it.

Held in early February, the by-election was staged in the gruelling wet heat of midsummer in the sub-tropics. It was a drawn-out dogfight of a campaign. Everyone who was part of it remembers the searing heat, the worn-out bad tempers and the malevolent mood of the electorate. The public were sick of election campaigns; they were resentful that this one was interrupting the lazy, cricket-filled days of their summer break; and they seemed angry about everything. In the end, it was a campaign that we lost – and with it we lost our parliamentary majority, we lost our government and we lost our leader when Wayne resigned.

The proposed Boggo Road justice precinct that had inspired such strong opposition in my electorate was killed by the incoming conservative government and the site would lie idle until Labor returned to government in 1998. One of my first local projects on our return to government was to put the site forward as a major urban renewal opportunity. Warwick Marler and other locals joined the government planners and over many years helped design a new knowledge precinct, now home to major research facilities and university laboratories, surrounded by new residential apartments and serviced by a new public transport hub.

*

With the defeat of Wayne Goss and his government, my world turned upside down. Peter Beattie was elected as the new opposition leader and he turned his mind to forming a new team. Like all new leaders, Peter wanted to break with the past. He wanted his team to reflect a new face for the Labor Party, and he wanted a younger shadow cabinet with more women in it. Peter recruited me to his frontbench team in February 1996, just seven months after I was elected. My plan to sit quietly on the backbench of a third-term Labor government, learning the ropes as my family and I adjusted gradually to my move into politics, evaporated.

Peter expected us to travel constantly and in a state the size of Queensland that is no easy task. He expected us to develop new policies and programs to take to the next election and to meet with as many stakeholder groups as possible, as often as needed. With only one seat keeping the government in power and us in opposition, Peter liked to remind us that we were only one heartbeat away from government. It was knife-edge politics and these were hectic, exciting years in the parliament. They were also hectic and tiring years at home.

Of all the senior responsibilities I took on over my seventeen years in parliament, those two and a half years stand out as the toughest on a personal and family level. For our family, there had been no gradual getting used to the idea of politics and public life. It felt like a turbo thruster had taken our lives out of normal orbit and was driving us at hyper speed. We all struggled to keep up. But as Oliver grew and became a little more independent and as we became more used to the pace of it all, we found a rhythm for ourselves as a family. I learned the importance of being truly with them when I was at home. Even if it meant coming home a little later, I would do my best not to bring work and phone calls home with me. We went together to public engagements whenever possible. We learned to accept the help offered by friends and the tireless support of my mother. We learned the value of spending time together at breakfast, touching base every day. But the years rushed by us in a blur and Greg had more of those precious growing-up years of Oliver's – the years that never come again – than I did.

My first portfolio as the shadow minister for public works and public sector administration pitted me directly against the premier, Rob Borbidge, who had responsibility for the public service. Rob decided early on to undertake a root-and-branch reform of the public service with legislation that contained a number of draconian measures. I used them to launch a solid attack on him and his government. I was the most junior member of the opposition frontbench up against a premier who relied on just a one-seat majority to win votes in the parliament. During the debate on his legislation, I kept him arguing late into the night. On the crucial vote on the most controversial of his reforms, a member of his own team missed the vote. It was Rob Borbidge's first failure to hold a majority in the parliament.

I couldn't have cut my teeth as a parliamentarian in more high-profile circumstances, and it didn't go unnoticed. In mid 1997, the *Courier-Mail* ran a full-page profile article identifying me as an emerging talent in Labor's ranks. Emblazoned across the top of the article was the headline 'Rising Star'.

In every leader's journey there are moments when they feel themselves separate from the herd, when they realise they are moving beyond its warm comfort. You know the moment of separation because it comes with the envy and resentment of your peers. As you emerge and edge past them, you can feel the realisation distress them. You make a decision then, consciously or not, to keep going or to retreat to the herd. We are pack animals and emerging from the safety of numbers feels unnatural. But this moment of emerging is an absolutely critical one in the development of leadership, and it is intensely uncomfortable.

With the two words 'rising star' I had pulled away from the herd. Instantly my colleagues lampooned me. The headline became my nickname for the remainder of our time in opposition. It was said with humour, but tinged for many with envy and a subtle reprimand that I was at risk of getting too far ahead of myself.

Not long after the article, I was approached by a woman from my local ALP branch, someone who had known me for many years and had my best interests at heart. She told me that people were starting to talk about me and that I should know what they were saying. She went on to reveal that I was beginning to get a reputation for being 'ambitious', and I knew from her tone that this was not seen as a good thing. She had sought me out to warn me so I could curb my behaviour. I wondered out loud why anyone would want a member of parliament who was not ambitious, but I understood the message and rolled it around in my head for several weeks. I was scheduled to speak at an upcoming meeting of the Queensland Labor Women's organisation and resolved to put ambition on the agenda.

I told the group that ambition is a good thing. It's a good thing generally and it's a good thing for women. Ambition changes the world: it drives economies and creates prosperity, it sparks ideas and innovation and creative endeavour, it propels champions and feeds excellence. I told them that it is so self-evidently good that it was reasonable to wonder why I was even saying it. But I was saying it because the reality is that many women are often not comfortable with the idea of ambition. And those around them are sometimes even less comfortable.

Ambition is just not seen as a desirable feminine trait. If you ask a random group of men and women to list ten common feminine characteristics I doubt that 'ambitious' would appear on any list – but I bet a majority would list it as a masculine characteristic. It will be sometimes used to criticise – 'oh, she's so ambitious' – and when we hear that we all know it's not meant as a compliment. Make no mistake, it's said to hold you back.

I don't know what my audience made of my exhortation to recognise and claim their own ambitions. But I do know that in speaking about it out loud and acknowledging my own ambition I had made a decision to find my place outside the herd, to learn to live with the jibes and the criticism that would increasingly come as I pushed myself forward. I knew that no one, male or female, ever succeeds in politics, or indeed much else, without some healthy ambition. I knew that we would never get out of opposition without ambitious frontbenchers pushing themselves at every opportunity. Ambition is a powerful motivator. It drives you through the tiredness and complacency that sometimes sets in, and through the rough patches, the times when you want to give up, when it's all too hard. In the world of politics and public life, you have to have large measures of it and you have to be comfortable with it. As the 'rising star' article cut me from the herd, I resolved to get comfortable with my ambition.

FIVE

Show Business for Ugly People

The phrase 'politics is show business for ugly people', believed to have been coined by US political consultant Bill Miller in the early 1990s, is a funny way to capture an essential truth. Those of us who take on a political life often share the same drives and ambitions that propel people onto the stage and screen. Like Hollywood, politics attracts those who want to make a name for themselves. It offers the lure of public attention, a certain fame and influence, and it offers them to those of us who lack the talents and physical blessings to make it onto the big screen. Much of the work of politics is done on the public stage – it has its own theatre in parliament and creates a wealth of human drama.

If the currency of show business is money and celebrity, the currency of politics is power. The power to change, the power to regulate, the power to decide what will be done and what will not be done are all in your hands. However, the larger truth is that the public attention and recognition will accrue only to those who use their power and use it well. The public are quick to identify those who are only there for the show business and quick to tire of governments that are reluctant to act. There is little room on the stage for those whom Roosevelt called 'cold and timid souls', those too cautious ever to know victory or defeat. The exercise of power is a hot-blooded business. It is the core skill of a politician, and it is learned on the job. This learning is often hard and painful and is conducted in the full glare of public attention. If you're any good and the electorate gives you enough time, you learn. With every piece of legislation passed, every reform, every speech, every mistake, every triumph and every loss, you get better at being powerful. As I made my way into the Queensland Parliament, then onto the frontbench and into the ministry, I learned these lessons over and over again.

So politics offers the chance to make big and extraordinary things happen, but only if you can be popular at the same time. Elections, polls and political commentary, like box office returns and the reviews of film and theatre critics, provide a running tally on your popularity.

Losing the Mundingburra by-election and therefore power was a tough lesson in the importance of popularity. Loss brings grief and heartache and recrimination, and there was plenty of all that to go around after Mundingburra. I felt the loss as painfully as anyone. I watched in anguish as Wayne Goss, a Labor hero, the man who had brought down Bjelke-Petersen, packed up his office and left the stage. But it was equally true that I had gained something from the experience. For the first time I had sat inside the inner sanctum. I'd had the chance to watch and listen and learn as the leaders of the party and the government and the experienced old hands of political campaigning practised their craft. In that inner sanctum I got my first real insight into the complex chemistry of polling, research, focus groups and the development of political slogans, messages and advertising. It was a hands-on chance to learn from the big boys – and they were all boys. I was the only backbencher and the only woman in the room.

Until this point, my experience in the Labor Party had been largely outside the central machine. Sitting on the campaign strategy team for Mundingburra had been an incredible opportunity. It had opened my eyes to the hard, real-world decisions that come with political leadership, the daily balancing of ideas and ideology with the pragmatic imperative of appealing to the electorate and getting re-elected. It had exposed me to the strengths and weaknesses of polling, and I'd learned that results are only as useful as the question asked. Tony Mooney was indeed a popular mayor, our polling had been right about that. But he was so popular locally that they wanted to keep him as mayor. He was 'rolled gold' for that position, not for one that would take him thousands of kilometres away from local problems and concerns. The locals told our door-knocking teams this over and over again as they made their way from house to house in the relentless heat of an unforgiving tropical sun. We had asked the wrong question in our original poll.

Being part of putting the campaign together, as an idea progressed to a slogan, which was then rolled into a television ad and tested with focus groups, refined, remade and tested again, taught me to be mindful of the egos in the advertising world. I watched the creative directors argue about scripts and images, music, lyrics, colours, the candidate's clothes and the tone of the leader's voice. We needed ads that worked, but too often the creative stars were mesmerised by the aesthetics of the ads and their own artistic reputations. Each time they lost sight of our purpose, we party officials would remind them we were the client and relentlessly test the material until it hit the spot.

I learned a lot about the breakneck pace of decision making in the hothouse of a campaign. With less than four weeks to persuade the electorate, an election campaign feels like a plane in a tailspin. Almost every hour brings a new crisis demanding attention and action. Split-second decisions are demanded of the team. Tempers fray easily and sometimes there is just no way to avoid making the wrong call. You do what you can to undo the damage and move on as quickly as possible.

Just as powerfully, the campaign gave me the chance to build connections with key players from other parts of the party. I saw them in action, saw their drive and ambition. I began to appreciate that while I had sparred with many of them in ALP forums over the years, we were all driven by the same passions. There were people like Terry Mackenroth, a longstanding and toughened warrior from the right of the party. Terry and I would continue to argue about many ideas, both in and out of government over the years, but we began to find common cause in the oppressive heat of that sweltering campaign. Similarly, the party secretary, Mike Kaiser, with whom I had previously clashed at almost every opportunity, began to appear in a different light as we battled together in the airless trenches of that campaign to hang on to a Labor government. Equally, it was a chance for others to see me through a different lens. Their view of me as an intemperate hothead from the irresponsible left of the party was tempered as they watched me work with the same dogged determination for the same ends they sought. The connections I forged and the lessons I learned in Mundingburra were building blocks for my ultimate leadership of the party.

Long before that time came, these new relationships became important for the Labor Party's return to government. Terry, Mike and our polling team, together with the new leader, Peter Beattie, came back around the campaign strategy table in the 1998 state election. This time it was a winning formula. Terry would go on to become deputy premier to Peter Beattie in 2000 and I would replace him as deputy when he retired in 2005. Mike Kaiser would become my chief of staff when I became premier in 2007.

After Mundingburra, I sat on the strategy team for every one of the next six state elections and several by-elections, most of which we won. In every one, I learned more about the art and craft of political campaigning, more about the people who help bring it all together and make it work, more about interpreting polling, listening to focus group results and reading the electorate.

Queensland elections are conducted over a minimum of twenty-six days. In every instance, these campaigns have been among the most intense periods of my life. At any other time, twenty-six days can disappear in the blink of an eye, but in an election campaign an hour can feel like a lifetime and the days stretch ahead as far as the eye can see. The campaigns themselves are carefully planned months in advance, building up themes and ideas, positioning the leader, planning announcements and activities and travel plans for every one of the twenty-six days.

Just as importantly, time is spent war-gaming the opposition's likely tactics and understanding our own weak spots and vulnerabilities. But for the leader, no amount of preparation is enough to overcome the merciless pressure of those long days.

*

Within hours of being sworn in as a minister for the first time in 1998, I felt the gravitational pull of political power as my office began fielding calls from everywhere. I was the new Minister for Families, Youth and Community Care and also the Minister for Disability Services. These responsibilities have typically fallen to women ministers at every level of government, on every side of politics, yet I was elated to have them. I had extensive experience in the community sector and many of my new responsibilities went to the heart of basic human rights that I hold dear. It's a part of government that has a close and tangible effect on people's lives.

Working alongside me would be my new chief of staff, Bronwen Griffiths. I had met Bronwen through my husband, Greg, who had worked with her briefly. Like me, Bronwen had grown up on the Gold Coast, on a banana farm in the Currumbin Valley. She holds an honours degree in economics and had been recruited into the graduate program of the federal Treasury straight out of university. Bronwen has a fine mind, a strong heart and a burning sense of justice. Together we wanted to rattle cages and shake things up.

The three decades of the Bjelke-Petersen government had been characterised by neglect in social services. While the rest of Australia had been developing new and better ways to help their most vulnerable people, Queensland had been ignoring them. As a result, our state had invested woefully low levels of resources in services for people with disabilities, abused children, the homeless, those suffering mental health issues, those requiring family support and those escaping domestic violence, to name just a few. We'd not only invested significantly less, but in many areas we were relying on legislative tools thirty or forty years out of date. We were using outdated, discredited service models, such as large-scale institutions, to deliver many of the services we did provide. Overcoming this legacy was a critical part of our government's agenda to transform and modernise Queensland. We could not hold our heads high and join other Australian states, ready for the twenty-first century, while we lagged so far behind in these areas. Failing our most vulnerable held us all back. My friend and mentor Anne Warner had held this responsibility in the Goss cabinet, where she made significant inroads and real progress. I relished the chance to pick up the ball and keep pushing the agenda forward.

On my first afternoon as minister, my staff took calls from distraught mothers of children with disabilities wanting help, from angry parents whose children had been taken into state care wanting the decision overturned, from organisations wanting extra funds, from advocates wanting legislation changed, from churches and charities, mums and dads, workers and volunteers, all wanting to see me, talk to me and persuade me to use my newfound power in some way.

There were so many challenges, so many worthy causes. I felt galvanised and fired up by it all and immediately began to sort and sift and set priorities. One of the most persistent voices in my ear came from the Neerkol Action Group. They were a newly formed alliance of adults, many in their late middle age, who had been consigned as children to large orphanages and children's homes and were now finding their public voice. The group largely comprised of former residents of an infamous Catholic children's home in Neerkol, outside Rockhampton in central Queensland. The Sisters of Mercy, the same nuns who'd taught me, had run St Joseph's Orphanage at Neerkol for almost a century. It had housed more than four thousand children over the years before closing its doors in 1978.

Many of those who'd spent their childhood at Neerkol spoke of horrific abuse and neglect at the hands of nuns, priests and workers at the institution. They wanted to break the silence of a lifetime, they wanted the public to know what had happened to them, they wanted punishment for those who had perpetrated the abuse and they wanted justice for themselves. They had been raising the issue in the public arena in whatever way they could. Now they wanted me, the new minister, to hear their demands.

I met with a large number of Neerkol Action Group members and supporters late one afternoon. We sat around the table of the conference room in the ministerial office. Bronwen joined me, both of us only a few weeks in the job and still finding our feet. We listened as the group explained that they wanted a royal commission into past abuses at Neerkol and other places like it. They wanted an open and transparent forum in which to raise their grievances. They needed the powers of a royal commission to dig into the past, to secure the records of churches and the institutions they ran and to uncover the truth of their experiences.

My job that day was to listen. As the room dimmed with the pearly light of early evening, I listened to heartbreaking stories of childhoods lost and stolen. I listened to stories of beatings and rapes, of brutality and deprivation, of cruel punishments and terrible injustice. I listened to a man in his fifties sob as he told me of his wife and local church abandoning him since he talked about his experiences for the first time. I listened to stories of continued institutionalisation in juvenile detention centres, jails and mental asylums as these children had left the orphanages and tried to find their way in the world, uneducated and barely socialised. I listened to these brave men and women speak of the unspeakable, give broken, weeping voice to long-held secrets and vent years of shame. I listened late into the evening, until they had talked themselves dry. We were all limp from listening. As I left the conference room, shaken and distressed, Bronwen turned to me, ashen-faced. 'No matter how long we're here, no matter what else we do, we will never forget what we've just heard and we have to do something about it,' she said.

She was right. I have never forgotten what I heard that evening. Some things, once heard, can never be unheard. After almost two decades in political life, this meeting remains one of the most harrowing of my many experiences.

As a minister, I had the power to act. But establishing a royal commission is a big power play. It brings all the weight and authority of the state to bear on an issue. It is not to be used lightly, capriciously or vindictively and is always a big decision for a government. Your actions can change lives, and along the way these actions can change you too. When you pull those levers of power, they start to define you, and the choices you make, the risks you take and the chain of events you set in motion will all leave their mark on you and colour the lens through which others see you. Our government was less than a month old and I was the most junior minister in the cabinet when I convinced the premier, Peter Beattie, to take this royal commission on. I have wondered since if we tackled it because we were so new and not bound or worn down by the weight of years in office.

The churches that would be investigated by the commission did not welcome the decision. With few exceptions, church leaders opposed the establishment of the inquiry, some even preaching against it from the pulpits of their churches. They were fearful of the exposure, defensive about their role over many decades in caring for children at the state's request and worried about the cost of possible compensation. As we established the inquiry, I met with the leaders of churches on many occasions and had to hold my nerve as they brought the considerable weight of their institutions to the table. These were very different meetings from the one I had held with the former residents of the institutions run by these churches. At these gatherings, it was lawyers at ten paces. Eventually, the major players reconciled themselves to the inevitability of the inquiry. To their credit, most of them began to understand the healing power of the truth. But it was a hard beginning for us all.

Less than a month after meeting with the former Neerkol residents, we established the Commission of Inquiry into the Abuse of Children in Queensland Institutions. I knew the inquiry would succeed or fail on my choice of commissioner. The issues to be considered by this inquiry would require someone with just the right touch, a sharp legal mind and a big caring heart. Leneen Forde was a lawyer and the recently retired governor of Queensland, our first female governor. Her career had won her the admiration of the public and the respect of the legal profession. Of course, I had never before established a commission of inquiry or appointed a commissioner, so this was an important call. Calls like this one stay with you. I phoned Leneen very late one night, because she was visiting family in Canada and I had to take account of the different time zone. I had only met her on a couple of occasions at official functions, and she was surprised to hear from me. She listened as I outlined the need and was then quiet at the other end of the line. I was wondering if the line had dropped out when I heard Leneen exhale heavily.

'Oh dear, this will be a heartbreaking task,' she said. I knew I had found the right person.

Leneen was appointed commissioner in August 1998. She had spent enough time working in the legal system to understand that sometimes those who most need its protection are those least able to cope with its adversarial nature. Leneen brought gravitas and compassion to the task. She gave those who wished to make statements the ability to do so in either public or private hearings. The inquiry investigated one hundred and fifty-nine institutions and had access to all the records of churches and government departments. It took sworn statements from more than three hundred former residents, many of whom told of their experiences for the first time. And for those who had told their story before, this was the first time their story had been listened to, believed and acknowledged. The inquiry brought the hidden experience of thousands of children to light and was the first of its kind in Australia.

Some will always say that commissions like these are nothing more than talkfests, that they achieve little and the past cannot be changed. It is true that a lost childhood cannot be recovered, but watching the Forde inquiry do its work, I was struck by the power of truth. The public was shocked by much of what they heard. They were horrified to hear that the institutions they had trusted the most, the state and the church, had betrayed that trust so profoundly. They were sickened to learn that the victims of that betrayal were children, the most vulnerable and most precious among us. For the victims, giving evidence to the inquiry was liberating. It was an affirmation of an unforgivable trauma, and many of them felt empowered for the first time. Many had kept their painful secrets hidden all their lives and speaking of them became the first step in their healing. The commission had unlocked a large and powerful truth, and in the unlocking had lifted a heaviness from many hearts. Churches and government agencies, and the many who had worked in these terrible places, were as unshackled as the victims, able at last to acknowledge and reconcile past wrongs.

The power of truth came early to Bishop Brian Heenan of Rockhampton. Neerkol was in his diocese and he had railed against the allegations by former residents, accusing them of being enemies of the church and fabricating lies to undermine its work. He circulated a letter to his parishioners saying the claims were scurrilous and scandalous, which caused great grief to those who had raised their voices against the operations of Neerkol.

But their grief did not hinder their efforts or their courage. They sought and gained a personal meeting with the bishop, where they gave him their stories, and he, like me, got a visceral understanding of what had really gone on behind the locked doors of his former institution. In a stunning and very moving reversal of his previous position, the bishop issued a public statement admitting he had been wrong and apologising for meeting the early claims with disbelief. This was no easy thing for a powerful figure in the Catholic Church. But as the truth so often can, it increased and enhanced his stature. His acceptance of the truth was all the more powerful because he had resisted it so vociferously. His actions had an incredible ripple effect across the church and for the Neerkol victims. The truth can change us all.

The power of the commission came home to me one night after a local ALP branch meeting, when a long-time party stalwart stayed behind to speak with me. He spoke quietly and thanked me for the inquiry, telling me that after much hesitation he had given evidence and it had been the most liberating experience of his life. He told me he felt freed from a burden that had weighed on him since childhood, and he now had the strength to share his past with his wife for the first time. I had known this man for years but never known that he had spent his childhood in an orphanage, never had an inkling of the load he carried. I realised that there were thousands of people in our community just like him, having the same extraordinary experience, and I knew that this great unburdening was good for all of us.

The commission was also a vehicle that reunited people; past residents who hadn't seen each other since they left the institution were now back in contact with the only people who knew the truth of their early lives. Many of those who started the Neerkol Action Group and others who came together through the commission have continued to work for the interests of former residents, running regular support groups, keeping people in touch with each other, helping others find their official records and keeping an eye out for one another. From time to time our paths cross and we relive some of the moments of those extraordinary months as the commission methodically did its work, giving them back their lives and helping them create new futures for themselves. They are different people now, stronger, happier and full of purpose. I doubt the anger will ever fully evaporate, but it no longer seems to consume them as it did when we first met.

I think of one man, in particular, who would drop by my office unannounced. He had been so full of rage when we first met that his efforts to speak about what needed to be done were often incomprehensible, his anger and pain choking his throat and filling his words with venom. He was loud, angry and sometimes very frightening, and he had numerous brushes with the police as a result. Now when he visits he has only one real purpose, to show me the latest photos of his grandchildren, who have arrived in recent years and filled his life with love. I am always moved by this new softness in him, gladdened to see how lightly his past now weighs on him. Sometimes when we talk I think, this is what it means to reconcile with a terrible truth and find a way to live with it. This is what it looks like when you find the right place for it in your heart, a place where you won't forget it but that lets you breathe more easily.

Something of the power of the commission is captured in the opening remarks of its final report:

> This is no ordinary report. This was no ordinary
> Inquiry. For the Commissioners and staff of the
> Inquiry, the experience has been deeply moving and
> deeply disquieting. We have heard repeated reports
> of physical and sexual abuse in government and
> non-government institutions over decades, which
> have resulted in irreparable damage to the lives of
> many Queenslanders. Why did this happen? How
> can anyone possibly repair the damage done? How
> can we as a society ensure that such violations never
> again occur to children whose care we have entrusted
> to the state?

The final report made forty-two recommendations, calling for redress of the abuses of the past and laying out a blueprint for reforming the current system. Chief among its recommendations were the calls for an increase of $103 million into our services for abused children to bring Queensland into line with the systems in other states, and for both the government and churches to consider compensation for past victims. Gaining the support to implement these recommendations was a huge challenge for me as a junior minister. I had only limited success at that time, securing an immediate initial injection of funds of $10 million into these services, with a commitment to increase this in every subsequent budget, and the establishment of a $1 million fund to assist and support former victims. Sometimes in politics you have to recognise an opportunity and rush to seize it, while other times you have to play the long game. When I became Treasurer in 2006, seven years after the Forde inquiry had finished its work, one of my most rewarding decisions was to establish the $100 million Forde Inquiry Redress Scheme, which made financial compensation payments to almost 7500 people.

The commission gave a forgotten group of Queenslanders and their experiences a proper place among us. It also gave an early shape to our government. We were sloughing off the past and building a new future, a modern state unfettered by our history. The Forde inquiry held a mirror to some of the worst in our past and helped define our government's emerging social agenda.

*

Exercising power usually means changing things, and disruption unsettles people. In government, you are required to act in the public's best interest. Of course, there is endless debate about what this best interest is. Even when agreement exists, there will always be those who feel the effects of change more harshly than others.

All too often, the reaction to change will be depressingly predictable. In 2000, I had carriage of the domestic violence protection legislation. It was long overdue for an overhaul, and I was shepherding a raft of amendments through the parliament. This legislation already included powers for the courts to make protection orders prohibiting violent spouses from contacting their victims. The amendments would extend these orders to other vulnerable people in violent domestic relationships, such as elderly people relying on family for accommodation and being mistreated by them. The amendments would also extend these protections to those in same-sex relationships. This amendment was the first major step our government took on same-sex relationship law reform, and I knew that many of the conservatives in parliament would vigorously oppose the new laws. At this time, the Queensland parliament included eleven members of the One Nation Party, an ultra right-wing fringe party that had burst onto the Australian political stage with the election of Pauline Hanson some four years earlier. Along with the Queensland National Party, these members hollered and raged about the evils of these amendments. The debate was one of the most fiery I encountered in all my seventeen years in parliament. One by one, these members rose to their feet and accused me of being an agent of Satan, of forcing children to live with transvestites, of doing the devil's work — and worse.

I had understood that I was taking a step too far for some, but I was nevertheless shocked by the vehemence of the response these amendments received. They did not seek to tackle what were then very difficult issues of marriage or adoption of children by same-sex couples; they simply made it possible for a man or woman in a same-sex relationship to seek legal protection from a violent partner. The speeches opposing these protections belied a visceral hatred of gay people. As I listened to the venom and bile that spat from parliamentarians' mouths, I realised that they would be pilloried for speaking like this about any other group in the community, but they felt they had licence to make these vicious attacks on gay people. Clearly, there was much more work to do on that front.

*

Another change I'd long been passionate about was to improve our education system, and as the new education minister in 2001 I was determined to make education the heartbeat of our government. Education is always close to the core of any Labor government agenda, as it gives people the chance to make their way in the world unhindered by the circumstances of their birth. Education had been a truly transformative experience in my own life, ensuring that I would have the independence and freedom that my mother had lacked for so long. Peter Beattie wanted to position Queensland at the forefront of research, learning and technology. As premier he wanted to make Queensland the smart state of Australia. Our drive to transform and modernise Queensland would be built on innovation, knowledge and science.

Given how far we lagged behind in these areas, it took quite a leap of faith for people to imagine this new Queensland. As a government we had to put real meat on the bones of this idea to convince Queensland and the rest of the country that 'Smart State' could be more than a slogan. As Peter set about working with our universities and research institutes, I turned my attention to our schooling system. With two young sons in local public schools, I knew there was much to be done, and I knew I had the power to do it. I also knew that change had to start at the very beginning.

Our early education system had a strange history. In 1953, a state government that was under pressure to provide public high schools for baby boomers reaching their teenage years found an intriguing solution. Mid-year, they abolished the first, preparatory year of schooling, known as Prep, and declared all Prep students to be Year One students, and all Year One students to be Year Two students and so on up the line, so that Year Seven students, overnight, became Year Eight students, immediately creating a high school. The net result was that Queensland children started their first year of schooling younger than their interstate counterparts and had one less year of education. After the abolition of Prep, a program of preschool education grew up in an ad hoc manner. In 2001, it provided a half-time program to less than forty per cent of the children in that age group, meaning that the majority of our children began school without any formal early learning. Unsurprisingly, their results in national literacy and numeracy tests were the lowest in the country. It would be very difficult in these circumstances for us to claim the mantle of Australia's Smart State.

The global research we studied agreed that the best place to invest in education is in the early years. It is in these years that children's development is accelerating, that learning is at its most powerful and that essential foundations are laid. Dollars invested in these years reap dividends in every future year of schooling. As a mother, I saw firsthand in my own boys what the research was telling us about the value of early education. Like thousands of other parents, we had been unable to secure a place in half-time preschool for our eldest son, but managed to find one for our youngest son when his turn came around.

I saw the difference this had made for both of them. For our youngest, this foundation had considerably eased the transition into school. It seemed both unfair and ineffective for these early building blocks to be distributed on a first-in, best-dressed basis. Every Year One class in the state comprised some children who'd had the benefit of preschool and some who had not, making the job of Year One teachers all the more difficult. The structure of our preschool system was also causing problems. As more and more women were rejoining the workforce after having their children, and two-parent working families were becoming the norm, our half-time preschool was making it impossible for many families to make this option work for them. The problems at this end of the schooling system were a constant source of disgruntled discussion among the mums I knew. This was something I wanted to fix.

At the other end of schooling, Queensland had one of the lowest high-school completion rates in the country, and more young people per capita not at school, not in training and not in work than in any other state. Again the research told us (and we could see all around us) that young people who do not complete high school have constrained opportunities throughout their lives. This too was something that had to be wrestled with if we wanted to be the Smart State.

I resolved to issue a public discussion paper proposing two main changes. One: introduce a full additional year of early schooling, available to all in every primary school across the state. Two: lift the school-leaving age, requiring all young people to be at school until they turned seventeen unless they were in paid employment or full-time training.

Changing an education system that is steeped in decades of traditions is no easy task. Especially when you're attempting the biggest reforms the system had seen in half a century. My first task was to get the premier's support. I set about mounting a case for the reforms and sought meetings with Peter Beattie to talk them through. In government, it's easy to get the leader's attention when there is a crisis or when something can be checked quickly by phone, but finding time for a lengthy policy discussion is always a challenge. Several scheduled meetings were cancelled as the premier was called to more urgent tasks. As weeks slipped by, I became impatient. In frustration, I wrote a one-page summary of my ideas, with a closing paragraph claiming my reforms would enliven his Smart State agenda and be one of the great legacies of our government.

I went to his office late one Friday afternoon and told his staff that, despite having no appointment, I would wait outside his door until he left for the night, no matter when that might be. Almost an hour and a half later, I was called in as Peter was packing up and about to head out to a function.

'You've got five minutes,' he said.

'I only need two,' I replied and handed him the note. 'Read this over the weekend and give me the green light.'

After the cabinet meeting the following Monday morning, Peter took me aside and asked if I thought we could really make this happen. I told him yes, but I would need his support and we would have to put real money into it. He gave me the go-ahead to bring the proposal to cabinet for endorsement and then to go public with the discussion paper.

Big ideas need to be explained clearly, so the proposal had to be well written and easily understood by everyone from cabinet ministers to the average parent. As education minister, I gave the job of drafting the proposal to the education department. And while the department had many talented minds at its helm, I grew frustrated by their endless bureaucratic drafts. I needed a proposal that would pull together the research, the data and the rationale that were crucial to getting this formula past the gatekeepers in government, and to communicate its value clearly to the public.

Eventually, I conscripted a small talented group, largely from outside the education department, to get the job done. Among them was Lorann Downer, a former ABC journalist who was working as a media advisor in Beattie's office. The team worked brilliantly together and soon had the project's prose singing. Lorann coined the phrase 'earning or learning' to capture the program I was proposing for fifteen– to seventeen-year-olds. As versions of our reforms have been implemented in other states, the term is now commonplace in discussions about this group in education systems around the country. Lorann deserves the credit for it.

As the new school year began in 2002, I was ready to take a fully costed proposal along with a public discussion paper to cabinet, where my ministerial colleagues would debate and assess it. Such a big reform could not be implemented overnight. My proposal outlined the need for change and committed to trial a new full-time Prep year in almost one hundred primary schools over the following three years. Further, it proposed to gradually put in place new programs for fifteen– to seventeen-year-olds before legislating a lift in the leaving age in two years' time.

Cabinet can be a tricky place. Ministers hold the future of the government in their hands and have a responsibility to consider every proposal in a context broader than their own portfolio. But every minister also has their own self-interest and political aspirations to consider. Every time someone else's proposal is approved, it diminishes the prospects of your own projects being funded. Ideologically, I knew that my colleagues shared my passion about the transforming power of education, and I knew they understood the political significance of schools in every community and electorate. I also knew that my proposal, fully implemented, would consume a large slice of new budget funding, denying funds to plenty of other good ideas.

But I presented them with a proposal that was both good policy and good politics. This massive investment in our schooling system would attack two big failings – our hit-and-miss system of early childhood education and young people being at risk of dropping out of high school. Here was something that every single member of the government could use to engage with their local schools and with mums and dads everywhere. My colleagues backed me and I launched into the process of taking the policy to the electorate.

Launching a big new idea into the public arena is an exercise in careful media and information management. You have to make sure the journalists understand the issues sufficiently to report them accurately. You must publish the information online and make it available to the public as quickly as possible. And you absolutely need to ensure that all the relevant stakeholders – in this case, the parent groups, teacher unions, professional associations, university commentators and the non-government sectors of schooling – are well informed prior to your going public.

I got off to a bad start with the stakeholder groups. Immediately after the cabinet decision, my staff called a meeting to brief these education sector participants. The premier and I addressed them before heading off to a media conference to publicly announce our decision. Our announcement came as a revelation to the players in the room. Not only had news of our plans not leaked, but unbeknown to me, our cabinet meeting coincided with a half-yearly meeting of every Catholic bishop in Queensland with their leader, the archbishop. While Catholic education representatives were at the briefing, they had not been able to advise the bishops before the news broke. As the news of our proposals hit the airwaves, it took the bishops, who have responsibility for the schools in their diocese, by complete surprise. The Catholic education system educates almost one-quarter of all Queensland's schoolchildren. Like most people, bishops don't like surprises and a collection of bishops likes them even less. The bishops were embarrassed to have been caught without the facts in front of their leader.

Our discussion paper proposed that the reforms apply to every school – public, Catholic and independent – but that was not made clear in the news reports. In my determination to get the proposal through cabinet, I hadn't focused carefully enough on bringing the very senior players, especially those who operated the non-government schooling systems, into the loop. Thankfully, the displeasure of the bishops was communicated to me through back channels and I was able to quickly organise a meeting to brief the archbishop, who was not only relieved to find that his schools would not be left out, but became an enthusiastic supporter of the reforms. It was a good lesson in the importance of nurturing relationships to build support and momentum for reform.

What happens in our schools interests everybody. Schools touch hundreds of thousands of lives every day. I knew that any changes would have to be well understood by all parties and managed carefully. Nevertheless, I was surprised by some of the resistance to the education reforms and where it came from. Some of the teachers in our existing half-time preschools were appalled by the idea that their students would be expected to do a full week in the classroom and horrified that the curriculum they had used for forty years would need to change to accommodate that. In more than one selected trial school, the long-time preschool teacher took immediate stress leave rather than participate in the reform.

Similarly, many high school teachers were appalled that they would now be required to find an education or training option for every young person. They were unhappy that the difficult and disengaged would no longer simply be allowed to drop out of the system. Given the resistance of some of its members, the teachers union was muted in its response to the reforms. Both reforms would require the employment of significant numbers of new teachers, all of them potential new members for the union. But, entrenched in the status quo like many of its members, the union at no stage endorsed the reforms. I had to be content that it did not decide to campaign against the reforms despite the strength of views among some of the disgruntled members.

I thought the union's silence a great weakness and told its leaders so. Reform needs courage and I didn't find any there.

Thankfully, there were many in the education bureaucracy who were excited by the reforms. Ken Smith, the director-general of the department, worked across the agency to ignite enthusiasm for these ideas. Ken had been my departmental director-general in my previous portfolio and would go on to work with me in infrastructure and trade and ultimately become head of the premier's department. Political reform demands a strong partnership between the government and the bureaucracy, especially between the minister and the director-general. Ken and I were a good team. He shared my passion to get things done, was a very effective operator and brought determination and hard work to every task. As we worked side by side to deliver a strong education agenda for the government, we learned a lot about each other. We went into the negotiating trenches together and learned each other's measure. Our ability to rely on each other and get the job done was a powerful tool in delivering the reforms.

Many teachers too were excited by the reforms. Schools had to apply to be part of the trial program, which meant that every trial site had a school principal who supported the idea and wanted to make it work. These principals quickly became Prep champions. They used their influence in their schools and their communities to garner support for this new opportunity. The early enthusiasm of this group of school leaders was critical to our success. Their advocacy for the idea within the broader profession oiled the wheels of reform.

Understandably, parents, especially those of very young children, had lots of questions and were wary at first. But enrolments soon began to flood in at every trial school as parents voted with their feet. In many cases, parents moved the enrolment of their older children to a trial school to keep their children together as the younger sibling got the chance to be a Prep student. The Queensland Parents and Citizens' Association was a rock-solid supporter right from the start and showed real leadership. It took parents' concerns seriously and worked them through, but never wavered in its commitment to giving our children the best possible start to learning. I visited trial sites in many different schools, in vastly different communities and locations, but the story was the same wherever I went. Experienced teachers spoke passionately of the difference it was making to the children they were teaching, many expressing surprise at the extent of the difference. One long-time Year One teacher was honest enough to tell me that her experience in the trial had led her to conclude that our previous system had been holding children back.

The Prep trials were a resounding success despite the naysayers and resisters. The expectations of parents had created momentum. Our new challenge was to turn a pilot scheme into a universal reality. This would be the real test, and there were many who thought it could not be done. They had grown used to governments trialling an idea and backing off when real money was needed to make the program available to everyone. Providing Prep to every eligible child in every primary school in every sector of schooling, in even our most remote towns, seemed a daunting challenge. It would take a large commitment of funds, the training and employment of thousands of new teachers, the building of hundreds of new classrooms and the finalisation of a new curriculum. All that would take time and good planning, but mostly it would need a lot of money. As luck would have it, the second year of the trial was an election year, and if ever a government is going to make a big commitment to something important, it is during an election. As a member of the election strategy team, I was well placed to persuade the leadership that the rollout of a full year of Prep to every Queensland primary school should be the core promise of our 2004 election campaign, and I worked hard to make it happen. When we won that election, the full implementation of this reform became my happy duty.

Reshaping something as big as a schooling system is hard work. The effort consumed my days from beginning to end. Talking seemed to be at the heart of the effort. Talking at public meetings of parents or at teachers conferences, arguing with Treasury and Public Works bureaucrats about building costs, negotiating with unions about the employment conditions of thousands of new teachers, speaking with principals about leading the change in their schools. It was one long conversation, a seemingly endless dialogue to persuade, cajole and pull every player over the line. Like all big undertakings it had many twists and turns, many moments when we faltered, when I could feel the risk of the venture collapsing. But these moments were fleeting and always quickly overshadowed by the heady exhilaration of what we were doing. As I navigated the reform through the parliament, through the budget process, through the union negotiations, through the organised opposition of disgruntled preschool teachers, through the funding talks with the Catholic and independent sectors, through the haggling over building costs, every milestone added to the growing

LEFT: Aged about two, with my brother Stephen. As the oldest of four siblings, I learned early that responsibility was its own reward.

I grew up on the Gold Coast, where I attended local Catholic primary schools. This was my Year One class at Infant Saviour School with our teacher, Sister Mary Antonia. I'm in the second row, fourth from the left. My brother Stephen is in the back row on the far left. From Year Four I attended Guardian Angels, which was run by the Sisters of Mercy, who were passionate about girls' education and instilled in us compassion for the needy.

The Whitlam government's introduction of the Supporting Mother's Benefit in 1973 gave my mother the confidence to leave her unhappy marriage. It was the first time I realised how governments can have a positive impact on people's lives. However, when my parents divorced, the church wasn't so supportive, and at age fourteen I moved from a convent school to Miami State High. **LEFT:** In my Miami State uniform circa 1975.

RIGHT: Thanks to Whitlam's abolition of university fees, I was able to attend Queensland uni. There I became involved in student politics and attended the 1978 protest against then premier Joh Bjelke-Petersen's prohibition of the right to assemble. The brutality of the police that day exposed the ruthlessness of the repressive Bjelke-Petersen regime. By 1980, when this photo was taken, I was running for the leadership of the student union. Two years later, I joined the Labor Party.

In 1985 I took a job in a support program for young families living in Redfern's housing commission flats in Sydney. There I fell in love with Greg Withers, the coordinator of a housing cooperative. Here we are at Bondi after finishing the City to Surf fun run in 1986.

When our first baby was born in late 1987, Joh Bjelke-Petersen's number was up, following damning revelations of corruption. The former peanut farmer finally resigned within a week of my giving birth, and Greg and I happily named our baby Joseph. **TOP LEFT:** Leaving hospital with Greg and Joseph in late 1987. **BOTTOM LEFT:** With my sister, Mary, and baby Joseph.

BELOW: Greg and I had a second son, Oliver, in 1993. Juggling politics and family is tough, but somehow we made it work. Time away together helped. Here we all are in the mid 1990s on one of many annual family holidays on Stradbroke Island.

During 1990, I travelled the state as a trainer with the Trade Union Training Authority. The job was tough but it opened my eyes to a much bigger Queensland and the issues faced by those who live in regional areas. Here I am on one such trip, standing in a dry creek bed in central Queensland.

Following Bjelke-Petersen's ignominious exit from the political stage, Greg and I worked hard for the election of a Labor government. Our hopes were fulfilled when Wayne Goss led Labor to victory in December 1989. The Goss government contained a record six female MPs, including my friend and mentor Anne Warner. Six years later, Anne decided to retire and encouraged me to nominate for preselection. Here we are on election night 1995, when she ceased to be the member for South Brisbane and I became the new representative.

The first day of the forty-eighth parliament on 5 September 1995 and my first sitting day as a member. With (L to R) my brother John, my mum, Frances Tancred, and Greg. The Labor government had a majority of one, and following the loss of the Mundingburra by-election in February 1996, we lost government and Wayne Goss resigned.

Former lawyer Peter Beattie led Labor to victory in 1998. Here he is with deputy Terry Mackenroth and the burgeoning ranks of Labor women MPs after winning the 2001 election. I'm second from the left in the front row. In this second term, I became Queensland's first female Minster for Education and the first woman to serve as the Leader of Government Business in the parliament. PHOTO BY GLENN BARNES / NEWSPIX

ABOVE LEFT: Former ACTU boss and federal Labor minister Greg Combet has been a lifelong friend of my husband, Greg. Here I am with the two Gregs at a 1998 election fundraiser, not long after the notorious waterfront dispute, in which Greg Combet was a key player.

ABOVE RIGHT: With Greg and the boys at the June 2000 march for reconciliation as Minister for Families, Youth and Community Care and Disability Services.

LEFT: With Peter Beattie, Terry Mackenroth and other Labor ministers in 2004. Acutely aware of how education transformed my own life, I was determined to make it the heartbeat of our government in my new role as Minster for Education. At the time, Queensland lagged behind most other states in early education and school completion rates. Raising the state's standards would prove to be a hugely satisfying job. PHOTO BY LYNDON MECHIELSEN / NEWSPIX

When deputy premier Terry Mackenroth retired from politics in 2005, Peter Beattie suggested I throw my hat in the ring for the job, and on 28 July 2005 I was sworn in as deputy premier of Queensland by governor Quentin Bryce. PHOTO BY DAVID SPROULE / NEWSPIX

In 2007, as deputy premier, Treasurer, and Minister for Infrastructure, I was responsible for ensuring our then drought-stricken state didn't run out of water. **ABOVE:** On a visit to the new desalination plant on the Gold Coast on 11 September 2007, following Peter Beattie's announcement the day before that he was retiring from politics, I declared I would be standing for the position of leader of the Queensland Parliamentary Labor Party. PHOTO BY DAVID CLARK / NEWSPIX

On 13 September 2007 my family were there to witness my swearing in as Queensland's first woman premier. Joseph and Oliver were highly amused when my mother experienced a serious wardrobe malfunction just moments before this photo was taken: (L to R) Joseph, Mum, Oliver, Greg and me.
PHOTO BY PATRICK HAMILTON

ABOVE: I've been an early-morning jogger for years, and I didn't give it up when I became premier. Here I am in Sydney for a meeting of COAG in 2008, jogging around the harbour at dawn with my then Treasurer, Andrew Fraser.
PHOTO BY PETER MORRIS / FAIRFAX SYNDICATION

RIGHT: Participating in the Brisbane to the Gold Coast cycle challenge the same year.

momentum. It gave the whole government a sense of purpose. The education story propelled us forward and we were animated by the impetus of it.

As the school year began in late January 2007, all the work was done. From Coolangatta to Cape York, from our biggest urban schools to our far-flung one-teacher schools, even in our famous 'schools of the air', every public, Catholic and independent primary school opened its gates to Prep students. It had taken five years of work, months of political manoeuvring, endless hard yards every budget cycle, days and days and days of argument, debate and persuasion – and now it was finally real. The five-year-olds who walked through the gates that morning will graduate in 2019. They are the first of a new generation of Queenslanders who will have the same years of schooling and the same early-childhood education as other Australian children. I will raise a glass to them in the final months of 2019 as they walk out of their school gates and into the world. As I planned and negotiated and bargained my way through the effort of getting them their extra year, I learned much about leadership and the exercise of power. I learned the value of marshalling support for a big idea before launching, the importance of an influential group of champions to lead the charge and I learned, again, that everything works better when you work to bring others with you.

*

The task of modernising and transforming Queensland demanded action on many fronts. Our economy needed to diversify beyond mining, tourism and agriculture into technology, science, innovation and research, the new drivers of economic growth. Our infrastructure had to be overhauled to meet the needs of rapid population growth; education, health, welfare and transport needed money and attention; and government and the parliament had to become more accountable. On top of all this was the need to nurture a flourishing arts and cultural life for people across Queensland. We held dear the view that creativity in all its forms feeds the human spirit and that a renewal in the arts would mark us as a truly modern state.

Responsibility for this part of our agenda fell to me when the arts portfolio was added to my education responsibilities in 2004. It was an exciting time to take over the reins of the arts portfolio, as we had just begun construction of the major Millenium Arts Project, which saw new art galleries and performing arts centres in a number of regional centres, including Cairns and Maryborough, and the development of Queensland's Gallery of Modern Art (GOMA).

GOMA was first conceived by my predecessor in the arts portfolio, Matt Foley. Matt was a passionate lover of the arts and had fought tooth and nail for this investment. I was thrilled to have the chance to realise his vision but, as I contemplated my new duties, I was mindful of our recent experience completing Queensland's new football stadium on the grounds of the old Lang Park. This stadium, now much loved and admired, had proved deeply unpopular in the building. In a state besotted with rugby league, this had caught us off guard. For many people, the stadium became a symbol of a government with wrong priorities. The community felt we should be building new hospitals or schools or roads, not football stadiums, and we weathered quite a storm of discontent as the stadium rose out of the ground. It has since become one of the most popular sporting arenas in Australia, but that experience was very much on my mind as I took on the task of overseeing the construction of our new art gallery. I worried that if the football-loving public of Queensland had resented a new football stadium, they would likely take a dim view of the large investment in GOMA.

It came as a revelation to me that this new art gallery was loved before it even began to take shape. At no stage in its construction, even when the costs escalated and I had to announce additional money to complete the project, did the gallery become a beacon for discontent. There were no angry letters to the editor, no attacks on the government for wasting taxpayers' money. Australian governments of all political persuasions have traditionally been cautious and reluctant about investing in cultural institutions. New cultural facilities are only added to the architecture of the country every thirty or forty years, and yet they define and redefine us. GOMA, and the capacity it has given Queensland to attract significant exhibitions, has reshaped the nation's view of the state's cultural life and its contribution to that of the country. It has become the most visited museum in Australia and is widely cherished.

GOMA was the most visible of our efforts to reinvigorate the arts, but there were many others. It was a time of great creative flourishing. As I worked to secure a suite of international ballet companies to perform in Brisbane, or gained funds for an indigenous arts strategy, including the successful Cairns Indigenous Arts Fair, or committed new funds to our film industry, I was excited by the politics of the agenda and the momentum it created across the community. In art, in dance, in theatre, film and literature, our efforts were felt and noticed across the country. It remains one of the only unambiguously popular agendas for which I held responsibility. The experience also buoyed me, personally. I felt enlivened by the creativity blossoming around me. The chance to work with some real game changers such as Tony Ellwood, the first director of our new art gallery, John Kotsis, who led the charge to renew our performing arts centres and the performances they secured, former arts festival director Leo Schofield and many others was a gift. It fed my own hunger for creativity and beauty just as it fed the hunger of the community, and I felt that reflected in all the other work I was doing at the time.

When we invest in the arts and our community's cultural life we enrich everyone in a much, much deeper way than when we build roads and bridges. Nevertheless, fighting for these funds in a budget process is a tough business. Something always seems more compelling or urgent. But a failure to grow these parts of our public life impoverishes us all and I am proud to have been part of governments – first Peter Beattie's and then my own – that kept this agenda near the top of the list. They say that 'politics is short; art is long' and the arts and cultural landscape of Queensland are the living testament to that.

*

My own education in exercising power took a further step forward with my promotion to deputy premier. In 2005, Peter Beattie confided that his deputy premier, Terry Mackenroth, was considering retiring, and he encouraged me to nominate for the vacancy. When this opportunity came up, I had been a cabinet minister for seven years, and a member of the Cabinet Budget Review Committee and Leader of Government Business in the House for five of those years. I was the third-most senior minister of the government, and in many respects the natural choice for the next deputy leader. But in politics nothing is predictable and there is no 'natural choice'. Ascending the ladder is a tricky business, built on a complex, interwoven chemistry between shifting allegiances, ability and hard work, loyalties, factional support and a multitude of indefinable factors.

The position of deputy premier gave whoever held it a huge opportunity to develop as a person and as a leader. If I took on the role, I knew I had to be prepared to step up to the top job if required. There is never any certainty in politics and most deputies never become leaders. But I felt strongly that I shouldn't take on the deputy position unless I was willing to take the next step. When I stood for the vacant position of deputy premier and was elected, I became the first woman to do so in the history of the Queensland Labor Party. I broke through another part of the wall that holds women back from leadership and I sowed the seeds of all that was to come in my political career.

With the new position came increased power. It came too with new portfolio responsibilities – a shift into the big economic arms of government: finance, treasury, infrastructure and state development. I was now responsible for a budget of more than $40 billion and overseeing some of the largest construction projects in the country. I relished the challenge of these new duties. It was a chance to learn and to stretch myself. I was now at the heart of government and exercising considerable power across all our major decisions.

More power brought not only more opportunities but more burdens. I felt the extra burden of it in Gympie, north of Brisbane, in late 2006, as I arrived to address an angry group of residents from the nearby Mary Valley. The government had decided to build a new dam that would flood the valley of the Mary River, and more than two thousand residents and opponents of the dam had come to the Gympie Showgrounds to make their views clear. As both deputy premier and Minister for Infrastructure I was responsible for building our new water grid, including this dam, and was there to explain the implications of the finalised plan, including its new boundaries. Infrastructure is almost always controversial. People want new roads and pipelines but are rarely pleased if the plans affect their backyard. At its most fundamental, the job of government is to provide the basics, and it doesn't get more basic than providing drinking water. In the middle of our worst-ever drought, our existing major dam was proving that, alone, it was not up to the task. This new dam was part of a multi-billion-dollar plan to drought-proof our rapidly growing capital city and south-east region for the future.

Unsurprisingly, those whose farms and homes were to be resumed to make way for this new dam were distressed and angry, carrying hand-painted placards full of fury and hate. As I rose to speak, I was greeted by a wall of howling protest. Two thousand angry people crowded into a large hot shed is a dangerous thing. As I looked out across a sea of ill-tempered faces, I could feel them provoking and inflaming each other. I could see uniformed and plain-clothed police throughout the crowd, but knew that in numbers like this they could be quickly overwhelmed. I knew too that this region of Queensland was home to the most vocal gun lobbyists, some of whom were likely to be in the crowd. Most of the crowd looked as if they had never been to a protest of any kind. They were ordinary mums and dads, genuinely and understandably distraught because of the threat to their homes and their community. But together, they had become a lynch mob. During my flight in to Gympie that morning, I had been absorbed in getting the details right. It was dense technical material and the residents deserved accurate, factual answers. In revising the details, I had not thought to fear for my safety. But as I readied myself to stand on the stage, I could feel the undercurrent of danger as it rose and swelled through the crowd. It was a knife-edge situation that demanded calm but firm authority. I knew that I had to listen to them and absorb their anger, I knew I had to be respectful and understand their fears, but I also knew that any hint of fear or weakness on my part could see the day quickly get out of control.

As I took questions, the heckling, jeering crowd began to settle. Everyone understood that some in the crowd needed more facts, and they respected the right of their friends and neighbours to hear the answers. Early on, one questioner threw the accusation that I would be high-tailing it out of there as soon as I could, without listening to them or letting them ask all the questions they had. I countered instinctively, telling him that I would be on that stage until he and his neighbours ran out of things to say. The crowd took that as a challenge, and I took the last question five long hot hours later. It was a marathon day. The crowd had not changed the government's decision, but they'd had every chance to make their point, and they had made me earn my keep. The tenacious valley residents did eventually win the argument when the Rudd federal government overruled the dam some years later.

In facing this angry mob that day there were fearful moments when I felt I was at risk of some very serious harm. But I also felt I owed these people answers, that if the government was going to turn their lives upside down then being there and listening was the least we could do. If we couldn't face them and explain why we were building the dam, then in my view we shouldn't build it. So I drew my strength that day from duty and obligation. I could have left after half an hour, but that would not have satisfied this crowd's anger, or its questions, so I stuck it out. I also learned a lot about how the project was being managed and how people were being treated on the ground, which helped us to do it better.

The whole event, of course, was being reported as it happened. The sounds and images of angry, screaming faces and mob-jeering were irresistibly compelling. As I returned to my office and began to take calls, I realised how others had seen it. In the eyes of most, the protesters had overplayed their hand, their message swamped by their anger and aggression. There was widespread amazement that I had stood and taken it for as long as I did, and I was appraised in a new light, as someone who had 'plenty of guts'.

I felt I'd done plenty of gutsy things before I faced the ill-tempered folks from the Mary Valley. But this new public image of me standing there, alone, staring down a surly, boiling mob without flinching or running for cover, helped to cement the view that I could summon the courage to do the gutsy things that leaders need to do, that I had the grit and substance to balance the show business.

SIX

In At the Deep End

Twelve years after becoming a member of the Queensland parliament, I was sworn in as the first woman Premier of Queensland at Government House by the Governor of Queensland, Quentin Bryce. That day, 13 September 2007, was when I shifted from being a leader in my community, as every MP is expected to be, to being 'the Leader'.

It was a bright spring morning full of sunshine and a palpable sense of history being made. Everyone there felt part of something bigger than themselves. I was just one of many present that morning who had worked hard for years to improve the lives of women, one of many who had worked to ensure women were endorsed as candidates, who'd worked to get women elected in seats that no one thought they could win, who'd argued long and hard within the Labor Party and in the broader community for women to get a fairer go. It was a big day for all of us. Even others who don't support my side of politics told me that they felt proud that Queensland had taken this step. They would still campaign against me at the next election, but my swearing-in was a moment, rare in Australian politics, that transcended the political divide.

When I became premier, I knew that I had chosen a particular kind of leadership: high profile, political and very public. I felt the sting of fear and anticipation that comes when you put your hand up. I had raised my hand for a huge responsibility, the kind of leadership that lives under the limelight of public scrutiny and criticism twenty-four hours a day. It was a choice I wanted, a choice that thrilled and terrified me, and one that I grabbed with both hands.

*

Between Peter Beattie's announcement of his retirement from politics and my swearing-in as the new premier there were just three days. Peter had been contemplating his decision for months, and he and I had held many conversations about his possible retirement. Our discussions were sometimes detailed, and often philosophical, but for me they always had a slight air of unreality about them.

Peter Beattie strode large on the political stage of Queensland. Having risen to public prominence as one of the outspoken architects of major reform of the Queensland Labor Party in the late 1970s and early '80s, he had gone on to become party secretary and was elected to the state parliament in 1989. Peter was part of the tidal wave that swept away the conservative rule of the Bjelke-Petersen government and elected Wayne Goss as the first Labor premier of Queensland in thirty-two years. By the time Peter and I were having these conversations, he had been a member of parliament for eighteen years, had won the last four elections and been premier for almost a decade. It was difficult to imagine Queensland politics without him, and it didn't seem plausible that he would simply walk away from politics and public life.

My discussions with Peter were not the only ones he was having. He had confided in a few trusted colleagues and had publicly raised the possibility of his retirement a number of times. At the ALP State Conference in early June 2007 he had announced that he was thinking about his future and whether he would stand at the next election. He had spoken openly with a number of journalists in the preceding months, who had faithfully reported his deliberations. Despite all his tilling of the soil, it still came as a shock when he told me he had made his decision, set the date and would advise his cabinet when they met on Monday, 10 September 2007. He planned to call a media conference immediately after the cabinet meeting and, with his wife, Heather, by his side, make the announcement.

As the days went by, Peter's imminent departure became increasingly real. Proving the adage that the best place to hide something is in plain sight, I watched as he took steps to put his decision into action. I watched him clean out his parliamentary desk in the middle of question time. A full parliament and media gallery looked on without realising the significance of his actions. I watched as he emptied the drawers in his office while we talked through the issues we would face in the days ahead. And as I watched, the reality of this enormous shift started to sink in.

Contemplating the days ahead, I began to plan my own next steps. Greg and I talked at home, conscious that life for both of us, and for Joe and Oliver, could be about to change immeasurably. We agreed that it was too much to expect two teenagers to hold this confidence and decided to tell them just as Peter was making his public announcement.

I was determined not to let anyone see me as distracted or to hint that something extraordinary may be looming. In public life you learn quickly that the art of keeping a confidence is critical to your survival. Peter was entitled to a dignified exit from his political career, and I would not be the one to give the ravenous media pack a sniff of this story. This was easier said than done. As the days passed, my excitement and nervous tension grew in equal parts while I prepared myself for what might lie ahead.

Peter had arranged to visit Kevin Rudd, then federal opposition leader, at his home in Brisbane on the Sunday evening prior to the announcement. The next federal election was due in a matter of months and Peter wanted to ensure that Kevin was not taken by surprise. Within minutes of Peter's announcement, Kevin would certainly be asked to comment. When Peter sent me a message that night telling me that he had broken the news to Kevin, the wheels were in motion.

On Monday morning Greg and I spoke quietly about what lay ahead of us that day. What had been a possibility may be about to become a reality. It was not a possibility that Greg had easily embraced. He often spoke of his fears for me if I took this step. 'Australians are brutal to their political leaders,' he had warned me. 'And they are particularly unforgiving to women in public life. I don't want to watch you being torn apart.'

But now that the reality could be upon us, he encouraged me. 'You can do it,' he said. 'We can make it work.'

We knew that it would bring more big changes to our life, but we were ready for me to jump through the next part of the wall.

*

Peter told his colleagues of his decision to retire just before the end of the cabinet meeting. There was a moment of stunned disbelief and audible intakes of breath from several ministers around the table. I watched my colleagues struggle to accept the news as I had done over the past week. Again, despite Peter's many private and public statements about his likely departure, they were all unprepared for this moment. One by one, each minister spoke of Peter's many political achievements, of his personal support for them in the rough and ready world of politics over the years. Some around the table, like me, had come from opposition to government with Peter and been a member of his cabinet for all his years as premier. Others had only joined the cabinet in the past year. For all of us, it was a poignant moment. We understood that an era was ending, and some fought back tears as they recalled the highs and lows. It was hard not to be sentimental.

As Peter prepared to face the press conference, I called a meeting of my staff to break the news and outline our schedule for the coming days. Many of my team had been with me for a number of years, though some were relative newcomers. Some of the senior staff had seen Peter's retirement coming, if not the timing; others were taken completely by surprise. The rigours of politics, the daily trench warfare with the media, and all the ups and downs of public life forge fierce loyalty and firm friendships in political offices. Our close-knit team was full of excitement about what this might mean for me and what it might mean for them. In truth, not all of them would be able to come with me if I moved from the deputy's office to the premier's office. For such a transition to occur smoothly, I would have to pull together a blend of Peter's team, whose members had solid experience running a premier's office, and my own team, who knew me warts and all. This would not be easy for me or for them, but for now that process was some days away and we were all abuzz with possibility.

The minute the news broke, the phones in my office began clamouring. My staff took messages and told media outlets and persistent journalists that I wished Peter Beattie and his family well, but was not available for interviews and would not be making any further comment. Today belonged entirely to Peter and his family. This would be his last media conference as premier, his last moment in the full glare of the public spotlight. He deserved to have the day to himself.

I picked up the telephone and got to work. My first calls were to my boys, to tell them what was going on. 'Cool,' Joe said. 'Cool,' said Oliver. Teenagers. What did I expect? But I was relieved that they were genuinely excited.

My next task was to settle the difficult question of a running mate. Coming from the left of the party, I needed someone from the right for factional balance. There were two frontrunners, both senior ministers: John Mickel and Paul Lucas. I had to speak to both of them as quickly as possible. The right faction had to be confident that I would be a leader for the whole party and that they would be part of its leadership team.

Knowing this day was coming, I had been thinking hard about the team I wanted around me. Both John and Paul would bring experience and clout to the job. Paul is two years younger than me and we had briefly been at university together, so I had known him longer and a bit better than John. But this played little part in my thinking and was not what settled the matter for me. Ultimately, I felt that Paul was hungrier, would work harder and was hard-wired for loyalty. When I told John that while I recognised his ambitions, I would be supporting Paul for deputy premier, it was a difficult and awkward meeting. Despite my rising excitement about the prospect of becoming leader, this meeting was a visceral reminder that along with all the great decisions, leaders have to make the ugly decisions that no one thanks them for. To avoid a divisive ballot, I asked John not to stand against Paul. John was not happy, but agreed to consider it. I took this to mean that he would do his own soundings about the support he would have should he force a ballot. When John did not stand, that told me he didn't have the numbers he needed.

My discussion with Paul was much easier. Between us we set to work talking to our caucus colleagues, who would be called on to vote for a new parliamentary leadership team at a meeting scheduled for Wednesday morning, less than forty-eight hours away. We advised each of them that I would be running for leader and Paul for deputy and asked for their support. To my knowledge, there was no one else likely to stand and no one else who would secure majority support if it came to a vote. The most likely outcome was that I would be elected unopposed. But to take this for granted would be the biggest mistake I could make. If I began my bid for the leadership by assuming that I didn't have to work for every vote, it would signal the worst kind of arrogance and start my new relationship with my caucus colleagues in the worst possible way. I had to earn the respect of every colleague.

Many calls were short as people assured me of their support. Others took much longer. Some colleagues let me know through others that they didn't need a phone call, I had their support. Others sought to talk through their fears or ideas about the challenge and opportunity of Peter's departure, while others wanted to negotiate something for themselves in return for their support. I also called a number of senior people in the party: the party secretary, Milton Dick; members of the executive; and senior union leaders. The hours wore on as I made call after call. Slowly, I began to understand that I would indeed be the only candidate, that I really was about to become the next premier of Queensland.

On Tuesday, the day after Peter Beattie's retirement was made public, I joined my running group as usual at 5.30am. As we finished our five-kilometre route, we came back over the Goodwill Bridge at Southbank to find that a large media contingent, complete with TV cameras, radio journalists and newspaper photographers, had turned up to greet me. I had been running with this group for almost five years, and before that day, the media had never bothered to show up. Bemused, my fellow runners watched the antics and tried to stay out of the way of the cameras. I was sweaty, flushed and very self-conscious about being in my running gear. This hadn't been part of my plan, but it was now part of the show. It was a taste of how my life was about to change.

Later that morning, I was scheduled to visit the construction site of our new water desalination plant on the Gold Coast. As deputy premier, Treasurer and Minister for Infrastructure, I was responsible for this $1.2 billion project that would provide our drought-stricken region with a desperately needed back-up water supply. The timing of this project was critical. We had been in drought for several years. Wivenhoe Dam, our primary drinking-water supply, was verging on running dry. In order to begin digging a tunnel out to sea to access supplies of saltwater for treatment, engineers first had to bore a seventy-metre shaft down to the tunnelling point. My visit coincided with the achievement of this critical project milestone. I resolved to go ahead with my visit to the desalination plant, making it and my hometown of the Gold Coast the backdrop for my declaration that I would stand for the position of leader at Wednesday's ballot.

At the desalination plant, I was kitted out with steel-capped work boots and a hard hat. To illustrate the completion of this shaft and the start of tunnelling, I would inspect the work up close. I stepped inside a metal cage suspended over the shaft and was lowered into the depths. My journey down the tunnel shaft now seems an extraordinarily fitting analogy for the next step in my political career. For all that I thought I was prepared for what was coming, I was in fact embarking on a journey to a completely foreign place. After twelve years in politics and having held many senior positions I was about to learn, as every leader does, that the journey from second in charge to leader is the biggest leap of all. No matter how long the apprenticeship, and mine was longer than most, there is no way to understand the enormous responsibility of being the last one in the chain of command, the one whose duty it is to make the call. It can only be fully grasped and understood when the heavy, visceral reality of it settles on your shoulders. Like the journey into that tunnel shaft, my destination was perilous and precarious, and the ground would constantly shift beneath me. I was heading towards an environment dominated by men where I would often be an outsider. And when I arrived there I would be able to see extraordinary new frontiers opening up, but I'd need a shell as hard as the protective work gear I was now wearing.

The media expected the news of my candidacy for the premiership and the press conference was alive with an electric current of anticipation. My staff, the plant site workers and the journalists all shared the sense that tectonic plates were moving in Queensland politics. The reporters had been interviewing me for years, but suddenly I was both the new kid on the block and the next leader of their state. As I emerged from the tunnel shaft and we gathered for the media conference, they pushed and swarmed around me, trying to get the best shot for the television audience, the clearest recording of my words for radio, the defining photographic image for the daily newspapers. Afterwards I felt calm but alive with the knowledge that I had taken an irrevocable step.

The following day I made the next necessary move by standing for the leadership of the parliamentary Labor Party. Because the Labor members would meet at Parliament House, Peter Beattie and I decided to walk the few blocks there from our offices in the executive building. As premier, Peter was flanked by his usual team of special protection officers from the

Queensland Police Service. I walked slightly in front of him with my soon-to-be deputy, Paul Lucas, and another minister. We had the full media pack in tow, recording this historic walk. My head full of everything that was about to happen, my thoughts consumed with what I would say to my colleagues, I paid little attention to my surroundings.

With no warning, a man yelling at the top of his lungs rushed across the street and into our path. He charged straight at me, screaming my name. 'I want to walk the plank with Captain Bligh!' he shouted, in a bizarre reference to my famous ancestor, William Bligh, captain of the *Bounty* and an early governor of the colony of New South Wales. I was terrified. I didn't know who the man was, if he was dangerous or had a weapon. A police officer grabbed me and deftly moved me out of the way as the other officers brought the man to the ground.

The interloper may have been a complete stranger to me, but he was no stranger to the police or the media. I had been accosted by a man better known to the Australian public as the 'serial pest'. He's earned his nickname by serially interrupting public gatherings and events, including running on to the racetrack during a Melbourne Cup and disrupting play on centre court at the Australian Open Tennis Championship.

I felt the sweaty prickle-skin rush of fear, but I had to recover my composure immediately. TV cameras and the eyes of a full media pack were all trained on me. My pounding heart took time to slow. The serial pest's intimidating stunt was a sickening reminder that putting myself forward for party leadership would not only give me powerful opportunities, but potentially it would expose me, and those close to me, to real danger.

A few minutes later I walked into the caucus room with Peter Beattie and my fear fell away. My colleagues rose in a cheer-filled standing ovation. This meeting was both sentimental and exciting. Caucus members spoke with emotion of Peter's time in government, but they enthusiastically endorsed the new leadership team. At his last such meeting, Peter was generous and jovial. After so many years the weight of responsibility was beginning to lift and he seemed lighter on his feet. He spoke of how much Labor had achieved, how different the Queensland of today was from the one he grew up in. To illustrate the line of change and transformation, he contrasted the leadership of Joh Bjelke-Petersen – National, conservative and male – with the leadership of Anna Bligh – Labor, progressive and female.

The caucus tradition dictates that when a vacancy arises, all those wishing to be considered will stand in their place. As I rose to signal my candidacy for leader, I looked around the room, confirming that there were no others rising to their feet. I heard the chair of caucus declare that I was elected, unopposed, as the new leader of the Queensland parliamentary Labor Party. I felt a very wide grin crack my face open. After all the fear and nervous tension of the days and weeks leading up to this moment, I let myself feel the elation of it. I stopped thinking, very briefly, of what I needed to do next and just let the joyful, unbelievable reality of it course through me for a minute.

The minute was soon up. It was my turn to speak to my team for the first time as their leader. I vowed to live up to their expectations and to be a leader for all of them. I promised to lead them with drive and energy and not waste a minute of the opportunity. I led them through the challenges that lay ahead and drove home just how hard we would all have to work to win the next election. I urged them to optimism and a belief that our best years were still ahead of us.

*

As Quentin Bryce, then Governor of Queensland, administered my oath of office at Government House, she departed from the set text to speak movingly of the significance of the day. As a woman who'd spent much of her own life breaking through walls for herself and other women, she felt the force of the moment just as I did. She spoke simply but powerfully of the fact that swearing in our first woman premier was an honour for her, a substantial achievement for me and a milestone in the state's political history. The governor said that while my achievement was worthy of remark, she hoped it was another step in the unfolding history of women's struggle for equality, which would one day make such events entirely unremarkable. I felt the truth of her words. There's no point going through the wall unless it's an opening salvo in bringing the wall down.

I looked across at my mother, imagining what this day meant for her. We caught each other's eye for a second, but had to quickly look away as we felt the emotion of it all almost catch up with us.

To know you're making history is a huge and magnificent feeling. The walls of the anteroom, where I had waited before the ceremony, are lined with the photos of governors past. Except for one they were all men, most from a military background, decked out in full dress uniforms, complete with swords. Today was a first: our first woman premier, being sworn in by our second woman governor.

I felt elated and full of the honour and humility that comes with public office. There, in the grandeur and gravitas of Government House, I felt the arc of history and my place within it. The marble tiles and polished floors, the architectural majesty of a building designed to speak of the dominance of an empire, all gave weight to the day. And in the lofty spaces of the imposing old house, I also sensed the burden of being part of history. Leadership started to settle on me physically. I felt all the hopeful aspirations of those who had supported my elevation to the premiership and those who wanted me to succeed. I felt the expectations of a hungry public, who wanted fresh ideas from a new premier and another opportunity to revisit old issues with a new government. I felt the truth that already, within these bright desires and expectations, the first seeds of inevitable disappointment were germinating.

*

Media are permitted on the grounds of Government House to take photos and footage of an event. However, convention dictates that interviews are restricted to an area off the grounds, at the entry gates, to avoid any politicisation of the office of governor. Government House has a long curved driveway stretching from its entry gates to its front steps. It has become customary for a newly sworn-in premier to walk down the driveway, some of which is hidden from view by large shrubs, surrounded by their family. The entire media pack waits at the bottom of the drive, hoping for some comments and snapping away with huge long-range lenses.

After a day laden with ceremony and formality, we walked solemnly down the drive, still gripped by the requirement to conform to the conventions. We were happy, but full of the tension that always hovers close on a day like this. My boys had been remarkable, mixing with adult dignitaries, eating delicate sandwiches without spilling even a shred of lettuce and smiling cheerfully throughout. But I could feel the effort they were making to rise to the occasion. My husband gripped my hand tightly. Protective as always, Greg knew how easily a moment like this could turn on one wrong word, how one small slip could be used against me.

The one small slip happened without warning. At the precise moment we strolled behind the tall shrubs, my mother's skirt fell straight to the ground. The elastic in her skirt-band had snapped, and because she was holding hands with Joe and Oliver when it happened she could do nothing to prevent it falling down. We all stopped in stunned disbelief. A horrified silence fell over my media staff and the security officers accompanying us.

'Granny's dropped her dacks,' one of my sons wisecracked.

'She's worse than Grandpa Simpson, you can't take her anywhere,' said the other.

My mother laughed, hiking up her skirt and giving the rest of us permission to laugh our heads off. Hurriedly, I tucked my mother's skirt into the band of her tights and hoped it would hold. She had felt the weight of the day as much as I. Her loud giggles, as I made her respectable, covered her embarrassment and washed away the disciplined tension we'd all been holding onto.

We resumed walking towards the gates and emerged again into the full glare of the media scrum. Miraculously, Mum's skirt-fail had occurred at the one place in the long walk hidden from the view of the cameras. We had wiped away the tears of laughter, but nothing could wipe the grins off our faces, knowing that the reporters had missed the best photo of the day by a matter of seconds. Along with the gravity and meaning of the day, this small private moment defines the day for us. We are a family like any other, giggling our way through our nerves, relieved of the weight of my new responsibilities for one silly, happy minute. Most media outlets used the photos taken as we completed our walk to the gates to capture the day's mood. We looked exactly as we felt: relaxed, fresh from real belly laughter, thankful and happy to be together. My framed copy of the best photo, which sits on our mantelpiece at home, remains one of my all-time favourite family shots.

*

Later that day I held a full media conference with my new Treasurer, Andrew Fraser. Andrew had been my natural choice for Treasurer. He was well qualified, with degrees in law and commerce, graduating with first-class honours and a university medal. He has a razor-sharp mind, and with the political courage to match was a clear up and comer. But at the age of thirty, he was the second-youngest Treasurer the state had ever seen, and my decision to appoint him had raised more than a few eyebrows. This didn't trouble me. As a new premier I had to prove many things to the electorate, chief among them that after almost a decade of Labor governments, the government I led could be fresh and new. I had to raise eyebrows and shake up the joint from day one. A few surprising appointments went a long way to sending this message.

At the media conference I laid out some of our early priorities and started to set the tone of my ambitions as premier. Previous Labor governments had been criticised repeatedly for not anticipating growth, for not keeping up with demand for services and infrastructure. People were feeling the push and shove of rapid population growth. They were sitting in heavier traffic, waiting longer in queues for health services. I knew it was important to acknowledge that we needed to do better and that we needed to govern with a long-range lens.

I spoke of our enduring passion to transform and modernise Queensland – economically, socially and culturally – of my intention to look over the next horizon and see the future challenges coming before they overwhelmed us. I outlined my intention to be a builder, to meet the infrastructure needs – the roads, the bridges, the schools, the health services – of the fastest growing state in Australia. I stressed that my passion for education remained as strong as when I'd held that portfolio and that I intended to build on my record of education reforms with more focus on the early years of learning. I spoke of the challenge of climate change and committed us to renewed action to address it. I spoke also of the importance of an open and transparent government and my intention to deal openly with the media and the public.

As Andrew and I laid out the economic priorities we'd discussed and the journalists peppered us with questions, I could feel the beginnings of us becoming a team: me talking the big picture, laying out my desire to make sure Queensland was ready to seize the opportunities ahead of us; and Andrew, already comfortable with the detail, not fazed by the ham-fisted attempts by journalists to throw him off his guard.

And then came the second slip of the day. Asked what kind of Treasurer he wanted to be, Andrew replied confidently, 'I want to be a future-focused premier.' For a moment he didn't even realise what he'd said, but as the journalists started to joke about a first-day coup, the realisation struck him with a sickening thud. It was clearly a slip of the tongue, and an easy one for me to joke away as it came hot on the heels of my outlining what kind of premier I wanted to be. But, of course, it was just too good for the media to disregard and it played on every news program that night as an almost playful end to the package about my swearing-in. Andrew kicks himself about that moment to this day. But I was sanguine. There is rarely a wholly positive report about any government on any day. For Andrew's sake, I almost wished my mother's efforts to derail the day had reached the cameras. For my mother's sake, I was glad that it was Andrew's slip-up, not hers, that had provided the media fodder on this significant day for our family.

SEVEN

Tits-up In a Ditch

For me, leadership is an extreme undertaking. It's an all-consuming, adrenaline-pumping, white-knuckle ride like no other I've known. The life of a leader is not a normal life. It is a life lived at the edge of physical and mental endurance. It is in equal parts thrilling and frightening, always complex and impossible to reduce to easy rules or dictums. Even those who seek it most are shocked by its relentless, unforgiving demands. And by its effects, leadership changes you.

In politics and public life, your leadership is constantly on show, constantly being weighed and measured, polled and analysed. But this scrutiny reaches fever pitch during election campaigns, when all eyes turn at once to the leader.

In January 2009 I sat with my election strategy team around the large table in the meeting room of my office. We had returned from our Christmas break and were heading into an election year, an election that would be my first as premier. Our pollsters were at the table, outlining our first polling numbers of the new year. The numbers were depressingly low, and Andrew Fraser shook his head, looked at our pollsters and said, 'So, we're tits-up in a ditch, then?' Among his Christmas gifts, Andrew had received the Annie Proulx short-story collection *Fine Just the Way It Is* and the story 'Tits-up In a Ditch' was fresh in his memory.

'Tits-up in a Ditch' tells the joyless tale of Dakotah, a young girl abandoned by her teenage mother and being raised resentfully by her grandparents Verl and Bonita. The story explores Dakotah's bleak and lonely life in the harsh farmlands of Wyoming. On a cold and snowy evening, as Dakotah sets the dinner table, her grandfather tells her about a cow that tried to climb a steep, wet slope that slid out from under her, landing the cow on her back in a ditch. 'Goddamn cow got herself tits-up in the ditch couple days ago. Dead, time I found her,' he says. It is a phrase that sticks with Dakotah, and she will use it again when she needs to speak of a grim hopelessness.

None of the rest of us had heard Verl's colourful phrase before, but we knew exactly what he meant. The phrase reeks of desperation and evokes a feeling that anyone who has ever sat around an election strategy table will instantly recognise. Even during a winning campaign there are terrible days when every part of the game plan seems to fall away. 'Tits-up in a ditch' quickly became the catchcry of our backroom strategy team as we counted down the weeks to the 2009 state election. So many factors seemed weighed against us that we increasingly felt, and often looked, like that sorry bovine creature, politically stranded, our hooves out from under us, mired in the mud with our legs pointing to the sky. The phrase evoked the size of the challenge we had ahead of us.

As we headed into that election, Labor had been in power in Queensland for almost seventeen of the previous twenty years, and the electorate's hunger for a change was palpable. It had dogged Peter Beattie in the lead-up to the previous election in 2006, but he had been saved when the coalition of Liberals and Nationals fell into a fight on the first day of the campaign about which party would nominate the leader if they won a majority of seats. It was amateur and absurd for them to fight about this publicly during an election campaign, and the electorate had quickly fallen away from them.

Having been denied change in 2006, the electorate was hungrier for it in 2009. Further, the Liberals and the Nationals had recently amalgamated to form one party, the Liberal National Party, and for the first time in more than thirty years would be taking a united front into the election campaign. We had been working for months to slow the growing momentum for a change of government. As that challenge began to feel insurmountable, the US investment giant Lehman Brothers collapsed, triggering a massive quake in the world's financial markets that quickly became a global financial crisis (GFC). The economic mood soured, large-scale job losses began to roll out across the state's economy and people became fearful for their financial security and wellbeing. The state's own finances were not immune and as we struggled, along with every other government in the world, to hold firm our budget position, Standard and Poor's dropped Queensland's credit rating from triple A to double A plus. It was a terrible blow to our economic credentials. Moreover, I could feel the weight of history against me. In Australia's political history, only two other women had ever held the position of premier: Western Australia's Carmen Lawrence and Victoria's Joan Kirner. Both, like me, had assumed the premiership mid-term after the retirement of their predecessors and both had lost government at the subsequent state election. If I won this state election in my own right, I would be the first Australian woman to do so. On all the indicators, it looked highly unlikely.

As I prepared to face my first state election as leader, feeling in good shape physically and mentally, I knew the odds were against me, but that stiffened my resolve. I had returned from my Christmas break full of resolute purpose. I had spent much of our family's Sydney holiday thinking about the challenge ahead. The GFC was continuing to wreak havoc across the economies of the world, and the election was shaping up as a contest about who was best placed to steer the state through the choppy economic waters ahead. On one bright, sun-filled day, Greg and I had walked the cliffs and headlands that frame the beaches of Sydney's eastern suburbs and talked for hours about what needed to be done. We knew that unemployment was the looming fear for many people as we headed into 2009. As we walked, we designed an employment strategy, including the setting up of a jobs taskforce in conjunction with the private sector to counter the unemployment threat. It was this strategy that filled me with purpose and I began to put it into action the day I returned from leave.

When Andrew Fraser declared to the election strategy team, a week later, that our re-election chances were 'tits-up in a ditch', I felt at once the fear of losing and the excitement of proving them all wrong. As we drew closer to calling the election, both emotions would drive me to just keep going.

In late February, I called the election for Saturday, 21 March. Some hours later, Kevin Rudd, by then the prime minister, phoned me. Kevin told me there were only a handful of people in the country who had faced what I was about to endure and that, having won his own election just eighteen months earlier, he was one of them. He went on to say that I would face the most gruelling experience of my life, that the demands would seem inhumane and the weight of it would feel unbearable at times. He reminded me that it was a marathon, not a sprint, and that I should pace myself. He wished me luck and counselled me to get plenty of sleep, advising me not to accept any night-time functions unless absolutely necessary. 'You don't win elections at night-time,' he said. He was right in all respects.

More than a year earlier, a man had stepped out of a crowd at a community barbecue in Cairns and told me he liked what I was doing but knew it was a hard job. He handed me a note and said he hoped it would help. Putting it quickly in my pocket, I didn't read the note for some days, but it turned out to be the 'Paradoxical Commandments' by Dr Kent M Keith:

1. People are illogical, unreasonable, and self-centred. Love them anyway.

2. If you do good, people will accuse you of selfish ulterior motives. Do good anyway.

3. If you are successful, you will win false friends and true enemies. Succeed anyway.

4. The good you do today will be forgotten tomorrow. Do good anyway.

5. Honesty and frankness make you vulnerable. Be honest and frank anyway.

6. The biggest men and women with the biggest ideas can be shot down by the smallest men and women with the smallest minds. Think big anyway.

7. People favour underdogs but follow only top dogs. Fight for a few underdogs anyway.

8. What you spend years building may be destroyed overnight. Build anyway.

9. People really need help but may attack you if you do help them. Help people anyway.

10. Give the world the best you have and you'll get kicked in the teeth. Give the world the best you have anyway.

I had never read them before, but they touched me as a profoundly accurate reminder of the reasons I was drawn to politics. They recognise, too, how easy it is for those reasons to be eroded by the unforgiving nature of the work. I kept this small note in my wallet and pulled it out on many occasions when I felt under siege. As I read it again on the day before I called the election, I thought that my staff might also find comfort and inspiration in it. With a quick note to them all, I left a copy on every desk late in the evening. I knew we had a battle ahead of us and that my team were facing a wall of resistance. For much of the campaign, we would have little regular contact and I would have few opportunities to lift their inevitably flagging spirits. I hoped this note would keep them focused on breaking through the wall.

*

Throughout a campaign, the party takes sample polls every day to track the mood and voting intention of the electorate. This tracking poll is complemented by regular focus group testing of ideas, policies, slogans and planned advertising. The picture is rounded out by larger polling samples taken in key electorates, and is further supplemented by the published polling of news media and lobby groups. When things are going well all this feedback serves to reinforce the campaign strategy and build confidence and morale. When things are tight or going miserably, and all the information is negative, it feels like a dead albatross around your neck. The leader is the public face of the campaign and that puts her on the road or in the air every day on a punishing schedule. It also puts her a long way from the strategy team. It requires enormous trust for a team to work in these circumstances. On the one hand, I needed to know when our polling had slipped or something I had said or done had missed the mark. On the other, I needed to be protected from a deluge of negative information that would chip away at my confidence. For the twenty-six days of the campaign, strategy meetings are held early every morning and late every evening and pulled together quickly in between if necessary. Sometimes my schedule would allow me to be at these meetings, but more often I participated at the end of a phone line or had to be quickly briefed between events and media conferences. When time was tight and the polling wasn't moving our way, the message more often than not was simply that we were 'tits-up in a ditch'. I didn't need to know every miserable detail. With those few words I knew I had to work harder, do a better job, find a clearer way to get our message to the electorate.

My first 'tits-up' message came sooner than I expected. On the first day of the campaign, seeking to set the focus on employment, I announced a new program to train more apprentices. In doing so, I mistakenly quoted a wrong number in answer to a journalist's question. I had a reputation in the local media for knowing my facts, always being well prepared and being able to accurately recall data when needed to illustrate my point. Two things underpinned this reputation. First, I find facts and figures easy to remember and do my homework to make sure I really do know my stuff. Secondly, and perhaps more importantly, I also have a personal rule that if I don't know the answer, I won't pretend I do. I simply say, 'I will have to get back to you on that one.' In this case, I broke my own rule. I knew when the journalist asked his question that I wasn't absolutely certain of the data he requested, but in the nervous tension of that first campaign press conference, I gave an answer anyway. It was a small mistake, but it had to be corrected, and in the feverish heat of a campaign the mistake took on an amplified significance. My first day quickly became about our campaign getting off to a bad start. As I travelled that night and missed the first television coverage of our campaign, Andrew's post-news message said, simply, 'tits-up'.

The terrible start affected our whole team and I could feel their disappointment and their fear about whether I was up to the task. This in turn had a terrible effect on me. As I felt their confidence slipping I focused inwards and got busy kicking myself for my mistake, a horrible own goal. There are few, if any, political leaders who don't have a moment like this, most often and most spectacularly in the full public glare of election campaigns. It is a sickening feeling that knocks you sideways, just when you need to be at your best. The task is to right yourself again as quickly as possible, but after forty-eight hours I was finding this hard going. As I battled with the voice in my head that was still taking me to task for a stupid mistake, I became more serious and earnest in my determination not to repeat it. I looked unhappy and sombre and was miles away from being the uplifting leader I needed to be to convince people that I was the best person to guide them and the state through the economic difficulties that lay ahead.

Neil Lawrence, the talented advertising director of our campaign, had developed an entire strategy based on my personal qualities and the importance of leadership in uncertain times. I had to find a way back to being the strong, optimistic woman of my own advertising. It was Mike Kaiser, my chief of staff, who snapped me back into the game. Mike is a campaign veteran, whose strategy work I'd admired since we'd first collaborated on the Mundingburra by-election of 1996, and he understands instinctively that elections are as much about mood as they are about facts. He resolutely decided on day three to change tack and go off the original plan. He cleared my diary and declared to the team, 'She has to find her smile again, get her out among people and away from earnest media conferences.' The team quickly scheduled a visit to a shopping mall where I could meet and greet voters as they went about their day.

These events always make campaign teams nervous. They are high risk, impossible to plan and impossible to control. But when a high-risk move works, it pays a high dividend. As I made my way into the air-conditioned cool of Chermside

Shopping Centre in Brisbane's northern suburbs, calmed like other shoppers by the soft music, I began to respond to the people who were seeking me out. The hour I spent in this shopping centre was an important emotional turning point for me in that election. I moved through the mall and spoke with mums and dads, with elderly pensioners, with shop owners and small business proprietors and with young people working in part-time jobs. It jolted me out of my embarrassment and made me refocus on the real fears and problems of voters. As we talked about their worries, I found my footing again. Politics is a profoundly people-oriented business, and it helps if you like people and find their company fascinating. This has always been part of the pull of politics for me, and I was recharged by it in the bright lights of the shopping centre. Those first days of that campaign were a very useful lesson about the powerful impact a leader's mood exerts on her team. As a shoal of fish moves and shifts to an unseen hand, so too my team swung back into formation, driven and lifted by the invisible force of my own restored confidence and optimism.

As the campaign drew to an end, I went into the final week of campaigning neck and neck with my opponent, Lawrence Springborg. From the very first days of the campaign, we had understood how important the last week would be. We knew that many voters would make up their minds in the last few days, and we had to make those days count. By law, a blackout on all electronic campaigning takes effect on the Wednesday evening prior to polling day on the Saturday. All radio and television advertising stops, and voters will only see the candidates or hear about their last-minute campaigning on regular news bulletins.

Mike Kaiser had begun thinking about a last-week strategy several months earlier, before we headed off to our Christmas break. As Greg and I were devising employment programs above the cliffs of Bondi Beach, Mike was putting the finishing touches to his last-week 'barnstorming' strategy.

Mike understood that part of the chemistry of a campaign comes down to who looks hungrier for the victory. The electorate wants leaders who want the job and are prepared to fight for it. I knew that my opponent wanted the job. Lawrence had been in parliament for twenty years, and in opposition for almost eighteen of those years. He had lost to Peter Beattie at the two previous elections and this was likely his last chance. As the campaign pulled into the home straight, the polls had Lawrence and his party just slightly ahead of us. He decided to stay in Brisbane for the last three days and campaign in vital city seats as well as begin to plan his new government.

It was a fatal error. Lawrence looked like he had taken victory for granted, that he didn't need to work for it and wasn't hungry for it. In contrast, Mike's plan had me announce on the Wednesday, just before the electronic blackout took effect, that I would finish the campaign by visiting thirty electorates in the last three days. These electorates would stretch from the far north to the far south, and I would not rest until the polls closed on Saturday evening. I would work for every vote and take no one and nothing for granted.

We told no one, including the large media contingent travelling with me, which electorates I would visit and when. It quickly became a guessing game as the media wondered aloud if it was physically possible to visit thirty electorates in a state the size of Queensland in the timeframe we had set ourselves. These travel plans had been laid well in advance, and while it was an almost impossible schedule, we made it.

As we visited the vast and varied places of Queensland, the images of our odyssey were full of colour and action and movement. I started each day at dawn on beaches and riverbanks, met schoolchildren and their parents, and visited workplaces. I climbed to the top of the hill overlooking Mount Isa in the far north-west, ate breakfast with local workers on the esplanade in Cairns and fed lorikeets at the Currumbin Bird Sanctuary as I revisited my hometown of the Gold Coast. As we traversed the state, we created momentum as we drew towards polling day.

But the polls continued to call a tight race and our sense of progress was dented when, on the morning before election day, the *Courier-Mail* predicted on its front page a landslide against me in Brisbane and an election loss. Their prediction was based on their own polling taken earlier that week. The article was compounded by the editor's decision to break with tradition and publish his recommendation that day instead of the usual Saturday morning. It was a move that I believe was calculated to weaken our position on that final day before polling, and it was a vicious and very personal editorial that recommended a vote for the conservatives. However, Labor's own daily polling had us drawing closer as the week progressed, and undecided voters were still making up their minds.

I knew that I couldn't be blown off course by the *Courier-Mail* in the last twenty-four hours of the campaign. As I faced the media that Friday, they saw a woman determined, not a woman defeated. Among my many stops that day was a visit to my old high school, Miami State. Our local member, who had held the seat for almost a decade, joined me at the school. After a long, hard month of campaigning, she was agitated and worn down by nerves and the newspaper's front page had added to her anguish. I grabbed her hands and told her without hesitation that she was going to make it over the line. I was saying it as much to convince myself as to convince her. It was Churchill's sentiment, 'If you're going through hell, keep going', that kept me fired up for that entire last day.

*

As election day 2009 unfolded, we braced ourselves for a tight result, one likely to be so close that we might not have a clear outcome on the night. After voting and spending time at polling booths across Brisbane, I settled in the quiet shade of the late afternoon to finish writing the speech I would give later that night. It is no easy task preparing for an unknown outcome. I concentrated on getting the tone right, looking for humility in the face of an electoral backlash that may wash us out of government, anticipating the questions about another woman failing to win government in her own right.

After the close of voting, Greg and I gathered in the premier's office with senior staff and some close friends to wait for the results. Greg's close friend John had travelled from Sydney to be with us at every election I had faced. His presence had become a tradition, and we were glad to have him with us again.

As the results began to trickle in, we were surprised to hear that the numbers were going our way. On early results we were polling strongly, much more strongly than we had expected. Mike Kaiser was at the tally room and he rang me, urgently cautioning me against taking any heart from these early results. In his view, the numbers were too early in the count to be trustworthy. But within fifteen minutes of his call, ABC commentators were announcing that, against all the odds, Labor had won. We lost eight seats, all held by good, hardworking people, but it was clear by 8 pm that we would hold fifty-one seats, giving us a clear majority of six in a parliament of eighty-nine seats.

The weight and truth of it all hit me when Lawrence Springborg called me to concede defeat. Our mood shifted from quiet gloom to disbelief to sudden exultation in a short but heady half-hour. I realised that my speech notes were all wrong. I would have to quickly transform my demeanour from a cautious wait-and-see approach to one of strong and confident authority. In a flash, all was movement in my office as I rang the governor to advise her officially of the result, Nicole Scurrah, Lorann Downer and I hurriedly amended my notes and Greg organised for Mum and the boys to meet us at the tally room where I would soon arrive to claim government.

For the months leading into the campaign and throughout each of the preceding twenty-six days, a clear victory had seemed the least likely of all the possible outcomes. As I took the stage that night, flanked by my mother, Greg and our boys, what people saw was a woman joyfully accepting the unexpected. My surprise and my gratitude were clear and real, so too my relief and my elation. As I finished thanking my team and committing myself to serve Queenslanders without letting them down, I began to take questions from the journalists gathered on the floor of the tally room. It was only with their questions that the gravity of the achievement began to dawn. They peppered me with questions about the fact that I had just made Australian political history, that I was the first woman to win a state election in her own right as leader. A question about whether I ever expected Queensland to be the state where this would happen was the one that brought it all home with force. I answered truthfully, saying that growing up on the Gold Coast I could never have conceived of it, that on becoming a young woman in the long shadow of Bjelke-Petersen's government it was beyond my imagination – and it still seemed remarkable that it had actually happened. But I also noted that it was the mark of a new and modern Queensland, one that had been taking shape over the past two decades, and was a further challenge to the persistent stereotype of Queensland being a redneck backwater.

I looked out from the stage at my deputy, Paul Lucas, my Treasurer, Andrew Fraser, my campaign team and the shining, happy faces of Labor party members and supporters. We had defied political gravity. As we slipped like that poor cow down the steep, wet slope of electoral politics, it had miraculously held firm, and we had found our footing. Now we found ourselves, our udders and our hooves all pointing in the right direction and steadfastly planted on firm ground, 'tits-up' no longer.

*

With this victory came my own electoral mandate and all the political authority that comes with that. I could feel a new strength in it. It gave me a renewed sense of purpose and a more commanding presence as I took up the reins of a new term of government. For leaders, the jubilation of victory is quickly over. The day after an election is always a tough day. It is a day that usually starts with the sad task of calling those who have lost their seats. This sorry duty is quickly followed by the painful business of putting a government together. There are big calls to be made with little time for contemplation. A new government has to be formed, cabinet ministers chosen and other positions of influence and power filled. A government has to be sworn in within days of an election. Those days are full of careful manoeuvrings and machinations as hopes are dashed, careers are made and lost. In our case, a government re-elected against the backdrop of a powerful electoral mood for change, I knew that first among my responsibilities was to renew the cabinet, to bring in some fresh new faces, younger members, ready with ideas to challenge us all and guard against our becoming stale.

The flipside of this task was to create some vacancies for these new faces to fill. The task of moving some ministers out of their cabinet positions involves a series of difficult conversations. In our hearts, we all know that we reach a use-by date, but we rarely recognise ours when it comes. Elections are like birthdays; every one brings you a little closer to death. With every election, a government is one step closer to its demise, and the decisions I made in those early days of our fifth term were decisions that would come to count. With a couple of exceptions, those who were not returned to the cabinet held their pain as a grudge, allowing it to fuel a growing distance between themselves and their loyalty to a party that had given them their every chance in public life. When things were at their toughest for us in the years to come, it would be some of those I disappointed on that first day who would let us all down as they took their revenge on me, leaking to the media and betraying the party.

Within a week of winning the election, I received a letter from the former prime minister Paul Keating. Ever one with an eye to history, Paul began his missive with:

> All congratulations. Your victory puts you and me on a unity ticket: the only two Labor leaders to have won a fifth election.

He went on to say:

> As you must well know, when you get to number five, the party is less hungry for the victory and the bullocking is left almost exclusively to the leader ... Can the Queensland Labor Party maintain the degree of hunger and discipline to give it a sixth term? If the answer is no, you should give this term everything you have. Better to use the power and the leverage than to sit playing media games to maintain 'popularity'.

Paul concluded his letter by exhorting me to have a go:

> Better to have a go, thrills and spills included, than to end up on that grey list of long-term Labor premiers who have already slipped from the public's consciousness and its enduring regard.

How prescient his words were to prove over the next three years. As we battled the economic fallout of the GFC and struggled to hold a battle-weary party together, it would be a testing term of government. How often I would feel myself doing all the 'bullocking' from the front, as I tried relentlessly to have a go.

*

After the painful process of renewing the cabinet in 2009, our first task as a new government was to turn our attention to repairing our budget and our financial circumstances. We had called the 2009 election just four days after Queensland lost its triple-A credit rating from Standard and Poor's. A credit rating is an important measure of a government's financial health. It calculates the ratio of the government's revenue to its debts and judges its ability to meet those debts. In 2009, Queensland had a big infrastructure program, the largest in the country. We were building roads, railways, schools and hospitals at an unprecedented rate to meet the fastest growing population in Australia. State revenues are largely made up of levies and taxes from consumption and economic growth such as GST, property taxes, payroll tax, vehicle registrations, mining royalties and gambling levies. When the economy slows, this revenue slows too. People stop spending, they stop buying new homes and investment properties, they put off buying a second car and decide not to go to the club on Friday night and play the poker machines. When the economic downturn is global and catastrophic, as it was in 2009, international demand for minerals and commodities also slows, tourism evaporates and businesses start going backwards and cutting jobs, reducing royalties and decimating payroll taxes. Within months of Lehman Brothers collapsing, Queensland's ratio of revenue to liabilities no longer met the credit agencies' triple-A standard, and we were downgraded.

A credit rating of double A plus is still very healthy; many banks, for example, are rated double A minus or lower. But a downgraded credit rating cannot be ignored. It determines the rate at which a government can borrow money, and when you have a big infrastructure and borrowing program, a downgrade adds millions of dollars in interest costs. These are millions of dollars that could be better spent on schools and hospitals. Further, there are major investors, including many central banks, which have lending rules that prevent them from lending to anything other than a triple-A borrower. We had to reduce our spending, increase our revenue and reduce our liabilities to rectify our credit rating or risk a further downgrade.

There were very few avenues open to us on the spending and revenue side, and none that would not cause significant pain. Queensland was the only Australian state that subsidised petrol. At eight cents a litre, the subsidy was costing taxpayers more than $400 million a year and was escalating as our population grew. Increasing payroll tax and royalties at a time of rapidly escalating job losses across the economy, especially in the mining sector, was not an option. We had no control over GST as it is a federal tax redistributed to the states. In any case, it was falling as people stopped spending. We had already increased vehicle registration fees in the mid-year budget review, six months before the election, in an effort to stem revenue loss. We could consider increasing property taxes, but the property market was catatonic, so an increase would net us little or nothing.

We had to take action on the liabilities side of the ledger. We had gone to the election with a central promise: to protect jobs. Almost all of the biggest jobs-generating projects in the state were government projects. We were building massive water pipelines, major bridges, new hospitals and large extensions to our electricity grid. For almost every one of these projects, the funds had already been borrowed, workers already employed and construction was already underway. It was theoretically possible but simply not tenable to stop the projects. To do so would have caused massive unemployment, exposed the state to untold penalties and taken further life out of an almost lifeless economy.

One solution lay in getting some of our liabilities off the state books, by transferring some of the current and forecast debt from government to private hands. In 2009 Queensland owned more government utilities and government enterprises than any other state, including some, such as the coal division of our state railways, that was not owned by government anywhere else in the country. A large portion of our infrastructure program was being spent on big projects to expand the capacity of these enterprises, from export infrastructure such as commercial rail and ports to the energy network. These government-owned enterprises borrowed on the government books, benefited from government rates of borrowing and contributed a large portion of our debt and financial liabilities. These companies' forecast borrowing needs also counted against us. In the case of the coal and freight division of our railways alone, this amounted to an estimated $21 billion over the next eight years just to keep the company functioning at capacity. It would take more to make it truly competitive against its new private sector rival, Pacific National, which had recently been granted third-party access to the rail network and was already winning contracts.

And so, within weeks of winning the 2009 election, we were presented with the ugliest of choices. Do nothing, watch the state slide further into financial crisis and face the very real prospect of a further downgrade, or do something and take the tough decisions needed to get us back on track. We chose to do something. We chose to assume the mantle of leadership and the responsibility of government. It was not the easy path. We abolished the petrol subsidy, knowing that it would cause pain, but were unable to justify it any longer. We announced that we could no longer own all our government enterprises and that we would examine which were the most appropriate for privatisation. We knew, as we sat around the cabinet table making that decision, that asset sales would not cause pain to anyone's hip pocket as the abolition of the petrol subsidy would. We knew it was the most sensible way to rebalance the state's finances without slowing a sluggish economy any further. We knew also that it would cause real, gut-wrenching heartache within the Labor Party and the union movement. We understood that many would feel betrayed that a Labor government would reach for privatisation, even in these dire circumstances. But we took our decision determined to protect the jobs of as many workers as possible, a foundation Labor principle that we held dear and hoped that our colleagues would similarly hold dear. We believed the economic circumstances to be so self-evident that our colleagues would understand our predicament. We were wrong.

The strength of the unions' ideological commitment to public ownership overwhelmed their loyalty to our government and they began a strident campaign against us. Spearheading their opposition was the allegation that I had 'lied' about asset sales, that I'd had some secret plan and had duped them during the election campaign. It is true that I knew drastic financial action would be necessary, and I had said this many times during the campaign. In fact, when I was asked once whether this might include asset sales, I'd replied that it could not be ruled out. But it is not true that I, or the government, had a secret plan. It is easy now to forget the uneasiness of the early days of the GFC. The ground seemed to keep shifting, and even the most seasoned economists were gripped by fear about where it might all end. The only certainty in February 2009 was the prospect of relentless uncertainty. It would have been impossible to tackle the challenges of the GFC without a mandate or to have contemplated in detail the tough decisions that would be needed with the election looming. I cast the election as a choice about who was best placed to lead through the difficult times ahead. The only battlefield on which an election in that context can be fought is one of leadership.

*

Mine was not the first Labor government to privatise publicly owned assets. The Hawke–Keating government sold Qantas, the Commonwealth Bank and the federal airports. Peter Beattie

the Sunday Mail

MARCH 22, 2009 $2   THESUNDAYMAIL.COM.AU

SHE DID IT

Anna Bligh has made history as the first woman in Australia to be elected Premier, leading the ALP to a fifth straight easy win over Lawrence Springborg's LNP

TRIUMPHANT: Anna Bligh leaves the Brisbane Tally Room last night with Deputy Premier Paul Lucas and Treasurer Andrew Fraser.
Picture: Bruce Long

| LNP CLAIMS MINISTER'S SCALP P2 | HER SECRET STRATEGY P4 | BATTLE FOR THE COAST P10-11 | SEAT BY SEAT RESULTS P14-15 |

Our polling numbers in early 2009 were so tight that Andrew Fraser, quoting writer Annie Proulx, described us as 'tits-up in a ditch'. It was exactly the kind of challenge I relished and I was determined to prove the pundits wrong. In the last three days of the campaign I visited thirty electorates and on 21 March 2009 became Australia's first popularly elected woman premier. **LEFT:** The front page of the *Sunday Mail* the next day. BY NEWS LTD, 22 MARCH 2009 **BELOW:** Greg gives me the thumbs up as I'm sworn in by Governor Penelope Wensley. PHOTO BY WILLIAM LONG

TOP RIGHT: With the new Queensland Labor caucus after our win in 2009.
PHOTO BY DARREN ENGLAND / NEWSPIX

BELOW RIGHT: At the launch of the Cairns Indigenous Art Fair on 20 August 2009 with artist Lorna Shaun, Minister for Aboriginal and Torres Strait Islander Partnerships Desley Boyle and artist Linda Jackson. I had been the Minister for the Arts since 2004, and the CIAF was part of our Backing Indigenous Arts program. It has become Australia's premier Indigenous art fair.
PHOTO BY DAVID CAMPBELL, COURTESY OF ARTS QUEENSLAND

TOP: The year 2010 was a tough one politically. Nevertheless, on Bastille Day, 14 July, when I turned fifty, friends and family attended a French-themed party at Brisbane's Montrachet restaurant. There Greg and the boys presented me with 'Parisanna', a map of Paris that featured all the significant people, places and events in my life.

ABOVE LEFT: Greg had spent months working on the gift, a re-envisaging of the city we have visited together on more than one occasion.

RIGHT: On the Île Saint-Louis with Greg and Oliver.

A week after my fiftieth birthday I was awarded an honorary doctorate by the University of Queensland, the institution where, as a young undergraduate, I first discovered the power of politics to make a difference. PHOTO COURTESY OF THE UNIVERSITY OF QUEENSLAND

When Queen Elizabeth II was scheduled to visit Brisbane's Southbank in 2011, one of the countless questions that came up was 'What to wear?' In the end, red seemed a safe bet, but sporting a larger hat than the Queen may well have been flouting protocol. Of course, her Majesty was too polite to comment, and we got on very well. PHOTO BY LYNDON MECHIELSEN / NEWSPIX

In late 2010 and early 2011, Queensland experienced devastating floods. By the second week of January 2011, the state was three-quarters under water, including parts of Brisbane. But, as I said in media briefings, the disaster might 'break our hearts' but it would 'not break our wills'. After all, we were Queenslanders. Sure enough, we pulled together and pulled through. On 19 January I visited Ipswich with the head of the flood recovery, Major General Mick Slater. Here we're surveying the damage with Brassall State School principal Peter Doyle and community members. PHOTO BY JEFF CAMDEN / NEWSPIX

Hot on the heels of the floods came a second disaster with the arrival of category-five cyclone Yasi on 2 February. The next day, acting prime minister Wayne Swan and I visited devastated Cardwell in far north Queensland. I call this my 'ugly' photo, but Queenslanders just saw a leader who was clearly more concerned about them than her appearance. PHOTO BY GLEN HUNT / FAIRFAX SYNDICATION

With Oliver, who was voting for the first time on 24 March 2012. In the lead–up to the 2012 election, the government's focus had been on rebuilding our damaged state. But by the time the election came around, Queenslanders were looking for a change, and Labor suffered the worst defeat in the state's history. That miserable day was my son Oliver's nineteenth birthday and his first chance to vote. 'Who else gets to vote on their birthday for their mum,' he told a journalist, a comment that played on radio throughout the day. PHOTO BY MICHELLE SMITH / FAIRFAX SYNDICATION

New Year 2013 felt like a fresh beginning, and I was ready to start a new chapter of my life. As it turned out, that new chapter began with a cancer diagnosis and ensuing treatment, which included chemotherapy. When *The Australian Women's Weekly* ran a story about me, editor Helen McCabe convinced me to pose without a headscarf or wig. After all, thousands of women have to deal with the effects of chemo every day, effects that too often remain hidden. PHOTO BY PETER BREW-BEVAN, FOR *THE AUSTRALIAN WOMEN'S WEEKLY*

With Joseph, Greg and Oliver during my cancer treatment in 2013.

As well as joining the boards of Medibank Private and Bangarra Dance Company, in 2014 I became CEO of the YWCA NSW. One of Australia's oldest charities, the YWCA provides services to more than 20,000 women, children, young people and their families. I also got my motorbike licence and bought *Audrey* the Vespa to ride around Sydney. **Above:** Here I am with *Audrey* in the CEO parking spot of the YWCA. PHOTO BY BEN WALTON, COURTESY OF YWCA NSW

Right: With Oliver (volunteering, dressed as a gondolier) at the YWCA's Mother of All Balls in 2014. PHOTO BY BEN WALTON, COURTESY OF YWCA NSW

privatised the TAB and Queensland's electricity retail companies. In each case, these leaders did so without the blessing of the union movement, but without a trenchant campaign against them either. In each of these cases, most of the employees were white-collar and female, as were their unions, none of which held powerful positions within the ALP. In the case of my government's privatisation of Queensland Rail's coal and freight division and our ports, the employees were male blue-collar workers and their unions large and powerful affiliates of the Labor Party. I was a female leader tackling the most entrenched industrialised male power bases within the party. I met with all the unions involved around the big table in my office late on the afternoon of the cabinet decision. It was a meeting charged with emotion but, as the light faded from the room that evening, the emotion was not anger. It had all the grieving sickness of a relationship break-up, and we all felt it. Everyone around the table, government ministers and union leaders, were sorrowful and ashen-faced. I can still feel the heart-heavy sadness of that evening as a new chasm opened up between us.

Just as it does in a relationship break-up, the sadness soon turned to anger. The unions emptied their war chests on us. Billboards targeting individual members of parliament went up in their electorates, television and radio ads assailed us and petitions began within the party and across the community. It was a knock 'em down, drag 'em out fight, all the more painful because long-time friends found themselves on opposite sides. The charge was led by the Electrical Trades Union (ETU), renowned for their destructive tactics. Despite being affiliated to the Labor Party, they had become regular donors to the Greens and felt no compunction about destroying a Labor government. The official stationery of the ETU declares 'Sometimes you have to burn the village to save the village', and they set about burning the village with a vengeance. The irony that huge numbers of ETU members were employed on major government building projects in the construction and energy sectors, their jobs all being protected by our asset sales, seemed lost on the ETU leadership, but it was never lost on me.

I met with union leaders over and over again, together and separately, determined to find a way through our difficulties. On many occasions some of the cooler heads sought me out, offering a compromise to resolve the dispute. I was willing to agree to many of these compromises, but none of those who proffered them had the standing or the authority to broker the deal and bring their colleagues with them. All of the major blue-collar unions had experienced a change of leadership in the previous two to three years. These new leaders were publicly flexing their muscles. They moaned privately about the destructive militancy of the ETU but none were able to stand up to it.

I had worried that many in the unions had become too comfortable to understand that these businesses, especially the coal and freight assets, would wither on the vine without continued government borrowing as their private sector competitors outstripped them. But during the talks they made it clear that they did indeed understand what was at stake. They understood better than most that without a massive injection of funds for new trains and new rail lines, the business would not survive. Worse, they understood that the government simply couldn't afford to keep up with the capital injections needed.

But the unions would rather watch these businesses go quietly and inevitably out the back door, taking all their members' jobs with them, than lose the union power and control they believed came with government ownership.

It was an epic fight for power between the new and old guards of the Labor Party. It was an awful tug of war between those who could not see a role for government that was different from that of the 1950s and those who wanted to create forms of government that would suit present circumstances; between those who believed that being true to your principles meant holding steadfastly to the way things had always been and those who understood that the world, especially the world of work, was constantly changing. And the incessant grind of this tussle wore us all to the bone.

Against all the odds and all the predictions the government held its nerve. I pushed through another wall, and Queensland Rail's coal and freight division was publically floated on the Australian Stock Exchange on 22 November 2010. In the end, this public float was the second largest and one of the most successful public floats in Australia's history. It created a new ASX Top Fifty company, headquartered in Queensland, in which all employees were granted shares. Now called Aurizon, the company has been able to raise capital, extend its reach across the country, expand into new markets, gain new contracts, lift its profits, deliver to its shareholders and employ more people in more secure jobs. More importantly, the sale liberated the state budget from the borrowing requirements necessary to keep the company growing. The coal and bulk freight division of Queensland Rail had never served a public purpose. It had been created in the 1970s to assist the fledgling coal industry to get off the ground. This industry is now dominated by some of the world's largest corporations and there is no longer any policy justification for Queensland taxpayers to underwrite the transport needs of BHP, Rio Tinto, XStrata and the like. These needs are now well served, as they should be, by Aurizon, and the passenger division of Queensland Rail continues in public ownership better able to serve the needs of the public. It remains an important economic reform that will stand the Queensland economy in good stead for decades into the future.

It also remains a terrible, heartbreaking wrench that tore an irreparable hole in the fragile relationship between the labour movement and the Labor Party in Queensland, just as similar debates have done around Australia in the past twenty years. As Labor struggles to reshape itself to reflect the changing face of 21st-century Australia, it is this relationship that has to be rethought and remade above all else. In Queensland, the decision by affiliated trade unions to campaign against a progressive Labor government went a long way towards ensuring we would be tits-up in a ditch when the next election came around.

EIGHT

Parisanna

'Paris is always a good idea.'
Audrey Hepburn as Sabrina Fairchild in *Sabrina*

Fifty is one of the big numbers on life's pendulum. Unlike eighteen or twenty-one, brimming with the possibilities ahead, or thirty and forty, full of babies and career and still looking forward, fifty is a moment that invites reflection and looking back. And more than these others, it has the feel of a fulcrum to it, almost but not too late to change tracks if reflection finds the course wanting. In 2010, as I looked back on five decades of living, I looked back on fifty years as a daughter, twenty-five years – literally half my lifetime – of sharing my life with Greg, twenty-three years of motherhood, fifteen years as a member of parliament and three years as premier. On all fronts it was a big year, and in the midst of all the busy demands of my political life we decided to celebrate it in style.

Bastille Day, France's national day, falls on 14 July, as does my birthday. I knew little of Bastille Day growing up, but as I got older it began to shine a special light on my birthday.

Every year the universal romance of France hangs a little magic over our celebrations. For decades now, it has shaped how we celebrate the day and that, in turn, has inspired an interest in French history, culture, language and food for me and Greg and our boys. As my fiftieth birthday drew near, there was no debate that we would be celebrating at Montrachet, our favourite French restaurant in Brisbane, and the theme would be French.

Greg and the boys took on my fiftieth birthday as a major project. Each had their role to play and they spent many hours in secretive scheming. They booked out Montrachet for the Saturday night nearest my birthday, invited fifty friends and family and encouraged them to embrace the French theme. Excitement mounted as the day drew nearer, plans fell into place and the boys regularly disappeared on mysterious, unexplained errands.

At work, I was navigating a difficult political landscape. In the wake of the GFC, the economy remained stubbornly in the doldrums and the state budget needed drastic remedial action. Our decision to privatise the freight division of Queensland Rail was gnawing away at the critical but often tenuous threads that bind a government to its party membership. I was working overtime to hold them together. It was a time fraught with constant political arguments and the personal pain that comes when the hard business of governing butts up against the dashed hopes of friends and supporters. My parliamentary team was fighting a backlash at every branch meeting, at every union meeting and around the dinner tables of friends and family. We were a mid-term government, hunkered down in the trenches, juggling tough and unpopular decisions, and no one was enjoying it. The pain was exacerbated by the heartbreaking federal leadership struggle in which Julia Gillard deposed Kevin Rudd as prime minister in June 2010. We all knew that a federal election was looming and that it would be a grim and difficult campaign, a campaign in which Labor's stocks would take a beating in Queensland, further diminishing support for our government locally.

As the morning of the party dawned that July, Julia Gillard headed to Government House and called an election. With the happy buzz of party preparations humming through the house, the contrast between my domestic life and my public responsibilities could not have been more sharply drawn.

*

Thierry Galichet is a French chef straight from Central Casting. He's passionate about food, and his guttural French accent matches the swift gesticulations of his hands as he draws us all into his restaurant. His girth precedes him and speaks of his long love of food, wine and all that is good in French cuisine. Montrachet, his restaurant, is named for his family's vineyard in France's Burgundy region. Nestled among the old shopfronts of Given Terrace as that long shopping thoroughfare winds its way up the hill of Paddington, it brings a little of Paris to Brisbane. While small and intimate, it manages to bring some of the grandeur of a classic Parisian bistro to this strip of restaurants and cafes. Tonight it sparkles as it fills with friends and family gathering to celebrate my birthday.

We have each taken on the French theme in our own way. I have chosen a simple red dress and have my hair curled in an effort to capture the French chic of Audrey Tautou, while Greg has adopted the beret of a Left Bank intellectual. The boys have decided to go all out and hire full costumes. Joe, now almost twenty-three, is magnificent in Napoleonic uniform and Oliver resplendent in the full regalia of a French courtier, complete with a long white wig. We are thrilled to see that others have taken up the theme in style. Striped sweaters and artist's berets mingle easily with Marie Antoinette gowns; French intellectuals with Moulin Rouge dancers. Our close friend Bronwen arrives in a cropped blonde wig as Jean Seberg in *Breathless*. Mum has joined in the spirit with her fingernails painted in the blue, white and red of the French national flag. All are ready to enjoy the night. There is a certain licence given when we don a costume, a permission to set aside our more serious selves, to relax and become more playful. Soon, even those who have simply tied on a red neckerchief fall into a bubbly party mood. Old friends and new, some arrived from interstate, along with family and close members of staff fill the room with laughter and cheerfulness.

The air is full of the irresistible aromas of wine, cream and garlic wafting from the kitchen when Thierry steps out into the crowd, brandishing a bottle of champagne and a sword. With one swift and astonishing stroke of his sword, he takes the top off the bottle and with a dramatic flourish glasses are filled to laughing gasps of admiration.

I watch Greg as he moves about, checking that everyone has a full glass, that people are introduced when necessary, that all is going well at this party he has planned with such care.

He has less hair now, but to me seems otherwise unchanged from the day in 1985 when I walked into that Redfern office and he asked me out to a Leonard Cohen concert.

Leonard Cohen's songs and lyrics have remained a constant touchstone for Greg and me and, along with thousands of other fans, we were deeply moved when we saw him again, twenty-three years after our first date. We wept as he took the stage in Brisbane and began his concert with the beautiful 'Dance Me to the End of Love', the song that we'd played at our wedding. It was a very different Cohen from the jaded man we had seen on that first exciting night together in Sydney in 1985. In 2008 Cohen had been renewed in his gift by the loyalty and love of his fans, buoyed by our joy in seeing him after more than twenty years. He was humble, grateful and, just like us, so happy to be there.

As I watch Greg play party host it is hard to remember my life without him in it. His constant presence has shaped and stretched and formed me. Together, we have navigated a life that is emotionally charged and intellectually rich. As he battled with a blender to make pesto that day in Redfern, it was the workings of his mind that captured my attention, and it has held me in its thrall every day since. Like others who love each other deeply, we have had our share of pleasure and pain. With him, I have had the worst arguments of my life. He has tried me and tested my patience almost beyond endurance. We have caused each other grief and brought each other matchless joy.

Greg and I share values and views in a way that is important to both of us, but we are very different in many ways. For all its frustrations, that's why it works. He brings me into the world of his hungry, searching mind and opens doors to new places for me. He knows everything there is to know about sport, even the obscure sports in which he has little or no interest, and can bring together the sporting facts and statistics with the economic and political context in which they occurred. I am endlessly astonished and entertained by this ability. He has spent a decade teaching himself about deep space and the workings of the cosmos. He brings me tidbits from the frontiers of mathematics and physics. He is a constant riddle to me, and I hope I am one to him. At Montrachet, I look at him with our friends and I want to hold his hand as we look back on all this living and laughing and fighting and loving. We are, at once, still those two young people in the kitchen in Redfern, feeling the first tingle of romance, and two new and entirely different people who have grown and changed each other as we've wrapped our lives together.

All those years ago, Greg was sharing a house in Sydney with his lifelong friend Greg Combet. The two met on their first day of kindergarten at Eastern Creek Public School in Sydney's western suburbs, and their friendship is a part of our family's life. That they share the same name has caused endless confusion over the years, but it somehow seems right to me. They don't share a surname but are like close brothers who know each other's strong and weak suits, and their time together from childhood has cemented a deep bond. Greg Combet is family to us and he has flown across the country to be here tonight. The young can never imagine being fifty, but as we all got to know each other in the back kitchen of their old house in Sydney's Dulwich Hill in the 1980s, we had no way of imagining this night, years ahead of us, when Greg Combet would take a moment out of his hectic duties as a federal Labor minister and I would steal time from mine as Queensland premier to celebrate my five decades. Of all the possible futures we dreamed for ourselves, this would have seemed the most improbable.

As the party glitters around us, Greg and the boys briefly disappear. They reappear carrying a large rectangular object covered in a sheet of material. This, I guess, is my birthday present. Greg briefly takes the floor and speaks of the significance of our Bastille Day theme, how much he loves Paris and how much he loves me. He then pulls the cloth off with a flourish to match Thierry's sword trick and reveals a large framed map. It is clearly a map of Paris, and at first I think it is a beautifully framed vintage map of the city. I lean closer and realise that while the map does indeed contain the bones of the city of Paris, it is a map of an imagined city, a city called 'Parisanna'. It is a city that maps my life.

Parisanna is conjured up from the dreams of my husband's heart. She brims with the allure of the world's most romantic city, a city he fell in love with on his first visit, and intersects with the life of the girl he fell in love with so many years ago. Every line of Parisanna sings the lines of my life and of our life together. Parisanna is an astonishing act of love. She has an imaginary, otherworldly quality to her that is not easy to paint in words. The map itself has been exquisitely drawn by Peter Edwards, a talented architect colleague of Greg's. It faithfully outlines the streets and parks and metro lines and monuments of Paris. But there the similarities end. Each metro line maps one of the lines of my life. And true to the Paris metro, each station on every line holds its own history. In Parisanna, each is renamed to capture the events and moments of my life, from the momentous events to the smallest pleasures, from my first election campaign to my love of knitting and drinking tea. On these lines are the first words of my eldest son side by side with my election campaign slogans; my mother's eight siblings have a whole line to themselves and mingle with the towns and places in which I have lived. Fourteen metro lines in all, these lifelines range across every part of my life.

On Line One, whose stations chart the moments, sayings and places, the funny memories, the family holidays and the favourite foods that are the backbone of my family life, I find 'docdile', Oliver's childhood word for crocodile, his favourite animal. I find 'lost passports', a shorthand reference to our trip to Europe during which Greg lost the family passports, not once but twice, setting off a crazy chain of events first in Bologna and then in London. On Line Five, where each station maps my political achievements, I find the royal commission I established, the education reforms I put in place, the water infrastructure I built. From Line Four, which celebrates my closest friends, emerge people like Jackie Trad and Di Fingleton and Anne Warner, who have stood with me and shared my life, while on Line Seven, the line that holds the big moments of my 2009 election campaign, each station holds treasured memories.

Beyond the metro lines, each monument, each bridge, each park and street is renamed to capture and celebrate a moment, a pleasure, a place, a friend. In these places I find my hairdresser, my favourite designers, my cherished authors. In Parisanna, the Louvre becomes GOMA, Queensland's new Gallery of Modern

Art, built while I was Minister for the Arts. The Pont Sully becomes the Kurilpa Bridge, the ultra-modern footbridge I built while premier to connect Brisbane's cultural precinct with its CBD. The welcoming space of Place Bienvenüe becomes Place Quailey in honour of Greg's uncle and aunt, George and Kath Quailey, who happily welcomed me into their family and filled the shoes of grandparents on his side of our family.

This beautifully drawn map is perfectly held in a wooden frame intricately hand-carved by Jack Barnes and his father, Ross, makers of fine church furniture. Hewn into it are the hearts and stars of the City of Love and City of Light. Magically, it has a secret drawer carved into its side. This drawer glides open to reveal a slender hardcover guidebook to the city of Parisanna, which Greg wrote. Its pages outline in loving detail the meaning of each station on each metro line and the connection each person, place and event on the map has to my life.

Opening with an inscription from Leonard Cohen's 'If It Be Your Will', and complete with photos and illustrations, the Parisanna guidebook documents the interwoven lifelines of my first fifty years. It takes the reader on a journey that slides effortlessly between the personal and the public, the political and the romantic, the ridiculous and the sublime, as they all beat together to make a city and a woman come to life. Page 13 will tell you that Châtelet Station on Line One is named after Le Grand Châtelet, the fortress that used to occupy the site and that, located at the centre, secures the stability of the entire metro system. It will tell you that in the city of Parisanna, this station is named for my mother, the emotional anchor of my life, the source of profound comfort and love who has nurtured our little family as only a grandmother can. On page 136 you will find that the Bourse, the French Stock Exchange, has been renamed for my Treasurer, Andrew Fraser, 'the young abacus' of my government. Page 35 will tell you that Cité is a station built on the spot that has long been thought of as the birthplace of Paris; hence in Parisanna it is named for Greg Combet, at whose share house our life together found its genesis. You will learn on page 38 that my friend, the author and poet Lily Brett, now occupies the Montparnasse-Bienvenüe station, originally named after a Greek mountain dedicated to Apollo, god of poetry and beauty. On page 12, you will find that the station Champs-Élysées–Clemenceau is named for Greg himself, because he is a man who 'knows that his Elysian fields are all around him'.

And on this birthday night in 2010, I can feel my own Elysian fields, my fields of heaven, all around me. Here on the map of Parisanna and here in the cosy hearth of Montrachet restaurant are my origins, my life's central players and supporting cast, all my twists and turns, my passions, my inner life and my public self. Here is my mum, enjoying the attention of our friends. They all know about the tight knots that bind me to her and love her because of them. She regales them with stories of my birth, of how reluctant I was to make my appearance, of how the nuns in the convent next door prayed for us and of how close we both came to not pulling through. She tells stories of how I insisted on walking at nine months, of how I would struggle unsteadily onto my chubby legs and run straight ahead until I hit a wall, then pick myself up and start all over again. She reflects that I haven't changed much!

Here are Stuart and Jo, Bonaparte and his Josephine. Jo and I met as feisty young women in Queensland's first women's policy unit, set up by Wayne Goss. We have shared our pregnancies and our years of learning to be mothers. Stuart was one of Greg's first new friends in Queensland, their son Hugo is one of Oliver's best friends and our families have shared holiday happiness and hospital terrors with each other.

Here is my brother John, the only one of my siblings who can be here, who remembers, as I do, when things were hard and we struggled to find our place in the world. I find his station on Parisanna, Le Pré-Saint-Gervais, recognising his gentle good humour and connection to me.

Here too my work colleagues: Steve Keating, whose media advice has got me out of more than one scrape; Dana Jackson, who has navigated the hellish twists and turns of my diary with a cheerful smile. Those who have served as my chief of staff, that most difficult and thankless of offices: Bronwen Griffiths, Murray Watt, Mike Kaiser and Nicole Scurrah – all are here to celebrate the friendships we have forged in fire together.

The night is a rare moment in a public life, a moment when those dearest to me can come together in love and friendship away from the prying eyes of a curious public and a ruthless media. We can have that extra glass of champagne, laugh a little too loudly and get sentimental. Parisanna becomes the centre of attention and people pore over her all night, delighted to find themselves somewhere in her streets and stations and to read in the guidebook the clever way that Greg has connected their lives with ours.

Late in the evening, I look up to see two faces pressed against the front glass of the restaurant and Greg realises it is

Andrew and Lucy, two young artists who helped him design and print the Parisanna guidebook. They were so moved by the project, they have been drawn to walk past and catch a glimpse of Parisanna revealed. We quickly welcome them in, introduce them to the great applause of the party and envelop them in our celebrations. The making of Parisanna is a story in itself. A team of people pulled together through friends and acquaintances, each bringing their own unique talents, never having worked together before, all beavered away in secret over many months to bring Greg's dream to life. Andrew and Lucy, along with all the others who had a hand in this remarkable act of creation, now have a place in our lives.

As the dinner plates are cleared, Joe and Oliver rise to share the job of the birthday speech. As they speak, they come close to eclipsing the halo of light being cast by Parisanna. Both boys have a good knack for languages and accents and both have studied French. They give a mighty speech, taking turns in English and French, and capturing some of Parisanna's lifelines perfectly. They start by drawing correlations between Bastille Day and my life in politics, painting a line between the hopes and dreams of the French revolutionaries as they stormed the Bastille and my radical, youthful determination to storm the barricades of the Bjelke-Petersen government. They compare those heroes of Bastille Day with the Australian Labor Party, 'a bunch of angry Catholic workers' who share the same quest for representative democracy and a fair go for all. They make the point that I share a birthday with the great British suffragette Emmeline Pankhurst, a fact I did not know before this night. Emmeline founded the Women's Social and Political Union in

1903 to campaign for the enfranchisement of women. She was arrested many times for her efforts and force-fed after hunger striking for her cause. Her perseverance paid off when British women were granted the right to vote in 1928 after more than twenty years of campaigning. Her name is synonymous with the twentieth-century struggle for women's rights.

'Emmeline received a great deal of criticism from those around her throughout her long career,' the boys explain. 'However, she pushed through adversity to procure more rights for women and to shake the foundations of patriarchal society. Anna shares many of the values that Pankhurst was renowned for: perseverance, determination and a strong desire for equality.'

As the mother of boys, I have often wondered what they make of my feminism. We have had our share of debates around the dinner table about what's fair for boys and what's fair for girls. They often felt in primary school that the girls in their class were allowed more leeway from teachers than the boys, protesting that girls got off easier when mischief was afoot. As they grew older, they were amazed to hear my stories about how recently women had got the vote; how, not long before the boys were born, women were forced by law to resign from work when they married; and some of the things that I repeated from old-time Labor Party meetings astonish them. They have grown up in a different world, one where their mother, along with the mothers of their friends, works and influences the world beyond their home. Their world is one where female friends are confident young women who expect equality and will call them on any signs of sexism. They are not frightened of this debate with me and I am often taken by their thoughtful consideration of gender issues. To hear them speak so openly and proudly about this aspect of my life is a warm and special moment for me.

Both boys look so young and handsome in their French costumes. How I have loved being the mother of boys. As I swelled with my first pregnancy, I found it hard to imagine anything growing inside me that wasn't a smaller version of myself and felt certain that I would deliver a dark-haired girl. It came as some surprise, then, that Joseph arrived with a headful of red hair and very much a boy. I wondered about the job of mothering a boy, but my doubts disappeared as I quickly fell in love with him. It is their maleness that I have relished as I mothered them, watching the mystery of them unfold, catching my breath on the raw energy of them and breathing in their difference.

To parent is to worry, to listen to a small voice in your head that maintains a daily tally of the perils that menace your children's lives. From the hazards of being fed solids too early to the ever-present dangers of cars, germs, spiders, falling buildings, swimming pools and angry words, parenting is fraught with the constant juggling of risk and safety. How often have I worried and fretted about how the choices I made might affect these boys? How searing the wrench as I dropped them at childcare or left home to travel? How many times have Greg and I feared for them and their future? As my life became more public and high profile, we became more anxious about the inevitable scrutiny of their lives. We knew that they would be judged harshly and unfairly for any of the normal mistakes that teenagers make. We feared the front-page frenzy that would follow even a minor transgression such as skipping school or being caught smoking.

In his second-last year of high school, when I was Minister for Education, Joe and his friends headed off to the school semi-formal dance, loaded up with backpacks full of cans of beer secured for them by a mate's older brother. Of course, they were caught at the door by the security officer doing bag checks. When our home phone rang at 8 pm, I was surprised to hear the voice of the deputy principal, Mrs Underwood, who was embarrassed to have to tell me what had happened and to ask me to come and collect Joe. All the boys, rightfully, were given a heavy suspension from school. This was unacceptable behaviour, and Greg and I let Joe know of our disappointment in no uncertain terms. He had never before been in any serious trouble and was generally a good kid. But we knew how the media would treat this. We expected it to be a front-page sizzler: 'Minister's Son in Illegal Booze Heist' or similar. I thought it too good a story for the teachers at the dance to keep to themselves and we braced ourselves, and the boys, for the onslaught. We waited in dread for our fifteen-year-old son to be dragged through the mud.

To the great credit and professionalism of the teachers and other staff at Brisbane State High School, this story never saw the light of day. Thankfully, my fears about possible loose lips or, worse, a deliberate leak from school staff were misplaced, and I will be forever grateful that they let Joe take his punishment without the double penalty of public exposure. But we all lived with the cold bite of fear in our stomachs for weeks as we waited for the media call that never came. It made me sick that my life choices had potentially exposed my boys to this unfair level of scrutiny. This misdemeanour is now ten years in Joe's past and we can all laugh about it. His view now is that highest on his list of crimes that night was the remarkable stupidity of trying to walk into a five-star hotel with a backpack full of beer cans, and he's right about that.

I knew also that my choices had exposed us all to possible violence and retribution from people angered by government decisions and from people with serious mental health problems. During my fifteen years in ministerial positions, my office received regular threats of violence, including death threats. On occasion these threats, including threats of sexual assault, were targeted directly at my children. Some threats were more credible than others, and police would brief me whenever they held genuine concern that a threat may be carried through. These threats are the dark underbelly of a life in politics. I refused to let them cower me, but Greg and I always discussed them, worried about them and feared for our boys.

Early in my political career, when I was Minister for Families, Youth and Community Care, a seriously mentally ill couple who'd had their five children taken into foster care found out where I lived and began turning up at our home unannounced. These calls culminated in a frightening late-night visit when they screamed and kicked at the lattice door on our verandah and came close to tearing it off its hinges. The police arrived quickly and took them into custody, but it was a terrifying experience for us all. Oliver was only six years old and had been asleep in our bed when the disturbance began. He was teary and frightened by the behaviour of these very disturbed people.

I was reluctant to press charges, feeling some pity for this couple and their unhappy lives, but I knew their own children had been removed from their care because they had recklessly endangered them. So I accepted the police advice and gave evidence against them. The husband spent a brief time in jail and his wife was committed to the care of the psychiatric ward of Princess Alexandra Hospital. They were both placed on protective orders prohibiting them from coming within a two-kilometre radius of my home, my office and the boys' schools. This provided some comfort, but I was always mindful that they were no respecters of the law. Their photo and the direct phone number of the local police station were always pinned on the door of our fridge.

And now, after all these dramas and all our fears, here are our boys, so young and handsome and accomplished. They are not without their faults or their own troubles from time to time, but in this moment they glow with happiness as they entertain the crowd and talk about their mother. Greg and I catch each other's tear-filled eyes. We adore these boys.

As their speech draws to a close, Oliver tells the party, 'Our mother has had an astonishing career, made great friends and changed society for the better. However, we're sure she would agree with us in saying that her biggest contribution to society was and is ourselves!' And he is right about that. Joe goes on to say, 'Our mother has always been exactly that to us. A mother. She is there when we call, interested in what we are doing and loves nothing more than coming home to some sea-salt chips, a glass of red wine and her family.'

My boys bring us all to laughter and to tears. Their laughing presence and their happy, joking ease with each other and with our guests remind us all that it is some three decades since we shone with the promise of youth. But their words and the intricate history so beautifully mapped in Parisanna make me feel that I have lived up to that promise, that I have grabbed life by the throat and given it a mighty shake, that I have made these five decades matter.

In July 2010, my political fortunes are at a terrible low. Our polling is depressing and nothing we do seems to lift us out of the doldrums. My public life is a source of despair for much of my fiftieth year, but on this night, as I reflect on those fifty years I am full of love and hope. I feel my friends and family find joy in each other. I can feel our lives and histories tie us to each other, and I can feel how much these ties matter to us. Our lives are richer for them, better for them. In Montrachet that night, I feel cherished as we all bask in a warm honey-gold moment, polling and politics far from our thoughts.

*

In the hard years that are just around the corner, Parisanna is always there, hanging on the wall above our dining table. She looks over our meals together, and she reminds me of who I am. In her lines I see my life reflected, a life of hard work and jumping hurdles, of dreaming big dreams and having big adventures, of learning hard lessons and looking fear in the face, of making friends and loving family. When I glance at her, I know that I am woven into the lives of others and they are woven into mine, that our lives criss-cross like the metro lines of Paris itself, sometimes heading in different directions but always connected. I find a woman who loves and is loved, who knows who she is and can do what has to be done. This map of my life is an ever-present reminder of my husband's devotion and enthusiasm for me and for our life together. There are few things that give Greg more pleasure than to introduce someone to Parisanna or, better still, to welcome someone whose name is woven into the map who has not yet seen it. He comes alive with not only the map and its significance, but with the exuberant pleasure of retelling the story of the project to create her and the sparkling party where she made her entrance. Parisanna is a solid, grounding touchstone in my wild and crazy public life.

NINE

Water, Water Everywhere

I've been riding in the back seat of the taxi for five minutes before the driver makes eye contact in the rear-view mirror.

'Love,' he says, 'I gotta tell you. You were bloody magnificent during those Queensland floods.'

I smile and thank him, though I'm at a slight loss, not quite sure how to accept the praise. I hope I accept his compliment graciously. His words are very familiar to me. Variations of them have become a regular part of my life. They turn up in unexpected and unlikely places. They come from the change room next door to mine when I'm trying on a dress. They come when I'm in a corporate boardroom. When I'm drinking tea at my local cafe. In planes and on buses, in places where I am known and at moments when I think I am anonymous. Despite their frequency, I rarely see them coming. It isn't always said with quite the same vernacular informality of a Sydney cab driver, but always with a deep sincerity, and so often with a sense of pleasure at having the chance to tell me this personally.

'From the moment I watched you doing all that, I've always wanted to tell you how I felt,' the taxi driver says. These friendly exchanges often come with an anecdote about a personal experience of those terrible disasters, or a story about a friend, a father, a sister, an aunt or a son who was caught up in the chaotic tragedy of it all. But just as frequently they come from someone with no personal connection, who tells me how touched they were, how connected they felt to me as we all lived through the floods and battled our fears together – even those from the other side of the country tell me this. Although four years have passed since those frightening raging waters finally subsided, the remarks often come with a choke in the voice, with tears hovering nearby.

Some people instinctively hold my hands while they look me in the eye and speak. A young photographer at a function in Sydney reached for my arm as if to steady herself and told me that, worried and frightened about her frail elderly mother in the floods, she had drawn comfort from watching me. A large man who crouched down beside me at a restaurant table told me that he'd only cried twice as an adult, once on his wedding day and the other time listening to me during our floods.

Through these very personal interactions, I am constantly reminded that in those long days and weeks of January 2011, when Queensland battled one of Australia's worst recorded disasters, something extraordinary happened. Something touched people in a way that politics doesn't usually touch them. The floods and cyclones that threatened to overwhelm us that summer were prolonged and terrifying. They veered from the menacing predictability of slow-rising rivers to the desperate horror of raging flash floods and harrowing cyclones, all tearing apart homes, communities and lives. The appalling force of nature hit us all with a sickening full-fisted punch, and we watched transfixed, collectively sharing the suffering, unable to tear ourselves away from it. It was no surprise to me that the event was etched in people's minds. The surprise was that it was also etched in their hearts.

Often, as we experience something, we can feel it changing us. As I gave birth to my first son, Joe, I knew that I was becoming a mother and that my life, and my sense of who I am, was being forever reshaped. As Greg and I waited through the long hours of contractions we knew our relationship was being altered, that we were becoming a family. I understood on the day I was sworn in as Queensland's first woman premier that I was making history. I could feel it. I was full to the brim with the sense that I was living a moment that would redefine me forever. But as those wild, flooding rivers tore through that summer I did not feel a history-making moment or that I was in the midst of another, even bigger, defining moment. I was too anxious about the frontline, too worried about what was next, to see myself and everyone around me being changed by what we were living through.

What was it about these events that penetrated people emotionally and moved them in some deep and lasting way? I didn't begin to feel the effect until near the end of that summer. For here is the thing: when you are smack-bang in the middle of managing a crisis, when you have to lead the response to a catastrophe, it's impossible to see yourself from the outside. The heart-racing pace of the crisis excludes all else. The looming danger grips you, and the heavy responsibility to lead people through it holds you still. You are seized by the compelling momentum of the events unfolding around you. Rarely pausing to look right or left, you keep marching forward, picking up the next decision and making it, moving to the next problem and tackling it, wrestling with the endless dilemmas that keep flying into your path. It is only now, some years after these unforgettable events, that I can see them more clearly. From this distance I can adjust the settings and see it all through a wide-angle lens.

*

The floods that came Queensland's way in 2011 were not my first as premier. Queensland is no stranger to the extreme weather that always lingers close to its tropical climate. In an ironic twist, I came to the leadership after years of drought. As Minister for Infrastructure, I had been responsible for building Queensland's biggest ever water projects, designed to drought-proof our future. Water supply to Brisbane was dwindling at a rate precisely equal to the speed with which our new dams and pipelines were materialising. The consequences of a delay to these public works could have been catastrophic. We had reached a point where people were using government-supplied egg timers in their showers to help minimise water use and conserve what little supply we had left. Footpaths were cracking as the scorched dry earth shifted below them. Trees were dying, tempers were fraying, dogs were listless, children were irritable and goodwill was wilting.

When drought-breaking rains finally came in January 2008, they were greeted with relieved open arms. But in a climate of extremes, they inevitably went too far in some places. In the regional mining town of Emerald, the endless rain overfilled the nearby Fairbairn Dam, which in turn broke the banks of the Nogoa River, flooding the town and surrounding mines.

I spent several days in Emerald, working with the heads of our frontline emergency response, learning about our hydrology capability, making decisions about allocating emergency resources. The local mayor, Peter Maguire, cut short a family holiday in Fiji to return to Emerald. Peter, who is better known locally as 'Maggot' – a fond nickname he embraces – is a colourful and widely respected character. As soon as Maggot got back and started to take charge of his team, I could feel the locals settle into a more secure response. Maggot knew the river and the surrounding properties intimately. Working alongside him for those few days was an instructive lesson in leadership. People trusted him because he knew his facts, knew his town and its river, and he told people what they needed to know. No frills, no sweeteners. This event was devastating for those who lost their homes and businesses to the floodwaters, but it was manageable and largely contained to this one regional centre.

Along with police and emergency workers, I became stranded on one side of Emerald as the floodwaters took out the rail and road bridges that crossed the river. I could have been evacuated by helicopter, but the town had lost power and communications were poor. Leaving just didn't feel like the right thing to do. I resolved to stay overnight in the evacuation centre set up in the local school, alongside the many families who had fled their homes. Of course, premiers always travel with a pack, with staff and police security, so if I stayed they all stayed too. These shelters are hurriedly put together and very rudimentary. They have what they need and little more: mattresses on the floor, shared school bathrooms, donated food prepared in the tuckshop kitchen. Sleeping there overnight, talking with displaced families the next morning, watching anxious parents trying to settle active children or help a frail, elderly relative, it was clear these were hard places to stay in. I would be returning that day to my safe home, but many of these families would be living at the school for weeks to come. It was an experience that never left me. The days in Emerald gave me an extraordinary opportunity to learn firsthand from Maggot's team, the state emergency responders and the affected families. Seeing the senior leadership of our frontline in action laid the foundations for what was to come three years later.

*

Because of the capabilities of modern weather monitoring, huge weather events rarely come unheralded. Through the autumn and winter months of 2010, weather patterns over the Pacific Ocean took a sinister turn. Weather experts began to see patterns not seen for almost half a century, registering numbers beyond anything previously recorded.

The language of weather has a certain romance to it. As scientists set their sights on the Pacific that year, they began to talk of La Niña, a weather pattern that brings rapidly changing conditions. La Niña, meaning 'little girl' in Spanish, sounds playful, light and innocent. She is anything but. She announces her arrival with a rise in surface temperatures in the western Pacific, in the waters to Australia's north, and a corresponding cooling of temperatures across the central and eastern Pacific. She whispers that she is coming with a shift in the pattern of air pressure between Asia and the eastern Pacific. Weather scientists measure the difference in air pressure between Darwin and Tahiti, and when the difference remains positive for a sustained period they know that La Niña is on her way. They use the Southern Oscillation Index to measure her approach by reading the oscillations, the small movements between one point and another, in air pressure. Way out over the deep blue of the ocean that is called the Pacific for its usual tranquillity, oscillations were bringing trouble. I thought about the Pacific Ocean oscillating far away to the north of Australia, of it quivering and vibrating across to Tahiti, and pictured a brooding, shifting sea, boiling with changing air pressures and giving rise to the massive, swollen clouds that came our way all through that winter. The 'little girl' had arrived and she was settling in for a long stay.

La Niña brings significant increases in rainfall along with violent storms and cyclonic events. Heavy rain began to fall in July and continued right through winter and spring. In 2010, Australia had its wettest September on record. These rains soaked Queensland for months. By the time the traditional summer wet season arrived in January 2011, water catchments across the state were full and the ground was saturated.

This La Niña was no ordinary little girl. She was measured in the highest levels since records of the Southern Oscillation Index began in 1876. The weather scientists started to bring their concerns to government. We were told to prepare for an exceptionally wet summer, a summer that could see as many as five cyclones cross the coast, a summer where weather would be unpredictable and extreme. We had no idea where or when La Niña might strike most fiercely, but we began to plan for what might lie ahead.

Emergency services dusted off rescue equipment that had been in storage during our long drought. Local councils stockpiled sandbags. Emergency alert systems were tested. Christmas holiday leave rosters were adjusted to ensure senior personnel were available at all times. Wivenhoe Dam, the large catchment that supplies Brisbane, had filled during the wet months leading up to Christmas. Stephen Robertson, our Minister for Energy and Water Utilities, took the unprecedented step, for a minister, of seeking formal advice from the dam engineers about whether water should be released in readiness for further downpours.

As schools closed for their long summer break and 2010 drew to a close, we'd had enough of the rain. Everyone hoped for sunny Christmas beach picnics. On Christmas Eve I met with the senior officers of our frontline, including the Queensland head of the Bureau of Meteorology, Jim Davidson, and the police commissioner, Bob Atkinson. We heard again from our expert scientists that our weather patterns were building to treacherous levels. We left with an ominous sense that we would be seeing each other again very soon.

*

Greg and the boys and I celebrate Christmas with great gusto. We love everything about it: the tree, the decorations, the exchange of cards and presents with friends and family, the carols, the food and feasting. We love the holiday, the days over Christmas when the whole neighbourhood is at home and the roads are quiet, followed by the mass exodus as everyone packs up and heads for a beach, a river, a family visit. When the long, hard working weeks and months of the year come to a close with the arrival of summer holidays, Australians not only expect little of their politicians but prefer them to be absent from their television screens and newspapers. It's the time when everyone downs tools and unplugs. For our family, it was the one time of year when we could truly relax, replenish and refuel as we spent easy time with each other, out of the public eye.

That summer we'd planned to spend Christmas at home in Brisbane and then head to Sydney after Boxing Day. Having booked a house in Rose Bay, near the beaches and close to friends, we hoped to settle in for three quiet, lazy, sun-filled weeks. I was now officially on leave. Deputy premier Paul Lucas had been appointed acting premier.

Christmas morning broke to the news that overnight a severe storm in North Queensland had been upgraded to a category-one cyclone and crossed the coast near the township of Gordonvale at dawn. Cyclones are categorised according to severity from one to five, with one being the least dangerous. Cyclone Tasha was mild by tropical cyclone standards, bringing very little in the way of gusting winds and causing only minor damage. Long-time locals in the north of tropical Queensland take these events in their stride, even on Christmas Day.

My morning was full of discussions with Paul Lucas and the emergency services minister, Neil Roberts, along with briefings from the weather bureau and emergency services experts. All confirmed that Tasha had wrought little damage and first responders had matters well in hand, but that sustained heavy rainfall was likely across the state. With a sigh of relief I returned to our family's unusually cold and wet but very happy Christmas festivities.

But Cyclone Tasha took no time off for Christmas. In the days that followed she dropped constant torrential rain on ground that was already waterlogged. Rivers began to fill at a disturbing pace. The small townships of Alpha and Jericho in the far west of the state flooded quickly. With reassurances from senior personnel that everything that could be done was being done, I arrived in Sydney for our family break early on the afternoon of 27 December.

Immediately on landing, I learned that the flooding was spreading and getting worse. The towns of Dalby, Chinchilla and Theodore were now under serious threat. I resolved to return to Queensland on the first flight the next morning. I had no choice but to recall senior staff, including the director-general of the premier's department, Ken Smith, from annual leave. Ken and I resolved to meet at Emergency Headquarters early the next morning at the first State Disaster Management Group meeting of the day.

*

Emergency Headquarters lies on the fringe of Brisbane's CBD and is a purpose-built disaster management centre. Fully equipped to oversee and manage emergencies across the state, Emergency HQ would soon become my second home.

Located in the grounds of a former school, Emergency HQ has an impressive technical capability. It receives a range of real-time information and responds accordingly. It simultaneously receives weather reports, hydrology data, flood maps, live video streams from cameras fixed to reconnaissance helicopters, active reports from police, fire, rescue and emergency frontline communications and information from live news channels. Multiple large screens display much of this information, which is constantly assessed and assimilated into strategic and tactical decisions about responding to a disaster. Although our government had funded a significant upgrade of Emergency HQ, the new facilities were still a few critical weeks away from being fully functional. For now, our efforts would be run out of the existing building, where we were all at least on familiar ground.

During a major disaster, every day at Emergency HQ begins and ends with meetings of the State Disaster Management Group. The membership of this group is legislated and includes the senior officers and personnel of all relevant government and non-government agencies. These meetings are formally convened by the director-general of the premier's department and attended by senior ministers, including the premier when available. Local mayors and disaster coordinators are hooked in by teleconference when necessary. This group brings together the most recently gathered intelligence and resolves priority responses for the day or night ahead. The issues considered by this group are generally high-level. Their decisions range from large and small resource allocations, such as the need for extra sandbags or extra police, through to major tactical decisions to evacuate a town, to invoke police powers to move people, to establish emergency evacuation facilities or pre-emptively cut off power and shut down public transport systems.

The real strength of Emergency HQ lies in its ability to seamlessly bring together all the senior players to form a team that can respond without the constraints that apply to any one particular service. Police, emergency services, health workers, defence personnel, fire and rescue teams, telecommunications and electricity companies, public and private, all levels of government, social service providers and disaster relief charities such Red Cross all sit around the same table. All work through the decisions using the same information regardless of which agency gathered or produced it. All bring their specialist expertise and personal experience to every dilemma. By the time someone becomes the police or fire commissioner or CEO of an electricity supply company, they have sat around this table a few times.

On that late December morning, as my ministerial car drove me through the gates of Emergency HQ, the full impact of Cyclone Tasha was becoming clearer. Three days after Tasha made landfall at dawn on Christmas Day, almost half of Queensland was underwater. One man had drowned when he was swept off a footbridge. Vast hectares of cotton crops in southern central Queensland lay wasted, and the state was already facing a $1.4 billion damages bill. The speed and scale of the devastation was shocking. We were in the throes of a major natural disaster.

Joining the familiar faces around the meeting table, I was surprised to see my director-general, Ken Smith, with his arm wrapped in a sling. He had slipped on his steep concrete driveway while emptying rubbish bins on our sopping wet Boxing Day, breaking his arm. He was clearly in pain and taking regular pain relief medication. He would oversee every day of this disaster in this condition, the constant but good-humoured butt of jokes about broken wings.

It was in these meetings that I learned what I needed to tell the public. It was here that we sorted out the information that was imperative and the directions to be issued. Good, clear communication saves lives in these events and, along with other senior personnel, it was my job to get people the information they needed as quickly and usefully as possible. Throughout the briefings by our technical experts I tried to translate what they were telling us into words that everyone could understand. I regularly stopped the hydrologists and weather specialists to suggest a plainer rephrasing of their information and to confirm that it remained technically correct. I also kept checking for clarity on what the data meant for each location. Many people were interested in the technical data, especially when it was breaking all known records. The readings from water gauges at various points in river systems, the likely rate of river rise and the gathering speed of gale-force winds were fascinating stuff. But lives were saved when people knew the approximate time a bridge would close, on which afternoon their access road might be cut, when their child's school would close or how many hours they had before their last chance to get to safety evaporated.

These overview meetings were followed by a series of operational meetings and teleconferences, attended by more frontline, operational staff. They focused on implementing the decisions and resourcing the response. Further briefings were provided to me, to local mayors and other decision-makers throughout the day on an as-needs basis and as situations changed. The meetings were also generally followed by a major media conference to provide the public with the latest information via the waiting media, who had also moved into the building. Emergency HQ was equipped with full media facilities to ensure that vital information could get out as quickly as possible, and most outlets assigned staff around the clock. The media pack waited hungrily for news, none wanting to miss out on any live coverage. Food breaks, phone calls and bathroom stops were all suspended while they waited for the State Disaster Management Group meetings to finish. It was all part of the rhythm and hum of Emergency HQ on full alert and in full swing.

That first day we issued official Disaster Declarations for Bundaberg, Central Highlands, North Burnett, Woorabinda and 'Maggot' Maguire's town of Emerald, where he was still mayor. A Disaster Declaration is a legal instrument that triggers a range of emergency powers for police and other authorised first responders, enabling them to take extreme action if necessary to manage the disaster. These include powers which would never be contemplated outside of war or an extreme emergency, such as the right to forcibly remove someone from their home or a public place and the right to destroy public property. A Disaster Declaration also entitles the designated area to disaster relief funds.

More towns followed the next day as I launched a disaster relief appeal, announcing a $1 million government donation to kick-start it. Later, I would be criticised for calling this appeal the Premier's Disaster Relief Appeal, as if I were using the name for political advantage. One journalist described the name as 'vanity' on my part. But the origins of this fund, including its name, do not reside with me and are, unlike much of political life, entirely altruistic. Establishing an appeal fund can take time, requiring a range of legal and financial documents and devices to underpin it. No money can be received into it until it has been legally established. Given the tropical nature of Queensland weather and the recurring need for such an appeal, the conservative premier Rob Borbidge, who took office when our Goss-led government lost its majority, had established an ongoing fund with this name. His decision meant that the fund lay dormant until an appeal was needed, when it could be easily and quickly reactivated. It was an act of great foresight on his part, one of those simple, small decisions that political leaders make that get little attention but make a great difference when it matters. His decision ensured that with just one signature and the agreement of major banks to collect money raised, a premier could activate an appeal in a matter of hours. But Borbidge could never have foreseen how sorely his Premier's Disaster Relief Appeal would be needed this time, nor how quickly and generously it would be filled.

After launching the relief appeal, I joined the deputy police commissioner, Ian Stewart, my staff and journalists to visit the flooded city of Bundaberg by government plane. Ian had been appointed the state disaster coordinator with overarching powers to direct personnel, equipment and resources as required.

Home to more than 70,000 people, Bundaberg sits on the Burnett River, which had broken its banks and reached its highest levels in sixty years. The famous Bundaberg Rum distillery sits on a small rise and was safe from the floodwaters. lying streets around it were full of small houses c for workers in the distillery. The flood-prone land and the houses reflected their humble beginnings. Hundreds of homes had been flooded, many totally destroyed. The local evacuation centre was full of displaced people and families. As we walked these streets, meeting and talking to those who had returned to see their homes underwater, I was struck by how many were already doing it tough and how few had any financial buffer to see them through a calamity like this. Many were pensioners or unemployed; others were working but on very low incomes and most were renting and had little or no insurance. The people I spoke with were losing everything they owned. Their stories would become a familiar refrain through the weeks ahead. Some natural disasters hit randomly, with no eye to wealth or privilege, but floods usually hit the poorest parts of town first and worst.

During a visit to the evacuation centre, set up in the council chambers, I sat and talked with those who had been displaced by the flood. For them, it seemed to have come out of nowhere and they were dazed with the shock of it. One day they were celebrating Christmas with their friends and families, and three days later they were homeless and living in an evacuation centre. It was a big thing to comprehend. At a personal level, the enormous shift in circumstances just could not be quickly understood. At a community level, it would shake up everything and everybody. Later, at a meeting with the local council, we were shown photos of massive road damage: parts of the nearby national highway had completely washed away and huge holes had opened up on major arterials, leaving many outlying areas isolated. It was clear that recovery in just this one region would require time and patience, a massive building effort and a big investment of public funds, and it would have a prolonged impact on the local economy.

As we were leaving, Ian Stewart received news that floodwaters raging down the Dawson River were again putting at risk the town of Theodore, some five hundred kilometres west of Bundaberg. Floodwaters were set to rise quickly, and roads out of town were rapidly being cut off. Ian decided to evacuate the five hundred residents and relocate them to the temporary living quarters of a nearby coal mine that had shut down for the Christmas break. Theodore would become the first town to be evacuated in Queensland's history. It would take all day to get everyone out safely. Most were airlifted by military helicopters, with the last ones taken out as night settled in and the town was lost to rising water. For us, it was a sombre plane ride back to Brisbane.

*

The next day, the floodwaters had begun to make their way south to the town of Surat on the Balonne River. It was clear that the small south-western town of Condamine also had to be evacuated. This time, there was no large mining camp nearby, and we needed to establish an evacuation centre in the nearby town of Dalby. Despite flooding in their own town, the local mayor and his community welcomed the displaced people of Condamine with open arms.

In Central Queensland, the Fitzroy River was also swelling and floodwaters had begun to make their way into the low-lying parts of Rockhampton. A city of more than 70,000 people, Rockhampton is a major regional hub. The Fitzroy River basin spans a massive 142,665 square kilometres of flood plain, Australia's second-largest river catchment system after the Murray–Darling. The city had seen floods before but this one was shaping up as a record-beater. Days before the Fitzroy River reached its peak, the highway to the city's south and the railway line were cut off by rising floodwaters.

By New Year's Eve, the flooding had slowed. I visited Bundaberg and Rockhampton with the prime minister, Julia Gillard. It was another day of grief and emotion as we talked with evacuees, held their hands and listened to their terrible stories of loss. The scale of human despair seemed overwhelming, yet there was more to come as many cities and towns had yet to see their rivers peak. However, the rain had eased. The hydrology and weather reports reassured us that it would be some days before we saw the next round of floods. Clearly, our swollen rivers had much grief yet to deliver, but for that weekend we had a moment to regroup.

That weekend was also my husband's birthday. Greg was still in Sydney on holidays with Oliver. During our daily chats I insisted on their staying on leave, though I was drained and missed them terribly. Tempted by the offer of a lift in the prime minister's plane, I flew to Sydney to be there for Greg's birthday.

It was a big mistake. I had been open and honest with the media, letting them know that I was seeing my family, that the floods had eased temporarily and I was only a phone call and an hour's flight away. But I had failed to remember that people in crisis were fearful, vulnerable and easily prone to believing that they were alone. I had let my own emotions and exhaustion come before theirs. This is not what leaders do. Having been away less than forty-eight hours, I returned on Sunday morning to a public mood that was sour and resentful. I had misjudged their needs and underestimated the importance and symbolic power of the premier's role and physical presence. I would not make that mistake again.

As the new week dawned on Monday 3 January, seventeen evacuation centres were in place across the state and more than 200,000 people had been affected in some way. Their homes, their businesses, their workplaces – all destroyed by floodwaters. Their communities were waterlogged and disconnected as bridges washed away and roads closed. For some, the cheerless clean-up had started. They had returned to their streets and neighbourhoods to be greeted with the mud and stench that the floods left in their wake. For others, the fearful waiting continued as rivers kept rising beyond all previous known levels, washing through streets and homes never before affected.

It was clear that the extensive damage to public infrastructure – our railways, our roads and bridges, our schools and sporting clubs, our ports and water treatment plants and our pipelines and parklands – was beyond anything we'd dealt with before. My mind began to turn to the logistics of recovery and rebuilding. As our weather returned to normal, so my attention would need to return to all the other demands of government. Recovery from this disaster would require the focused leadership of someone dedicated to this enormous task alone. It would require a coordinated effort across all levels of government, all government agencies, all sectors of the economy and the community as a whole. It was time for me to appoint a flood recovery taskforce and someone capable to lead it over the year ahead.

Ken Smith and I discussed possible appointments. Leading the recovery would require someone who could command authority and bring together all the disparate recovery agencies, along with the capability of the private construction sector. We were certain it also required someone who knew Queensland, who had lived here, who knew and understood the place; someone who could get the roads rebuilt but would also know something of what had been there before and could understand the grief.

After we made a number of inquiries, the prime minister confirmed that Australia's defence chief, Air Chief Marshal Angus Houston, was willing to make available Major General Michael Slater to lead Queensland's recovery operations. Slater, or Mick as we all came to know him, was a serving officer, at that time leading 7th Brigade, based at Gallipoli Barracks in Enoggera, Brisbane, one of Australia's largest military bases. He'd come to Enoggera after several years heading up Lavarack Barracks at Townsville, in Queensland's far north. Mick has extensive military and leadership experience, with Distinguished Service citations for his roles in INTERFET Command in the lead-up to Timor-Leste's independence and for earlier service in Kuwait. He holds master's degrees in strategic studies and business administration and has trained in mobilisation planning at the US Army War College. Happily, he is also a born and bred Queenslander. He was perfect for the job.

My path had crossed Mick's on several occasions, mostly ceremonial events where we both had official duties to perform, such as on Anzac Day and Australia Day. I didn't know him well, but in my brief contact with him I had been impressed by his capability and easy air of authority. Our ability to get along together was not a consideration for anyone, including myself, in his appointment to head the recovery taskforce. But as luck would have it, we hit it off from our first briefings. We did not know it yet, but our diaries would become synchronised for much of the next six months, including most of our weekends.

At a joint media conference on 5 January to announce his appointment, I got my first taste of Mick's no-nonsense style.

'Tell us, Major General,' said a journalist, 'why did you choose the task of leading this recovery effort?'

'I'm in the army,' Mick said. 'I don't get choices.'

'How do you think this assignment will be different to your wartime experiences?'

'I won't have a gun.'

Mick's style completely stumped the gathered journalists, but I could tell they liked him and respected his candour. I watched and wondered how a politician would go with the same blunt style and knew that these same journalists would judge someone out of uniform much more harshly.

*

The recovery effort would be a mammoth undertaking, as getting even one life back on track takes a remarkable effort of will and cannot be done quickly or alone. I knew firsthand that it would take most people much longer than they imagined to right themselves again after the uprooting dislocation of these floodwaters. Twenty years earlier, my mother had been living on a small hobby farm an hour or so west of Brisbane in the Lockyer Valley. On a day like any other, when she was in Brisbane visiting my sister and her new baby, that small farm burned to the ground. Mum had been left with nothing other than the contents of an overnight bag. In her early fifties, with all of her four children grown up, she had just started to enjoy the next phase of her life. She was financially secure, had three baby grandsons and was revelling in her newfound independence after working hard all her life and raising her children, for most of that time as a single mother.

We learned very quickly just how devastating a natural disaster can be. Gone were all the family photos, the photos of our childhoods, our birthday parties, our first days at school, our goofy adolescent moments. Gone too were all the photos of my mother's family – her parents, her brother and her seven sisters. I felt the loss of these as much as the loss of our own photos. The formal photos of my mother and her eight siblings together captured a very different time and a very different Australia, and I had always loved looking at them. The 1950s summertime snaps of the eight girls standing on the beach, eldest to youngest, all wearing old-fashioned swimmers with their long hair in plaits and ponytails, were now gone forever. I still miss them.

Gone too were all the quirky, handmade Mother's Day gifts and cards, the precious artworks and woodwork projects we'd all brought home over the years. Mum's jewellery, nothing of huge monetary value but many pieces holding memories of a special moment, had disappeared. It's strange the things you miss the most. Mum had an old enamel baking dish that she used for making baked custard almost every week of my childhood. It was battered and ordinary and no one would have given it a second glance, but her kitchen still doesn't seem right without that old tin in it.

But greater than the loss of any of these possessions were the invisible losses. Long after it was extinguished, the fire burned a hole in my mother's self-confidence and her sense of herself as a capable, independent adult making her own way in the world. The loss of her home meant she became homeless overnight. Of course, my brothers and sister and I, along with her own siblings, all helped out. But parents don't want to be dependent on their children. She mourned the loss of her independence. She also felt that this was a time in our lives when she should be helping all of us, not the other way around.

The familiar objects in our lives, the ones we carry from house to house and place to place, somehow orient us. Just as that old baking tin always marked a kitchen as my mother's, our much-loved, well-worn possessions mark a space as uniquely ours. Our tattered cushions, our beloved favourite books, the tablecloth passed down from our grandmother, the one-eyed, dog-eared stuffed toy panda bear – all add up to who we are and where we've come from. When every single familiar thing you've ever known is whipped away in a single moment, it is frighteningly disorientating. I watched my mother's disbelief and dislocation as her familiar world was lost to her. We all felt something of what she'd lost. Two decades on, any one of us might still ask, without thinking, to borrow, use or see something that no longer exists.

The task of replacing even the basics seemed overwhelming. Two days after the fire, I took Mum shopping to buy new clothes and some extra underwear. I can still remember our shock as the bill was calculated. It dawned on us that everyone gathers their underwear collection gradually and that to replace just that, all at once, was going to cost more than we thought, let alone everything else. We both felt heavy and old as we left the shop. The real size of the task was beginning to hit us.

My mother is now in her seventies and a very active, independent and lively woman. But she says that it took her close to five years to feel on the same stable footing, physically and emotionally, as she was before the fire. I know from watching and sharing her journey that new things can't replace the older, well-loved ones, but that inch by inch, the cracks left by a disaster can start to mend and seal over.

TEN

The Rule Book Runs Out

Mick Slater was on the plane with me four days later, returning from that visit to waterlogged Rockhampton, when we flew straight into lightning. He made the mistake of confiding that this was actually the third time he had flown into lightning, each time in a small aircraft, including once in a helicopter. Relieved by the opportunity to have a joke, all of us aboard immediately agreed that he was a dangerous lightning magnet, and we vowed to be wary of flying with him ever again.

While that flight ended in laughter, and the live telethon after it raised millions of dollars for the floods' rain-weary victims, the rain cell continued to menace the region overnight. Torrents of flooding rain began to pour into catchments that our scientists now described as 'super-saturated'. The rivers that fed Wivenhoe Dam, dry to the point of despair only three years earlier, were swelling. These rivers were now carrying a huge volume of water, which was on its way to overwhelm the dam and the towns and cities in its path.

When I woke on Monday, 10 January, to another gloomy, rainy day, I did not know that it would be the day when the warning of that lightning strike was realised, the moment in my life that would test my mettle as a leader like nothing else before it.

We had been so confident that events were taking a quieter turn that on the previous Friday we ceased the daily meetings of the State Disaster Management Group. On the Monday morning, the State Cabinet Disaster Recovery Committee met for the first time to consider Mick Slater's draft recovery blueprint.

But by mid-morning I learned that Bundaberg, to the north, and Chinchilla, to the west, had both begun to flood a second time. The same rivers had broken their banks again. Water had begun to seep into the same homes it washed through just two weeks earlier. The same shattered people I had met and listened to in evacuation centres, many of whom had just finished washing the stinking mud and debris from their homes, were having to return to the same evacuation centres. I wondered how their hearts would bear it.

At the same time I heard that a new front was opening up. The Mary River, flowing through the regional towns of Gympie and Maryborough, had broken its banks and would flood both places during the day. This news weighed heavily on us all. Any optimism we may have had that these disasters were slowing quickly evaporated. The State Disaster Management Group would reconvene first thing the next morning.

But then, to my dismay, I learned that a greater danger was emerging. The Bremer and Brisbane Rivers, which flowed through the region surrounding our capital city, were now in flood. The experts expected the floodwaters to devastate Ipswich in two days' time, and Brisbane in three. Between them, these cities were home to almost 3 million people.

After all that we had been through, this news was hard to comprehend. In 1974, floods had wreaked havoc in Brisbane. Wivenhoe Dam had been built in the late 1970s and early '80s to supply water to the growing city and to mitigate the damage of any future floods. But the sheer volume of water coursing down our river systems would overwhelm the dam. Learning that engineers would have to begin controlled releases of unimaginable megalitres of water to prevent a failure of the dam wall shocked me. I knew that it would also shock and frighten the people of the cities in danger.

I rang the mayor of Ipswich, Paul Pisasale, to tell him what I knew. He too was shocked but immediately launched his city's emergency plan ahead of further briefings. The lord mayor of Brisbane, the future premier Campbell Newman, had already been briefed by his water engineers. I let his office know that I was about to announce at a media conference the disaster that awaited us.

Once again, deputy police commissioner Ian Stewart and I prepared for a media conference. This would be a media call in which we would have almost too much news to tell people. We conferred on the key points, cross-checked our facts and predicted the likely questions. As we walked to the media room, Ian took a call. He told me quickly that police were receiving disturbing reports out of Toowoomba, a regional city to Brisbane's west. Reliable details were hard to get, but it appeared that all hands were on deck helping on the frontline of what sounded like a dangerous flash flood. His officers were assisting rescue workers with swift-water rescues in the main street of Toowoomba.

Toowoomba is my mother's hometown, and I visited it many times as a little girl to see my grandmother. As I well knew from the many trips up the winding range road, when inevitably one or more of us would get carsick, it's on top of a mountain, almost 700 metres above sea level. There was no river running through it. But Ian and I agreed that even with so little information to go on, we needed to break this news. We could honestly say that we had few details, but we could not keep this to ourselves. We had no real knowledge of how serious it may or may not be, but people were in danger and others would want to know what was happening.

When I announced renewed flooding to the north and west, and the floods on their way to Ipswich and Brisbane, the mood was subdued. The news was chilling even for these seasoned journalists. Suddenly, it was not just a news story. It was their home, their family, their neighbourhood and their city. As I spoke I could see that although they were recording and taking notes as always, they were also calculating how this one would affect them and the people they loved.

I turned the conference's attention to what was happening in Toowoomba. 'Police are making swift-water rescues in the main street,' I said.

Immediately as the words came out of my mouth, I regretted not checking the information. Ian and I had decided on the run to talk about this report. The idea of mountain-top Toowoomba's main street flooding, let alone its being the scene of raging torrents and swift-water rescues, suddenly sounded ridiculous and implausible. I was now very worried that a mistake this big would make me and the authorities look stupid and ill-informed. This was no time to cause the loss of public confidence in the disaster leadership.

En route back to my office, I continued to fret about the wisdom of raising the spectre of a dangerous flash flood in Toowoomba when I had not been fully briefed. I needed to talk to my media team about what we could do if the reports turned out to be wrong.

When I arrived in the office, my media team were glued to TV screens. I joined them in watching the first live footage out of Toowoomba. We saw cars being upended and carried off by huge waves. Families huddled on the roofs of their cars, screaming, as mud and water washed around them. People were trapped in trees on the main street as water swirled at their feet.

After weeks of seeing floodwaters photographed from every angle, from riverbanks and from helicopters, we should have been immune to the sight of more rushing water. But this was not rushing water like anything we'd seen. This water was furious. Trapped and raging, it was flying at buildings and cars in huge violent waves. Huddled around the television screens, we were mute with horror. Hands rose to cover our gaping mouths. Then gasps became cries as a rescuer's rope failed to reach a man clinging desperately to a tree. We fell silent again as we understood that we were watching people who may be about to die. Our eyes stung with tears as we watched a small boy trapped inside a car sinking into swirling mud, while his distraught parents on the car's roof desperately tried to reach him.

The television footage was so shocking, so unexpected, so frightening, so utterly different from the slow-moving rivers we had been watching take days to rise and peak. I knew these images would go global. The scenes were horrifying and compelling in equal part. I knew that everyone who saw them would feel the same. And no matter how many times I've now seen them replayed, I'm still mesmerised by the power of them.

As the images raced across our screens in scene after scene of appalling terror, I felt us hit a tipping point. Suddenly, we were in the middle of a different event. It was an upside-down, lurching through the looking-glass moment. We were now in a place where our capital city could flood despite the massive dam that was built to stop this, where major regional towns could flood two and three times in a matter of weeks, and where people could die in an angry wall of water on top of a mountain. I have heard it said that leadership is what you see when the rule book runs out. Standing in my office, watching a savage wave of brown water attack the streets of my grandmother's town, I felt the rule book run out. I felt all the known parameters for dealing with crises evaporate around me and knew that I, along with everyone in the leadership team, was about to be tested.

These images would play a pivotal role in this summer of disasters and how they were later understood. Until that afternoon, Toowoomba was not on anyone's radar. The Bureau of Meteorology had warned that morning that heavy rain could cause flash flooding in the south-east of the state. They could not be any more precise than that, but no one would have thought it possible in the elevated city of Toowoomba. And no one who saw the images that came out of the city that afternoon would associate them with the words 'flash flood'. These horrifying images captured an event that was simply beyond our comprehension and our vocabulary. They introduced a threatening air of unpredictability. For the first time in all those unsettling weeks of trouble, it seemed that we had truly lost control, that we could no longer even know what would happen next. Worse, it felt that all our knowledge, our science, our preparations and experience might be useless in the face of Mother Nature's new and incomprehensible behaviour.

These images, and the fearful effect they had on everyone who saw them, go right to the heart of why these disasters continue to find a place in our collective memory. As the event came without warning, only the local media were on hand. In the absence of any forecasts, the powerful capability of the major networks had not been deployed to the quiet city of Toowoomba. Most of the images we now associate with this frightening afternoon were captured on personal hand-held cameras and smartphones held by witnesses leaning out of office windows or standing inside elevated shops for shelter. In many cases, the images were accompanied by the panicked cries and distressed whimpering of those witnesses reacting to the terror of what they were seeing.

If this event had occurred even five years earlier, we would not have had the ability to capture it this way. Still photos from conventional cameras could not show us the rapid pace of it. Without YouTube and the internet, we could not have seen these scenes almost as they were happening, with all the shock and awe that comes with real-time experience. There was no professional editing, no polished cutting or splicing. If anything, the shaky images were more compelling for the immediacy the amateur operators brought to the experience. Nothing was censored, nothing was left out. We could imagine ourselves being the people who were washed away. As we waited for the surge of water heading to our capital city, these were the images we saw in our mind's eye, and they scared us half to death.

It was late afternoon when emergency services helicopters started to arrive on the outskirts of Toowoomba to assist with rooftop rescues. Television stations, having diverted their helicopters to the city to source more electrifying images, began broadcasting their footage. From their images and reports, we began to understand the full scale and horror of what had unfolded in the region around Toowoomba: a massive wall of water, rushing down the mountain range, had torn across the peaceful farming valley below it in a deadly surge.

The news helicopters brought us images of whole families perched on the roofs of their farmhouses or clinging to trees and the gutters of their rooftops as rushing water pulled at their bodies. Our hearts thumped as we watched people waving at the cameras, screaming at those in the helicopters for help. But news helicopters do not carry rescue equipment, and there were no ropes or winches and no staff trained to use them. Again, we were assaulted by images of people of all ages, all shapes and sizes, men and women who looked like us, like our mums and dads, on the verge of death. These televised images were almost all we had to help us understand what was happening. The raging water had taken out telecommunications towers and closed roads. Local frontline responders could not communicate with Emergency HQ. The weather had worsened and it was not possible to land emergency helicopters in any of the affected areas. Despite the conditions, emergency helicopters winched forty-three people to safety in less than two hours. It was a remarkable effort, unprecedented in Australian civilian history. Later, we heard many extraordinary tales of bravery and courage from these few hours of chaos. But as night fell, hundreds remained on rooftops without rescue. Our response was effectively grounded. Police and emergency services were trying desperately to piece together what was happening and pull together a response. I headed home to anxiously await further briefings as soon as more was known.

At home, I received early reports from some small towns in the Lockyer Valley – the fertile farmlands that lie between Toowoomba and Brisbane – of people swept out of houses, and survivors gathered in local schools with no phone coverage and little or no information. None of the authorities could find out any accurate information, but it was clear something terrible had happened and that more may come overnight.

I was relieved to know that Greg and Oliver would soon be back with me. In Sydney, still on holiday, they took one look at those images on their television and started packing. They knew the ground had suddenly shifted and they needed to be home. Joseph had already returned to his Brisbane flat from the Woodford Folk Festival and would also be visiting. Like every other family in Queensland that night, we needed to be with each other.

The snippets of information I received were horrifying. Up until then we'd been able to give some warnings and had largely been able to protect people. Now, suddenly, we had no idea what was going on, who was in danger, how many were hurt, how bad their injuries were. I was sick with worry. It seemed our formidable team was suddenly helpless and people were in extreme danger.

I worried that if Queenslanders woke up the next morning not knowing that all this had been happening, people would feel we had withheld information. If the media helicopters, which were bound to be out at first light, drip-fed footage in unreliable dribs and drabs, people might suspect we didn't even know it was happening at all. That would be worse, eroding their trust at the worst possible time.

I decided to call a State Disaster Management Group meeting for 8 pm. The leadership team was caught up in responding to their own agencies' priorities. We needed to regroup, to share the scant information we had, and to try to understand the whole picture. I directed my team to alert the media that I would do a live conference immediately after the meeting.

There was no time to wait for an official car. Driving through torrential rain, I picked up my media advisor, Kimberley Gardiner, on the way to Emergency HQ. The teeming rain was almost impenetrable, and both Kimberley and I were fearful driving on the slippery roads.

At the meeting, the representatives from every frontline agency pooled the available information. The picture we pieced together was shocking. We discovered that there had been numerous deaths, but didn't know how many. We knew that there were many small towns where whole families were on rooftops unable to be rescued. Little towns like Murphys Creek, Postmans Ridge, Withcott, Helidon and Grantham had been battered. Two of the worst-hit towns were completely cut off as muddy landslides washed out roads and caused bridges to collapse. We heard reports of whole houses being washed off their foundations with families still inside. We knew that power was out and phone towers were down. People in the most desperate of circumstances could not be reached. No access or communication were possible. And the rain continued unabated.

This media conference was an important one, allowing all media to put the most up-to-date information in the morning papers and on the first radio and TV bulletins. For me, this late-night meeting and media conference felt like a wresting-back of control from nature and they set the tone for our actions for the rest of that week. We would give people every piece of information we had as soon as we had it. We would give it to them warts and all. They would know we were telling them everything we could. That night I told them that our situation was 'grim and desperate'; I told them what we knew and what we didn't know. I told them that many had died and more were in danger. And I told them that worse was yet to come.

*

The flooding of a capital city is a major news event. All the national morning TV shows relocated their teams to hastily built outdoor sets, high on the cliffs of Kangaroo Point overlooking Brisbane's CBD. With a sheer drop down to the Brisbane River, the cliffs were a perfect vantage point from which to capture the drama of an unfolding flood. These sets became my first port of call each morning, as the cliffs were on the route between my home and Emergency HQ. After a telephone briefing around 4.45 am on each day of the crisis, I made my way there, provided as much of an update as I could for the media, then headed directly to HQ.

The water heading towards Ipswich and Brisbane was beyond all records and would do untold damage. The emergency releases being made from Wivenhoe Dam were the largest in its history and would cause damage as they tore through the area downstream.

At Emergency HQ, the mood was sombre as the State Disaster Management Group pored over data, questioned the technical experts, plotted the possible scenarios and considered extreme circumstances. The room was typically calm, considered and determined. These people were highly skilled professionals and disasters did not daunt them. There was always a sense of urgency but never an air of panic. The team worked methodically through each situation, resolving each dilemma, finding a way around every impasse with clinical precision. But there was also an easy camaraderie, the kind that comes from having been through the trenches together, a feeling of trust and confidence in one another's judgement and ability. There was often a good share of humour, an ability to laugh at ourselves, that lightened the mood when necessary. The jokes broke the tension when it threatened to escalate.

But the atmosphere in the group had shifted. We all knew that we were now managing a different event, at a new tempo, with so much more at stake. We were under siege on all fronts and we could feel it stretching us to breaking point. We needed to prepare people, we needed to communicate the flood map information so people understood which areas were at most risk, we needed to prepare two million people for flooding, for public transport shutdowns, road closures, food shortages and prolonged power outages. Our city dwellers were soon to have no communications, no electricity, no transport and, in many cases, no shops open. Massive evacuation centres needed to be established within twenty-four hours. The Red Cross swung into action and the city's showgrounds were activated. Huge sandbagging exercises began across the city to minimise damage wherever possible.

At the same time, the mighty wall of water that had been tearing through the Lockyer Valley to Brisbane's immediate west was still leaving devastation in its wake. More than one hundred people were missing and eight were already confirmed dead. Roads, rail, power and telecommunications were completely cut. Police declared Grantham a crime scene. The grim search for bodies would begin when they could gain access to the town. A major incident room was established to manage the police response to this event. A temporary morgue was also established.

At Emergency HQ, the air was heavy. I understood that the team was fearful of what we faced. That, like me, they wondered for the first time if we were up to the task. I knew they needed boosting, that we all needed to believe in ourselves and back ourselves.

I told the team that we were about to be tested like never before, that we now had a catastrophic disaster on multiple fronts, that lives would depend on our ability to rise to the demands of this next challenge. I told them the eyes of the nation were now on us. I told them I knew they had what it took. That I knew they would not fail this test.

As I left the meeting to convey the dire news to a hungry media, I felt a steely resolve not to be defeated by any of it. I felt the need to convey that resolve to my frontline, to my colleagues, to the media and, most of all, to the public. I wanted everyone to know that in the face of these overwhelming events, the leadership was strong. Thinking of a way to convey this strength, I quickly scribbled 'hearts, will' on the bottom of my handwritten briefing notes.

It would be the first time during these events that I risked speaking to Queenslanders in lofty terms, and I wasn't sure I could strike the right note. In the three minutes it took to walk across to the media room, I decided not to overthink it, to just go with my gut. I was convinced that the urgency and peril of the situation demanded words that would raise our spirits. This conviction outweighed my fear of the risk inherent in speaking to the community in an elevated language and tone. This was not the common language of Australian politics. Our citizens like it best when their political leaders don't get too far above their station, when they act and sound as much like everyone else as possible rather than using dramatic rhetorical flourishes. I didn't have much time to think about it and no time to confer with my staff, but I knew I was taking a personal and political risk. If I misjudged this, I would look foolish, and no one wants a fool leading an emergency.

At the press conference I concluded with the statement: 'This ... may be breaking our hearts ... but it will not break our will.' I said it as a battle cry, because that's where we were, in the heat of a battle against a formidable foe. As I said them, the words didn't feel awkward, but necessary to match the circumstances. These words became the banner headline in *The Australian* the next morning, 12 January.

Words are such powerful tools. They can bring simplicity to complexity and an intensity to our feelings and emotions. At the same media conference, the police commissioner, Bob Atkinson, called the wall of water that had swept through Toowoomba and the Lockyer Valley an 'inland tsunami'. He gave a name to something that had previously defied description. It may not have been meteorologically accurate, but it was a name that helped people to imagine and understand what had happened. From that point on, it was referred to as an inland tsunami, and everyone knew exactly what that meant.

The battlelines were now drawn on so many fronts, and the event changing so rapidly, that it was difficult to implement our decisions. Just as we decided that a river had settled, more rainfall put it back in contention. As we decided to evacuate one town, water began to threaten the town we were moving people to. The hydrology and weather data was changing so quickly that carefully constructed plans were thrown out before the ink dried on them. It had become almost impossible to manage the flow of accurate information to the public. As Bob Atkinson and I discussed breaking news about likely flood levels in Ipswich, we knew we could not wait for the evening media briefing to get this news out.

'Premier, I think we should move to two-hourly media briefings,' Bob said, thinking out loud. It was good advice.

My staff moved to confirm with media representatives that it was technically possible. Between myself, the Minister for Police and Emergency Services, Neil Roberts, Bob Atkinson and his deputy, Ian Stewart, we agreed that at least two of us would be available for a full media update every two hours, from 8 am until 8 pm, every day for as long as necessary.

On this basis, all media outlets switched their scheduled summer programming to full disaster coverage. They had the confidence to do this because they were guaranteed fresh material every two hours, and given that some of these conferences lasted forty-five minutes or more, this was a lot of material to work with. But just as importantly, every station had the technical capability to switch easily and affordably to disaster coverage. They had mobile satellite outdoor broadcasting capabilities parked outside Emergency HQ. They had reporters stationed in numerous hotspots across the state, in Dalby and Chinchilla, in Toowoomba and the Lockyer Valley, in Ipswich and several places around the capital city. They had helicopter coverage and their major breakfast program sets on the Kangaroo Point cliffs to broadcast from at any time.

Like the phone cameras that had brought us the terrifying footage from Toowoomba, this technical capability changed the tenor of this disaster. The event went national, and the coverage transmitted almost constant live broadcasts of every aspect of the disaster. It brought the deeply personal experience of it into every lounge room. The victims of this event were not numbers or faces shown briefly on the six o'clock news. We met them and got to know them as reporters spent time in evacuation centres and in their homes, interviewing them about what it felt like, how they were coping. Australians waited with the same fear-filled hearts as those Queenslanders in the path of these swollen rivers. They listened to the same updates, the same calculations and predictions. They knew, often before those directly involved, just who was in the path of danger and when it would hit. This disaster became a shared, lived experience like few others in our nation's history. These rains and flooding rivers were like an unfolding television miniseries. For hours and weeks, we all watched and waited for the next instalment, mapping the changes, counting the cost, reaching out to the damaged. Little wonder the event struck a deep chord in us and still lives so vividly in our memories.

As Bob Atkinson and I had wrapped up our morning media conference on 11 January, the raging wall of water in the Lockyer Valley had left Grantham and made its way to the small communities of Laidley and Forest Hill. I walked past Ian Stewart, standing with his phone glued to his ear. I heard him say, 'You need choppers to evacuate *how* many people?' He quickly told Bob and me that the roads out of these towns were now cut off and we needed to airlift people to safety. Emergency services helicopters were joined by defence helicopters and evacuated more than a hundred people ahead of fast-moving floodwaters. Among them was a toddler, trapped on a roof with her grandmother. This little girl was featured in the next day's *Australian* under that headline 'Break our hearts, but not our will'. She was wearing only a nappy and being carried by a uniformed soldier out of a Black Hawk helicopter. This dramatic and striking image captured the peril experienced in these towns. It was starting to look and feel like a warzone. What caught my eye was that this little girl had black writing down the side of one arm. We learned later that her grandmother, who was looking after her alone at the time, had written the child's name and her mother's phone number on her as she was being fitted into the harness to be winched to safety. The grandmother didn't know if she would make it out alive herself, didn't know if she would see the baby girl again. I am chilled as I think about this grandmother writing on this little arm. I imagine what was going through her mind and the sheer terror that drove her to make sure this baby could be reunited with her mother.

Tragically, other children and babies were not to return to their families. The wrenching stories of unendurable loss began to seep out. We felt the unspeakable pain of a young pregnant mother who fled her home carrying her toddler as the rushing waters tore through without warning, only to find the waters were too strong and the little girl was washed from her arms. Another family lost both parents as their teenage children made it to safety. A father and his young daughter drowned as he tried to rescue her. These stories pierced us with sorrow and fear. With many still missing, we knew that we would hear more stories like them.

The day darkened as driving rain fell from heavy black clouds. Major shopping centres in Brisbane's CBD shut down as their car parks started to fill with water. Public transport ceased. Power was being cut off in all city high–rise towers to prevent electrical fault fires as the water reached their electrical rooms, most located in underground car parks. The roads were at a standstill as workers poured out of the city.

Back in my premier's office, I was signing the paperwork needed to manage this next crisis when my brother John rang me. He was worried that our mother's ground-floor unit may be in the path of the Brisbane River as it swelled and flooded.

When I talked with Mum, she was anxious. The Brisbane City Council website had crashed under the weight of demand and she was unable to access the flood maps. I consulted my staff, who told me that the flood maps showed her unit to be in the direct path of floodwaters if the river's peak reached our worst predictions. John and I decided to get Mum out of there and relocate her to my place. John helped her pack up and my eldest son, Joe, went over to keep her company. Moving Mum added a new dimension to the event for me. While my home was on a hill and safe, our family, like so many others, now had a personal stake in where these waters ended up. I was relieved to have Mum with us. This was no time to be alone.

The city council's website had excellent flood map information, but I knew that if my mother had trouble dealing with it, then thousands of others would too. I called the Lord Mayor, Campbell Newman, and proposed that we make a joint approach to the local daily newspaper asking that it run full maps in the next edition. He agreed, as did the editor of the paper, and the maps ran the next day. But these were too late for the people of Ipswich, whose city had already begun to flood.

Throughout the afternoon of 12 January, Emergency HQ dealt with rising levels of distress and anxiety coming from the fearful people of Ipswich. The city had little time to organise the evacuation centres needed to accommodate the numbers of people pouring out of their homes. Neighbourhood centres and local churches started to fill the void and a massive effort was being made to get food, bedding and other supplies where needed as quickly as possible. The scale and speed of what was happening in Ipswich was threatening to unravel us. With less than forty-eight hours' notice, a city of more than 170,000 people was flooding. The logistics of this were on a scale bigger than anything we'd dealt with, and the usual air of urgency at HQ bordered on panic for the first time since the rain began. Without doubt, there was chaos and fear and the response in Ipswich scrambled to match the pace of the water. But it's a strong community and local leaders rose to the challenge in their own neighbourhoods. One way or another, the people of Ipswich were kept safe.

As busy as we were, with further disasters opening on new fronts, we felt no sense of progress. Every hour seemed to bring a greater sense that we were standing still or, worse, slipping backwards. These are the moments when leading means almost physically reaching down inside to pull out something more of yourself. In the maelstrom, you are on full alert, every muscle fibre twitching and bending to the purpose at hand. It is the doldrums that test your mettle. The long stretches, not where nothing is happening but where you can feel no progress, are the times that demand the most.

At the State Disaster Management Group meetings during that week, we had as many as forty mayors on teleconference. While the team kept focused on an orderly, precise rollout of assistance, it was becoming a disorderly event to manage. I knew that many of these mayors were grappling with issues beyond the resources of their small councils and needed a more personal response. The deputy premier, Paul Lucas, was the designated go-to point in state government for mayors and councils. Paul seized this responsibility with both hands and diligently made and maintained contact with the affected councils throughout the event and, importantly, beyond it. I credit Paul's very genuine approach to this work for the bipartisanship and goodwill that characterised the relationship between state and local governments throughout the long recovery and rebuilding process in the aftermath of the disasters.

The day before the Brisbane River peaked on 13 January, when we were losing hope of ever seeing the sun again, we had woken to blue skies and sunshine. This had added a further air of unreality to the already unbelievable. Under a clear blue sky, the filthy brown river was building and surging. It tore boats and boat ramps from their moorings and threw them downstream in their hundreds. It carried the debris from the communities torn apart by the inland tsunami. People lined the cliffs and riverbanks to watch astonished as fridges and freezers, cars and tractors, shipping containers, tables, chairs, trees and dead animals tore past in a fast-moving flotilla of jumble and crashed into the pylons of bridges. A whole floating restaurant that had dislodged from its moorings washed by. The rushing power of it held us awestruck. Outer suburbs of the city were fast filling with water, and people were making their way to higher ground. Friends took in friends, families moved in with relatives, and the streets were filled with people swapping food and blankets and stories as they bunkered down on each other's floors for the duration.

Large-scale evacuation centres at our showgrounds and the QEII sports stadium were rapidly filling. On the night of the Brisbane floods, they would house more than six thousand people. They would become a temporary home to people whose nursing homes and retirement villages were inundated, people whose homes were cut off by floodwaters, travellers who were stranded, families, singles, children, the aged, the frail and the sick. The scale of this mobilisation reflected an awesome community capability. The centres were set up and staffed by voluntary organisations such as the Red Cross and the Salvation Army, by good people who stand ready to turn out on request. Volunteers were deployed from across the state, away from their own families, at a moment's notice. They were ready to feed up to four thousand people with just twenty-four hours' notice. They came equipped with medical supplies and trained health workers. They were as handy with a portable generator as they were ready with a pot of tea. They were an army of willing worker bees and their stalwart, ready presence filled me with confidence and pride every time I saw them in action.

The clearing weather gave me the chance to get into the air and see the extent of damage, especially in the Ipswich area. Mick Slater and I headed off in helicopters from Emergency HQ to survey the floodwaters from the sky. We were soon struck by a scale of disaster beyond anything the TV cameras had been able to capture. In every direction, as far as the horizon, brown swirling waters engulfed everything in their path. Our central fruit and vegetable markets were underwater, our new multi-lane freeway between Brisbane and Ipswich was drowning. We could identify the suburb of Goodna only because the top of the pedestrian rail overpass was still visible. Street after street, suburb after suburb, houses were flooded to their rooftops. It seemed beyond possibility that people would be able to face this. The vastness of it crushed us. Our gasps of horror soon turned to silence. From up here, it seemed that this was finally beyond us. For the first time since the rain had started on Christmas Day, I was overwhelmed with doubt.

As our chopper landed, I knew that I could not head into Emergency HQ feeling like this, that I could not sit at the State Disaster Management Group meeting carrying this doubt. My sense of defeat would be seen in my face, in the way I held myself, and it would carry like a virus through the team. I squared my shoulders and drew myself up. It took a deliberate and conscious effort, and I knew it had to be done.

I walked into the meeting with Mick, and we shared with the team what we'd seen. We were clear, clinical and focused. I kept my doubts well hidden and we got on with planning the next round of action. The Brisbane River would reach its peak that night. We expected it to be close in height to that reached in 1974, but we could not be sure. In a city this densely populated, extra centimetres in water levels can draw thousands more people into the danger zone. We had some idea of what to expect based on that 1974 experience, but every flood is different and already our river had broken its banks at different places and in different ways than expected. And we were a vastly different city than we had been almost forty years ago. Our population had more than doubled. There were new suburbs and developments, new industrial areas where before there had been nothing. Whatever was coming, we knew that it would cause grief and hardship.

My home was across the river from Emergency HQ, and our worst-case predictions would see floodwaters cut the roads in between. I was advised not to return home that evening, so I stayed at the nearby home of my chief of staff, Nicole Scurrah. Another staff member, Don Wilson, whose home was in Goodna, near Ipswich, also stayed over. We watched the last of the television footage together and talked about what the next day would bring. My sense of being overwhelmed that afternoon was playing on my mind, and I knew that as people everywhere started to see images of the damage done to their capital city, as locals came back to their battered homes and neighbourhoods, they would feel this too. Just as I'd had to rally myself earlier that day, I understood that others would need rallying. My doubts about our ability to rise to this challenge would only be realised if we doubted ourselves. We were facing an extraordinary recovery effort and we would need to lift ourselves up and feel equal to the task. I understood also that this was a time for leadership. It would fall to me to elevate people from their despair and set them squarely to the task at hand. Again, I thought about the personal and political risks if I did not hit the right note. What I said the next morning would matter.

In Australian cultural discourse it is common to hear questions about what makes Queenslanders different. Why do we seem to breed and attract the larger-than-life characters, the florid and flamboyant, the wild crocodile hunters and the loudmouth politicians in big hats? I have come to believe that it is our status as a frontier that marks us in this way. European settlement occurred later here than in other major states, and it met with much harsher conditions. Blinding heat, raging floods, cyclones and searing droughts, combined with sharks, snakes, poisonous spiders and crocodiles, kept all but the most tenacious settlers at bay. Only the tough, the undaunted and the brash would survive and make it. It's a history that breeds a pioneering spirit and a fierce parochial pride that you can feel at a State of Origin football game.

In Queensland, this history has settled deep into our psyche. We may not know or understand all the pioneering history, but we all hold firm to the view that we're a little bit tougher than the rest of the country because of it. When Greg first arrived in Brisbane to make a new life with me in 1987, among the first things he noticed about his new home was how often the locals proudly referred to themselves as Queenslanders. He was right, but I had never noticed it. As a Queenslander myself, it was invisible to me until he drew my attention to it. Even those who move here from other states and other countries quickly fall into step. After all, they have often come to Queensland to build a better life. Our beaches and sunshine promise a lifestyle with new freedoms. In their own way, these newcomers are pioneers too.

We don't all wrestle crocodiles, wear big hats, shoot our mouths off or throw money at wild ideas, but in these big colourful characters we admire something bold and crazy-brave. They speak to a sense we have of ourselves as people who thrive on beating the odds, who stare down their critics. You can see a similar social and political culture in American states like Texas, for similar reasons. It may give rise to some overblown public identities, but it's also a mindset that encourages risk-taking and entrepreneurial zeal.

On this miserable night, as we waited for Brisbane to flood, I didn't spend any time on this analysis. This was the Queensland that had shaped and formed me, and I knew it instinctively. I knew that if I could appeal to this part in each of us, it would lift us. As I lay that night in a bed that was not my own, like so many others bunking down with friends, I knew in my gut that this frontier spirit was what I had to find in myself and ignite in others. I made some quick notes, thinking to polish the words further in the morning, and finally found some much-needed sleep.

On 13 January, again the morning broke bright with sunshine, and the welcome news that the Brisbane River had peaked slightly below our worst predictions. There was a sigh of relief, but it was short-lived. Despite reaching a lower peak than in the 1974 flood, the river had wrought much worse damage. We were a bigger city now and had been harder hit. Thankfully, people were safe, our frontline response having worked to protect everyone overnight. There would be a tragic death later in the morning when a young man attempted to return to his parents' home and was drowned in a stormwater drain, but given the size of the city and the size of the flood, our frontline was magnificent. Many people were yet to see their homes and neighbourhoods firsthand as roads were cut and they were stranded. But the media choppers were out at first light and soon started bringing us the images that rammed home the force of this water. The images showed a broken city. A CBD that was closed, eerily silent and empty. Suburb after heartbreaking suburb of homes and parks and playgrounds drowning in mud and great whirls of dirty brown water. A great sadness settled over us. We could almost hear and feel the sighs and tears in lounge rooms across the city as we watched and took stock.

And then, there on our early-morning television screens, was *Mavis*, the small river tugboat. Her owner, Doug Hislop, had heard that the city's floating walkway had been torn from its moorings. It had become a 300-metre, 1000-tonne floating missile rushing down the river, headed straight for the Gateway Bridge that spanned the river mouth. Police closed the bridge, fearing that the impact of this missile would cause structural damage and a possible collapse.

Doug Hislop had grabbed his mate Peter Fenton and took *Mavis* out into the treacherous conditions of the flooding river. With our hearts in our mouths, we watched as Doug and Peter fought the surging waters to manoeuvre *Mavis* alongside this massive piece of dangerous debris. Slowly, they began to force the debris away from the bridge and nearby marinas. It was an act of astonishing courage. Cheers went up everywhere as *Mavis* saved the day. We would watch *Mavis* and the pair's daring bravery again and again throughout the day and never tire of it. *Mavis* made us all feel ten feet tall.

Our State Disaster Management Group meeting that morning was one of the largest we held. As we began to assess the damage in south-east Queensland, a new front was opening up in the south-west around Goondiwindi, and we focused on a possible evacuation there. The huge floodwaters of the Fitzroy River in Rockhampton, to the north, were not receding as quickly as hoped and the city's airport, road and rail access remained closed. This was causing major supply and logistics headaches for the towns and cities north of Rockhampton. By now we had a full team of defence personnel, transport company operators and major grocery chains working on supply problems across the state, and this team was asked for a renewed effort on this front. I walked to the media conference with Ian Stewart and Mick Slater. I had a long report to give, and I stayed focused on getting as much information out as I could.

I then shifted from these facts and spoke, as I had planned, directly to the hearts and minds of Queenslanders. I hadn't had the chance to polish my words as I'd hoped. I hadn't had the chance to discuss these words, or the risk of saying them, with any of my team. Again, I went straight from my gut. I looked into the cameras and started by including everyone who had lived the agony of the past few weeks.

'Can I say to Queenslanders everywhere, wherever you are, and there are so many places to list, if you are in central Queensland, if you're in south-west Queensland, if you're in western Queensland, if you're in the Burnett region, the Darling Downs, Toowoomba, the Lockyer Valley, Ipswich or Brisbane, all of those places have been affected by floods and I say to every one of those people in those areas and to Queenslanders in other parts of the state: as we weep for what we have lost, and as we grieve for family and friends, and we confront the challenge that is before us, I want us to remember who we are.'

My voice broke. I gulped and my throat constricted with tears. I feared I would not be able to go on. My heart was sinking. I was totally captured by that awful physical process of trying to hold back tears while continuing to speak. As that hot, salty water starts to flow into your eyes, and your mouth and voice start to wobble, you instinctively try to stop the quivering by clenching your jaw. Your throat swells and you know that before long your nose will begin to run. A good cry can be a great thing, but a cry in public, in the middle of a weighty speech, is a horrible experience. I felt like a lousy failure as I forced back tears and struggled for air.

Suddenly, I felt Mick Slater fix his knuckle into the small of my back as if to say, 'Finish the job, soldier.' This did the trick. I straightened and took a breath.

'We are Queenslanders,' I continued. 'We're the people that they breed tough north of the border. We're the ones that they knock down and we get up again. I said earlier this week that this weather may break our hearts, and it is doing that, but it will not break our will, and in the coming weeks and in the coming months we are going to prove that beyond any doubt. Together, we can pull through this and that's what I'm determined to do. And with your help, we can achieve that.'

As a woman leader, I was always conscious of the need to be and look strong. Always deeply aware that the smallest falter, the finest grain of weakness, would be amplified by my gender. Always worried that deep prejudices about women being the weaker sex would activate at the first sign of emotional strain on my part. In a crisis, people look for strength; they need it like food and water, to sustain them. I left the media room certain that I had failed the task, certain that my tears and choking voice had crushed people's confidence, not lifted it.

I found a quiet room to overcome my embarrassment and pull myself together. To my mind, I had cried at the worst possible moment. Now, when people most needed confirmation of my strength, of my belief in myself and in them, I had fallen short. But my media staff rushed in, elated. They, and it seemed everyone else, had been lifted by what I'd said. Against all the odds, my tears came at a time when they stirred people's aching hearts.

It was the strangest of moments. These words, and the heavy emotion with which I said them, remain one of the public's strongest memories of me and my time in public life. In the months ahead, they would be printed on T-shirts and inscribed on the walls of sporting clubs. One woman sent me a photo of the words tattooed across her shoulder. They did exactly what I set out to do: ignited, inspired and united people.

So there it was, a golden, shining moment when I rose to the call of my office and completely missed that I'd done so. So certain that I had failed, I was bewildered by the reaction.

As my staff rushed off to answer the continuing media questions, Mick Slater sought me out to apologise for pushing his knuckle into my lower back. He was appalled that he had touched me like that. I told him that his action was prompted by his own gut instincts and those instincts had been completely correct. His action had helped me enormously. That insistent knuckle had physically straightened me up and pulled my mind back from my running eyes and quivering voice to the task at hand. So effective was it that I recently recommended to a friend that she have someone stand close to her, knuckle at the ready, as she gave the eulogy at her mother's funeral. She delivered a beautiful tribute to her mother with no need for the ready knuckle, but said she felt more confident knowing it was there.

Tears or no tears, my instinct to appeal to the parochial, frontier spirit of Queenslanders was the right one to follow. As history now records, Queenslanders rallied and mobilised in droves. They picked up mops and buckets and formed an army of volunteers. The Brisbane City Council coordinated a fleet of buses taking volunteers to the worst-hit places. In Brisbane and across the state, neighbours helped neighbours, friends reached out to friends and strangers came from everywhere to help whoever they could. These volunteers became known as the Mud Army, and the world marvelled at images of it marching through our streets and suburbs. For the thousands displaced and homeless, it turned a tragedy into an uplifting experience of profound humanity.

*

In the weeks that followed the flooding of Brisbane, massive clean-up operations took place across the state as we restored power and reopened roads. Suburban streets filled with convoys of army vehicles laden with young soldiers recalled from their Christmas leave for the clean-up task. Kerbsides began to pile high with rubbish as homes were cleared out, the precious possessions of a lifetime reduced to ruined, soiled mounds of jumble. Heavy garbage trucks criss-crossed cities and towns as the debris was carted away. Hardware stores were emptied of high-pressure water guns, and neighbourhoods began to brighten again.

January is peak summer in Queensland and temperatures soared as the floodwaters receded. They left behind oceans of steaming, stinking mud and everyone who lifted a mop or a shovel in those weeks will forever recall the stench of it. There is no smell quite like it. It pushed into our nostrils and clung to our skin, our hair and our clothes. Many places had been underwater and without power for more than a week and the sharp stink of putrefying meat and vegetables, the reek of the rotting flesh of dead animals and decaying vegetation mixed into a foul miasma. It smelt the same in Rockhampton and Condamine as it did in Brisbane and Goodna, and it rose in waves as searing heat turned the wet mud steamy and humid. At the Rocklea Markets, Brisbane's fresh produce distribution centre, the frozen coldrooms full of the city's meat supplies, now rotting and rancid, became a major public health hazard. The clean-up teams had to wear full-body moon suits and breathing masks to safely remove the spoiled contents. But there was a catharsis in the work. The relentless and unforgiving rains had almost sucked the life out of us. We all longed for the return of our real lives and this filthy clean-up took us a step closer to them every day.

Along with the clean-up came care and compassion. From one end of Australia to the other, people sent donations of money. Towns, churches, sporting clubs and local groups gathered up spare clothes, blankets, toys and household goods and hired the trucks to send them to us. In Grantham so much was received that the council had to open a warehouse and bring in a full-time coordinator to store it, sort it and distribute it effectively. People rostered themselves to cook communal meals in those places that continued without power for weeks. All of this happened organically, without government assistance or organisation, driven by real care and concern for those who were suffering. Social media brought people together, quickly linking those who needed something with those only too willing to help.

Whether the need was for a generator, some transport or some voluntary labour, it all came in bulk. Danielle Crismani, whose children were staying with their grandmother and were cut off by floodwaters, began to bake cakes for the SES volunteers who were out in the hot sun shovelling mud. She put out a call through her social media networks and within days had hundreds of mums, and others who couldn't join in the effort of physical labour, baking cakes. This in turn gave rise to the need for help to get the cakes out to the volunteers. Willing drivers answered her call. Her charity, Baked Relief, was born, and it continues to activate whenever a disaster looms.

My own electorate incorporated the Southbank reach of the Brisbane River, and many of my constituents had suffered the same fate as others across the city as the floodwaters took their homes. I spent time during those weeks being part of the local clean-up when I could. But most of my time was taken up negotiating with the federal government and local councils as we pulled together our recovery arrangements. We established a new reconstruction authority. We called a commission of inquiry into the management of the disasters, with particular reference to the operation of the Wivenhoe Dam in the lead-up to and during the events. It was a busy and hectic time, but one when every move, every decision, took us further away from the disasters and closer to normality.

*

Just as we all began to feel that we could take a little rest on the end of our brooms and shovels and breathe a sigh of relief, the

Bureau of Meteorology came knocking on my door again. On Friday 28 January, just a fortnight after Brisbane had flooded, Jim Davidson advised me and the senior emergency response team that two tropical cyclones were forming in the Pacific Ocean. Both were headed towards Queensland and both were likely to cross our coastline within a week. As Jim outlined this news with his usual care and precision, he was met with incredulity. After all we had been through, this news just didn't seem possible. It was preposterous. In fact, the first response around the table was snorts of laughter. 'Two cyclones in a week? You've got to be kidding!' As I made the news public, it didn't take long for social media to fill with jokes about plagues of locusts and alien abductions being the next afflictions to come our way.

Once more, Emergency HQ was activated and we began to plan for the next round of trouble. Cyclones are tricky things to predict. They have a measurable force and a definable pattern that help to plot their likely trajectory, but their own momentum can cause them to swing off this trajectory with little notice. They can come flying towards you with all the force of an Exocet missile, only to turn away at the last minute and dissipate out at sea. Queenslanders are used to planning for cyclones that ultimately veer away, leaving us safe and wondering what all the fuss was about. But these two cyclones were the work of the devilish La Niña, and given her recent form we couldn't take any chances. This time, it was the far north of our state at risk, with Cyclone Anthony expected to gather the force of a category-three event and cross the coast between Bowen and Cairns within two to three days. Its partner, Cyclone Yasi, was emerging as a much stronger event and was headed for Cairns within the next four to five days.

When the bureau first briefed me about these cyclones, they had barely formed. Anthony was in Australian waters and had formed enough to be named, but Yasi was still a circling cloud mass, drawing hot air from the warm waters off Fiji and had not yet warranted a name.

True to forecast, Anthony crossed the coast close to Bowen, near the Whitsunday Islands, late on the following Sunday night. Despite being a category-two cyclone by landfall, it did not bring the damage that was feared. Large trees were brought down and the coastal strip from Mackay to Townsville was battered with heavy winds and saturating rain, but people were safe and the event was manageable.

Cyclone Yasi, heading for Cairns in the far north, was a much more frightening prospect. It had loomed as a category-four cyclone, but as Cyclone Anthony battered the Whitsundays, Yasi gathered force and was upgraded overnight. Australians woke to the news on Tuesday 1 February that a category-five cyclone was now making its way towards us. According to the Bureau of Meteorology, a category-five event is defined as one that is 'extremely dangerous with widespread destruction'. The storm that threatened us had gathered pace and force over the Pacific Ocean and had now emerged on our radar systems. Yasi's destructive core measured some 500 kilometres, with associated weather activity stretching 2000 kilometres, bringing winds of over 200 kilometres an hour, with gusts of 285 kilometres an hour. This storm was larger than Hurricane Katrina, which destroyed New Orleans and killed more than 1800 people in 2005. Images of its huge, menacing white presence began to dominate news headlines around Australia and around the world. All jokes about disasters and Mother Nature's sick sense of humour evaporated as we moved to high alert. Cyclone Yasi was emerging as the largest in Australia's recorded history and we were once again in uncharted territory.

The mood of the State Disaster Management Group that Tuesday morning was grim as we examined the weather charts and listened to the briefings from our weather experts. With the news of Yasi's upgrade, our challenge lifted to another level. Mayors of local councils in the region joined our teleconference and we began to chart a series of evacuations. Our best forecast had Yasi hitting somewhere between Townsville and Cairns, within a 200-kilometre stretch between two of our largest regional cities. We had less than forty-eight hours to set up safe shelters and evacuate people in the cyclone's likely path. We knew that even a slight shift in Yasi's course could take whole towns in or out of the danger zone. Cyclones bring intensely powerful winds and flooding rain, but when they get to this size they also bring the threat of storm surge. Storm surge is a massive wall of seawater picked up by the force of the cyclone and moving at very high speeds. It was storm surge that caused most of the damage in New Orleans, and it was storm surge that occupied our minds that morning with our weather experts predicting surges of up to seven metres. Evacuation centres were quickly identified, additional personnel were dispatched and commercial airlines were drawn in, scheduling additional flights to bring visitors and tourists to safety.

When we regrouped at the end of the day, emergency responders reported a different challenge. Out on the frontlines, they were encountering a high level of complacency. Long-time residents of the tropics were greeting Yasi with a laidback scepticism and misplaced bravado. Many insisted on staying where they were, and those in coastal towns seemed unaware of the storm surge danger. A 'she'll be right mate' attitude was standing in the way of authorities' attempts to adequately prepare and protect many of these communities. The Bureau of Meteorology issued an overnight statement announcing that Yasi was 'more life threatening than any cyclone experienced in recent generations'. It was an uncharacteristically colourful phrase for the bureau and it hit the headlines. I authorised the necessary declarations to give police and others the power to remove people by force if necessary. Worried mayors took matters into their hands, assembling large door-knocking teams to walk through neighbourhoods and move people on. Bill Shannon, the mayor of the Cassowary Coast, personally walked the streets of Cardwell, a small town at the southern end of the coast, with a loudhailer to finalise the evacuation.

As Yasi got closer, it gathered more speed and more force. At our next planning meeting on Wednesday morning, we learned it had also slightly shifted course. The revised estimate of Yasi's trajectory was that it would now hit the city of Cairns or just north of it some time later that night or in the early hours of the next day. Cairns is a city of more than 150,000 residents. As the gateway to the Great Barrier Reef, it is also a tourism centre and its population regularly swells with visitors from around the world. It has many resorts and high-rise hotels along its foreshore.

Its foreshore is also home to the region's major base hospital. At the northern end of the esplanade that runs the length of the city, the hospital overlooks the wide blue Pacific. It was originally built with deep verandahs where patients could convalesce with peaceful views and the freshness of an ocean breeze. It was now in the path of the deadly force of a major cyclone.

In the southern hemisphere, the rotating winds of a cyclone spin clockwise. The winds are at their most dangerous to the south of the storm, as its spiralling arms pick up momentum. If Yasi hit north of Cairns, the damage would be even worse than if it met the city directly. We agonised about how best to manage this risk, but with time running against us we took the decision to evacuate the hospital. As I made the call, I felt the cold fear that comes with high-stakes decisions. Cairns Base Hospital was caring for some three hundred patients that day. Some of those patients were critically ill or injured; some, including newborns, were in the Intensive Care Unit; others were high-need renal dialysis patients; many were unable to move and still others were in the early stages of childbirth. Relocating these patients would put their health, and for some, their lives, at risk. All the major services for the hospital are located in its lower floors, including electricity substations and generators, radiology, blood supplies and pharmaceutical stores, and the hospital would simply cease to function if these were taken out by a seven-metre storm surge. On the one hand, the decision was clear and easy. We could not leave these patients in the expected path of this cyclone. But as I imagined these very sick people being uprooted, removed from their hospital beds with their life-saving tubes and drips and medical equipment, transferred to the Cairns airport, flown 1700 kilometres south to Brisbane and resettled in another hospital far away from their loved ones, I was terrified of the danger to them at every turn of that journey. It would be Australia's largest ever evacuation of a major hospital and largest medical airlift – an unprecedented decision.

Every leader has to make such high-stakes decisions, but some sit heavier than others. They can't be easily left behind as you move on to the next task. They sit like worry beads in the palm of your hand, and your mind rubs away at them, revisiting them until you know the result. The hospital was closed early that morning and a massive medical and logistics operation swung into action. I sought regular updates throughout the day, the operation never far from my mind, conscious always that someone – a child, a frail grandfather, a new mother – may not make it through. It was a decision that weighed heavily on the whole team, and Emergency HQ was quiet with worry that long Wednesday.

A temporary medical facility was established at a sports stadium some ten kilometres inland from Cairns for low-care patients. Emergency medical-staging facilities were established at both Cairns and Brisbane airports to stabilise patients before and after their journey. An RAAF Hercules was dispatched to Cairns with additional medical staff, and additional transport was sourced from the Royal Flying Doctors and commercial airlines. In total, eleven aircraft formed the convoy that brought these patients to safety. Brisbane hospitals moved quickly to make room for the incoming patients, cancelling elective surgery and hastening discharges where possible. Over the next eighteen hours, an extraordinary exercise proceeded to relocate critically and seriously ill patients, with the last airlift arriving in Brisbane in the small hours of Thursday, 3 February. That day, 202 inpatients left Cairns Hospital, among them eleven ICU patients, nine of them ventilated, seventeen newborns and eleven children. Every patient arrived safely. The staff of Cairns Base Hospital had no plans, training or experience for an evacuation of this scale. The story of their efforts endures as a remarkable testament to their skill, their ingenuity, their courage and their compassion.

Among the many accounts of this story are some priceless experiences. Along with other available aircraft, the nine-seat government jet was dispatched to assist the airlift. As a base hospital, Cairns provides maternity services to women who live in some of the most remote places in Australia. Given the unpredictable arrival dates of babies, most women travel to Cairns three to four weeks before their due date, just in case. On 2 February, nine women, who were all due to give birth within days, were evacuated to Brisbane on the government jet. I've flown on this jet many, many times, and the image of this plane laden with heavily pregnant women always brings a grin to my face. Regrettably, no one took a photograph, but it must have been quite a sight! Cairns Base Hospital also provides critical services to outpatients, among whom were a group of renal dialysis patients. While they did not need to be hospitalised, they had to be relocated to guarantee they received dialysis on time. The five-star Brisbane Sofitel Hotel opened its doors to accommodate these patients, many of whom had never stayed anywhere like it and couldn't believe their luck.

As darkness fell that night, I did my last live media conference before the cyclone hit. With a furious and fast-moving Yasi heading towards our coast, we couldn't know precisely where it would strike, but we knew it would be upon us within hours. There was now no chance that it would veer away from the coast and leave us alone, but even the smallest of shifts to the north or south could mean the difference between a manageable event and a catastrophic one. One of the last questions of the night came from a journalist about messages that were being received from a group of six people in a building in Port Hinchinbrook, just south of Cardwell, trapped and asking for help. I answered with the terrible truth. It was too late for help to come, because the wind and rain that were now battering the coast made it too dangerous for any vehicle to set out and impossible for any helicopter to take off. It was a sickening answer. I finished that night by telling people:

> As we close this update this evening, I say to all
> of those people who are still able to receive these
> broadcasts, whether it is on radio or on television, we
> are waiting anxiously with you. As we close tonight,
> we know that the long hours ahead of you are going
> to be the hardest that you face. We will be thinking
> of you every minute of every hour between now and
> daylight, and we hope that you can feel our thoughts,
> that you take strength from the fact that we are
> keeping you close and in our hearts. We look forward
> to seeing you safe and well tomorrow morning.

Along with all the senior members of the emergency management group and a huge contingent of media, I spent that night camped on the floor of Emergency HQ. None of us knew what to expect overnight.

After a fitful sleep, I was greeted pre-dawn with the news that, as forecast, Yasi had crossed the Queensland coast as a category-five cyclone close to midnight. Contrary to expectations, it made landfall on the Cassowary Coast, hammering the small towns of Tully, Tully Heads, Cardwell, Mission Beach and Innisfail. The large regional centres of Cairns and Townsville were safe, but nothing in a 500-kilometre radius of Tully had been spared. We greeted the news that there appeared to be no casualties with relief, but the early reports of destruction were little comfort. After an early-morning media conference, I headed into the cyclone zone. While roads into the area were impassable, and some of them had completely washed away, it was possible to fly to Townsville and go into the area by army Black Hawk helicopter. Wayne Swan, who was acting prime minister at the time, Mick Slater and Bob Atkinson accompanied me on the trip.

As the Black Hawk left Townsville airport, we flew into heavy rainfall. The destructive core of Yasi may have continued inland, where it was still wreaking havoc, but it was pulling a massive rain cell in its wake. The intensity of the rain became clear as it began to pour into the helicopter, the winds buffeting us from both sides. Only Mick had headphones connecting him to the pilot's communication system, and I could see from his intense concentration that the trip wasn't easy going. About twenty minutes into the flight, the Black Hawk dropped altitude and went into a stationary hover as visibility ahead fell to zero. The side doors were open and we could see dense, flooded bushland below us. We held this position for almost fifteen minutes as the pilots waited for the cloud to lift. I learned from Mick later that for much of this time the pilots had been planning an emergency landing, fearful that the flight could not be sustained any further. With a brief reprieve in the weather, they headed back into flight and we were soon flying over Cardwell. The town is located just over the steep Cardwell range and is a welcome rest stop for travellers on the national highway to Cairns. As we dropped low to land, it was clear that there was no longer a national highway. Yasi's storm surge had picked it up, smashed it into pieces and dumped most of it into the ocean. It was a terrifying sight.

As we stepped out of the Black Hawk, Wayne Swan removed his boots and poured a litre of water out of them. But any effort to keep dry was futile as rain continued to lash the little seaside town. Within minutes, I was soaked through and my wet hair whipped my face. Within an hour, a photo of me in this state made its way across the country. It is, without any doubt, the ugliest photo of me ever taken. But the minute it hit screens, my office started getting messages and phone calls from people excited and delighted that I was on television looking like this. It was another lesson in authority. While dignified bearing can add a commanding air, it doesn't need to be wrapped in a uniform or an imposing suit. People took comfort from my disarray. They knew in an instant that I was worried about them, not myself. Such is the cynicism about people in public life that public figures are assumed to rarely operate out of anything other than self-interest. As I surveyed the devastation all around me in Cardwell that afternoon, my grooming was the last thing on my mind and my dishevelment gave others reason to believe it.

We met with the local mayor, Bill Shannon, to get an idea of the immediate needs. Bill's efforts had saved many lives as he walked those streets with a loudhailer, cajoling and persuading his residents to leave. It was clear that we would need the support of the army to clear roads, set up temporary kitchens and provide other support. It was equally clear that the damage to the Cardwell Range road would prevent a convoy of army trucks getting in for several days. It was the first of many trips into far north Queensland that summer as we assessed damage, met with locals about rebuilding projects and again walked the long road to recovery.

*

Throughout these natural disasters, I saw the great healing power of laughter at work. I saw it at Emergency HQ when a well-timed joke would break the tension for a weary team. I saw it in country Queensland and in our cities as people prepared for the worst, and I saw it on social media as people shared simple human stories. I saw it in the most unlikely places, in washed-out houses and flooded streets, in local police stations and in evacuation centres. During the floods I visited the evacuation centre in Helidon where the displaced residents of Grantham were relocated while their town was locked down and their homes searched for dead bodies. It was the bleakest of visits. Only days before, many of these people had seen their friends and neighbours and families washed away in front of them. Most were traumatised and very fragile.

I spoke with an older gentleman and asked him his name, but as he began to speak it became too much for him and large tears rolled down his face. As I held his hand, a woman with no teeth walked up and put her arm around him. With the kind of rough humour that can come with many years of marriage, she said, 'Premier, this is my husband. We only had minutes to get out of our place when that wall of water came, and I had to make a fast choice between getting him out or going back for my teeth. As you can see, I picked him, and right now I'm not sure I made the right choice!' Despite his pain, his face lit up with laughter, and he was all right again for a while.

While visiting the towns of Tully, Tully Heads and Mission Beach early in the week after the cyclone, I was reminded again of the great healing power of laughter. The dry humour of the locals emerged as they searched for ways to cope with what had happened to them. Hand-painted signs appeared at the gates of properties, bravely flouting the devastation that lay about on all sides. In front of a house with no roof and few remaining walls, with a large volume of water across its garden, I read this sign: 'For Sale: With Air Con & Swimming Pool'. Outside a farmhouse, flattened to the ground and reduced to rubble, I read: 'Is that all you've got, bitch?' And on a store that was boarded up and without a roof: 'You can kiss my Yasi!' The last was so popular it was made into a bumper sticker, and as the region recovered and rebuilt it could be seen on cars and trucks everywhere, in defiance of everything that Mother Nature had dished up to these close-knit communities.

On the day I flew into Cardwell with Wayne Swan, the weather did finally prove too much for the Black Hawk. We landed at Innisfail airport, which is little more than a shelter shed and a toilet block. We were effectively stranded. There were no beds in town. Even the local police watch-house beds had been commandeered for people evacuated from their homes. The police commissioner phoned ahead to Cairns, and cars were dispatched to pick us all up. The tropical rain was coming down in great sheets by the time we began driving to Cairns. The night was impenetrable, visibility so low and the road so dangerous that I began to wish I was back in a leaking Black Hawk hovering over a flooded forest. As the police officer charged with driving us made his way slowly through the deluge, we could feel the pressure he was under. Things got worse as his windscreen misted up, obscuring his vision further. He was a typical knockabout north Queenslander and broke the tension for everyone when he gave up wiping the windscreen with a rag and burst out laughing. 'What are the chances, hey?' he roared over the pelting rain. 'The only time in me life I'm going to be in a car with the bloody acting prime minister, the premier, the police commissioner and an army general, and me bloody demister goes and shits itself!'

*

After six weeks in the grip of an escalating series of disasters, Queenslanders could finally stop in mid February 2011 and begin to count the toll. Before us lay the challenge of rebuilding almost thirty per cent of our railways and 19,000 kilometres of road. Around 45,000 properties had been damaged, many beyond repair. A further 500,000 homes and businesses had endured prolonged outages of electricity and suffered losses as a result. Fifty-four coal mines had been inundated and were temporarily closed. The banana, sugar, cotton and dairy industries had been devastated, with a full season's crops wiped out. Seventy-four evacuation centres had housed more than seven thousand people, hundreds of whom would need temporary accommodation for more than a year. Forty-one community recovery centres were established and remained in operation for more than twelve months. Almost three million Australians had been affected in some way. Thirty-seven people lost their lives and three remain missing.

We had lived through one of Australia's worst recorded natural disasters. It had knocked us down, but we were determined to get back up again. The Mud Army's volunteer efforts were matched by the energetic response of our recovery agencies at all levels of government, by our community agencies and by corporate Australia. Funds pouring into our relief appeal rose to $277 million. More than 40,000 Queenslanders would receive financial assistance from this fund and they would need it. We had a long road to recovery ahead of us, but at last we were on the way.

The unfolding of these disasters and the way they were captured, reported and experienced explain in part why they have penetrated our collective memory so deeply. There are so many features of the way this disaster was lived and understood that mark it as a rare and unusual episode for us all. It was a prolonged crisis, playing out for almost six weeks – six weeks that brought new devastation almost daily and were seemingly without end. It was a crisis sustained on many fronts. The span of catastrophic damage stretched from the far northern tip of the state through every one of its regions, from the central to the far west and into the capital city. The crisis played out during the summer holidays when more of us are watching our televisions than at any other time of year, and Australians everywhere got genuinely caught up in the unfolding drama. And more than all of this, these disasters were the first in Australia where continual live media coverage was augmented and complemented by the widespread use of social media. A rolling, ongoing human tragedy, with all the compelling visual force that Mother Nature could muster, was captured live in dozens of locations simultaneously and shared on a minute-by-minute basis by anyone with a mobile phone in their hand. It was a potent and emotionally charged mix that etched these events into the national psyche.

I became the public face of these extraordinary events. When people see me and meet me, whether on their television screens or through the rear-view mirror of a Sydney taxi, the tragic images of that time come immediately and unbidden to mind. It was a long wet summer and the memory of it lives with us all. For me, the memory holds the uplifting power of finding a new outer limit to myself. In those endless weeks of rain and misery, the hunger for leadership was palpable. In the most desperate and frightening of circumstances, people craved comfort and reassurance; they searched for motivation and inspiration. I knew in my bones that it was my job to provide it, my duty to lead and to do it in a way that had never before been demanded of me. With no rule book to guide me, I just decided to step onto the centre of the stage and to stay there until the job was done. As I did so, I felt a new reserve of strength build in me and had a new realisation of my own capability. As we battled on every front that January, Mike Kaiser sent me a message saying simply 'Cometh the hour, cometh the woman', capturing the truth that, as the event challenged me, I was rising to meet it and others could see something in me that they hadn't seen before.

Just as every other challenge and obstacle has built a stronger platform under my feet, the newfound strength of that summer has stayed with me. I now have a better, clearer view of what I can do when life throws the seemingly impossible at me. This learning was there to cushion the landing when the same people who had relied on my leadership in these disasters voted me out of office just twelve months later – and it was there in my back pocket when cancer came knocking at my door soon after.

ELEVEN

Lost – and Found

The floods and cyclones of January 2011 had come hot on the heels of the public float of the coal and freight division of Queensland rail. The goodwill and comradeship that swelled the hearts of Queenslanders in the wake of the flood disaster had dissipated much of the acrimony surrounding the sale, but the damage was done. Labor was a house divided – we had aired our divisions in the most public and painful of ways and it had eroded the electorate's confidence in our ability to govern as a united team. The union campaign to brand me a liar was a success and the electorate found it hard to forgive me.

Despite this, on 24 March 2011 *The Australian* published Newspoll figures that showed I had staged the biggest political turnaround in the history of the poll. A twelve per cent surge in Labor's primary vote in the three months since the last poll was unprecedented and a clear response from the electorate to my handling of our natural disasters. While this turnaround was gratifying, I had seen too much of Labor's own private polling to take much comfort in it. The electorate's mood for change continued unabated, and they had moved beyond any inclination to forgive the mistakes made by my government.

Inside Labor, the noise about asset sales had quietened to a low hum, but the bruises were still healing and the troops disheartened. More threateningly, the LNP had responded to the surge in my popularity by installing a new leader. In the absence of any strong talent within their parliamentary team, they chose the unconventional step of appointing a leader from outside parliament: Campbell Newman, the mayor of Brisbane. It was a move that would pay off for them as the electorate felt for the first time in more than a decade that the LNP were presenting them with an electable, proven leader.

For much of that last year of our term, our government's focus was on the gargantuan task of rebuilding our damaged state. We established the Queensland Reconstruction Authority to pull together the work of government agencies and the private sector. Major General Mick Slater, on whom I had relied during the floods, accepted the task of chairing the new authority, and Graeme Newton, an energetic, smart engineer, who was Queensland's coordinator-general and director-general of the Department of Infrastructdure, was appointed to lead it, in recognition of his big-project expertise. It was a successful formula and the seemingly insurmountable task of repairing 19,000 kilometres of damaged roads, twenty-nine per cent of our rail network and 45,000 residential and commercial properties, and getting fifty-four closed coal mines and the cotton, banana and sugar industries back into operation was tackled systematically and effectively. It was a remarkable achievement, requiring the combined effort of all levels of government, major corporations and local businesses, community groups and welfare agencies and the goodwill, hard work and patience of people from every walk of life. Queensland would never wish for these disasters again, but most would agree that we were strengthened by them. It was a year of recovery, and it brought us all closer together in ways that continue to hold true.

*

On other fronts, it was a year of hard slog for us as a government. The fallout from a failed payroll system in Queensland Health continued to plague us. The new system, badly installed the year before, had left thousands of nurses without pay or underpaid for months on end. While it had improved, it continued to fail throughout 2011. It became for many a powerful symbol of an old government. It was a technology failure that should not have happened, and while any government would have been marked down for it, there was no mercy left for a government that should have known better after almost twenty years in the job. We were not new kids on the block, we were not a young government finding our way and we should have got it right. In all our polling, this issue came up time and time again as a reason to change government. It hurt us more than asset sales in most parts of the electorate. There were many other examples of a government fraying at the edges, and every time they flared up they took their toll, reinforcing a growing sense that it was time for us to go.

Just one year after that remarkable Newspoll result, on 24 March 2012 we were thrown, savagely and unceremoniously, out of office. We had known the loss was coming, but the size of it was a shock to everyone. It was clear from all the polling that we were facing the loss of government. Labor had held power in Queensland for twenty of the previous twenty-two years, and the electorate wasn't just hungry for a change, they were ravenous. With a swing of just over fifteen per cent, Labor lost forty-four seats and was reduced to just seven seats in parliament, the worst defeat in the state's history. There was little comfort in the fact that I held onto my own electorate of South Brisbane, and I stepped down from the leadership and resigned from politics.

I have read and heard of many reasons for the malevolent, visceral nature of the result, but none has ever fully explained it. After our win against the odds in 2009, this time round voters really wanted to get rid of us. After three years of our making tough, unpopular decisions, they wanted a reprieve. After the economic hardships of the GFC, they hoped the other side could fix it quicker. Incumbent governments around the world from both the left and the right were thrown out in those years following the financial downturn. They didn't like the negativity of our campaign and marked us down heavily for it. The spectacle of a federal Labor leadership battle, in which Kevin Rudd unsuccessfully challenged Julia Gillard in a bloody battle for the leadership, playing out for the whole first week of our election campaign also eroded Labor's credibility. Some journalists claimed the electorate is still working out what it thinks of women leaders and was harsher in its judgement of us. All this and more came together and crushed us.

That miserable election day in 2012 was Oliver's nineteenth birthday, and also marked his first opportunity to vote. We headed off to the polling booth together as a family, knowing that we would lose the election. With Greg and the boys standing resolutely beside me, I faced a swirling media pack after we had cast our votes. I took their questions in my stride, but felt my hackles rise when one of the journalists singled Oliver out and asked him what it felt like to be voting for his mother when he knew she would lose.

It is a golden rule in politics that journalists do not put questions to the children of politicians. Moreover, it is a golden rule in decent, civil society that journalists do not bait the children of politicians, particularly in difficult and emotionally charged moments like this one. I drew myself up, ready to give it to this journalist with both barrels blazing, unfettered by any of my normally disciplined politeness, but Oliver stepped up to the microphone before I could open my mouth.

'Hey, I'm the lucky one here today,' he said, with extraordinary presence of mind. 'Who else gets their first vote on their birthday and gets to vote for their mum at the same time? That feels like winning to me!' He disarmed the journalist's surly rudeness with his easy youthful charm, and his comments played on radio bulletins throughout the day, diluting some of the misery of it. For me, 24 March will remain the day I celebrate giving birth to this remarkable young man, not a day to mourn an election loss. I will always be proud of Oliver for that moment.

*

There is less curiosity about winning than about losing. I am rarely asked about what it felt like to win. We can imagine ourselves in the shoes of a winner; we can sense the jubilation of it and feel ourselves in that exultant moment. Although I think that most, in this imagining, feel only the lightness of a win rather than the weight of it. I have been surprised to find so much interest in what it feels like to lose, curious myself that the intrepid questioner is brave enough to broach the subject. Losing an election is so public and such an immediate and spectacular fall from power that people are genuinely intrigued by the human experience of it. The fascination of it overrides any polite hesitancy they may have about exploring it.

In the lead-up to the 2012 election, months of bad polling had given me plenty of time to think about losing the election and to steel myself against the brutal heaviness of it. I thought it would have the adrenaline-rushing drop of freefalling from a twenty-storey building and hitting concrete. But it never felt like that, not like a fall. In the first days and weeks it was a kind of nakedness. I felt raw and unprotected, as if I was walking in a crowded street with no clothes on, skinned and exposed by some excoriating chemical. The sour taste of failure sat smouldering in the back of my mouth. I could not think of my colleagues who had lost their seats without feeling the burn of shame. Humiliation is an awful burden. Of course, I replayed events and conversations and decisions and thought about how I could have changed them, made them work in the government's favour. But not for long. It was done and no amount of replaying could change any of it. It is inevitable that some of my loyal staff and supporters felt a fierce anger at the electorate, a raging sense of injustice that all our efforts and hard work were so poorly recognised and so badly rewarded. I am grateful to have been spared the rage of injustice. I'm not sure why I felt so little anger, but it's a corrosive emotion that I've seen eat away at the hearts of good people, and I'm relieved not to be one of them.

I did not finish my time in public life with regrets. It is a rare thing to be a member of an Australian parliament for seventeen years, even rarer to spend fifteen of those years as a cabinet minister, and unique in Queensland for a woman to spend any of it, let alone almost five years as I had done, as premier. While there are always judgements that would play differently with hindsight, I feel satisfaction that I didn't waste a minute, that I seized opportunities and made them count. I have a list of achievements that has changed the fabric of my home state forever. The mission and purpose that propelled me into politics, the desire to transform my home state, to reshape it as a modern, energetic and exciting place to live and work, were well and truly reflected in our efforts.

Along with the introduction of Prep to our schooling system, my early decision as premier to introduce fluoride into Queensland's drinking water is a long-term, over-the-horizon reform. In our fifth and last term, I took Paul Keating's words to heart and had a go. In those three years, we lifted kindergarten places from twenty-eight per cent of four-year-olds to ninety-four per cent. We implemented a solar energy program that lifted the number of homes with solar panels from just one thousand to over 200,000. We modernised the adoption laws to provide for open access to information. We introduced groundbreaking laws in political accountability, becoming the first Australian government to ban political lobbyists from sitting on government boards and limiting political donations; we passed Australia's first laws to recognise same-sex civil unions; and we bid for and won the 2018 Commonwealth Games for the Gold Coast. Along with managing the economic and financial fallout from the GFC and the natural disasters of 2011, it was quite a term, and one that broke through the wall on a number of fronts.

*

When you lose an election, you lose government, and along with it you lose the form and fabric of your daily life. Beyond the grief of the loss, there is a feeling of being all at sea, of being somehow lost in the world. All the familiar habits and rituals that pinned your feet to the ground go missing and leave you feeling mislaid and disoriented. In the first few weeks after the 2012 election loss, I felt all the confusion that you would expect those suddenly empty days to bring, days stretching out in front of me without appointments, meetings and functions to fill them. Those days held the sensation that comes with time wagged from school – a guilty feeling that there was something I should be doing or some event I would be in trouble for failing to attend. In a way I felt the dazed hesitancy of the canary beholding the world when the door to its cage has been flung open.

Those days brought with them a positive taste of liberation. For the first time in almost two decades I could begin to imagine a life beyond the twenty-one square kilometres of my electorate, beyond the strictures and constraints of public responsibilities and expectations. The lost feeling was disorienting but not unpleasant as I gave myself up to it and began to indulge in the simple daily joys of my new freedom. Now I had the freedom to read for as long as I wanted, to spend hours cooking with my sons, to make music playlists, to drink tea with old friends, to dream of new plans and reimagine my life. I was physically exhausted; the disasters of the previous summer meant I'd had no leave for two years. I also knew that reimagining my life would take time. Everyone in my family had been making room for me for twenty years; I now had the chance to make room for them. I had watched other colleagues leave politics and rush with too much haste to a decision about what to do next. I resolved to take twelve months off from everything to recover and renew. I told friends I was taking a sabbatical. My sons laughed and said I was taking a gap year.

Within a fortnight of the election, Greg and I drove south to Sydney for Easter. We had not taken a long road trip together for more than a decade and never without our children. Oliver had finished high school the year before, and my release from public duties coincided with a big shift in our parenting responsibilities. Our nest was emptying and our boys making their own big steps into adulthood as we were stepping into an unfamiliar world as private citizens. We took off with the magnified anticipation of teenagers heading out in their parents' car for the first time. Only our friends knew we were going. There were no security arrangements, we had no itinerary and no schedule. The mild golden sun of early autumn warmed the car as we played old favourites on the stereo and talked about all that lay ahead. As each kilometre slipped away, Queensland felt like a shoreline disappearing behind us. The lush heat of home gave way to the rolling green dairy country of New South Wales's northern rivers, and even some of the feverish heat of

Queensland politics seemed to cool. Driving south, this trip seemed a harbinger of our lives to come, with the freedom to be spontaneous, to live without carefully laid plans, to experience the world in a new and different way.

As we enjoyed the Easter break with friends, our discussions kept returning to the idea of living in Sydney, Greg's hometown and the city of his childhood and adolescence. It had been agreed between us for some time that after my political career came to an end, whenever and however that might occur, the next big family decision would be his. Greg had left his home, his friends and his family to move to Queensland with me in 1987. While he had happily made a new home there, Sydney was always first in his heart. It was no surprise then that the idea of returning to live there began to take root in our minds that weekend. It was still just an idea, and we wanted to talk with Joe and Oliver about it, but as we walked the city's streets we began to fill with the excitement of a newly minted possibility.

Talk of travel also filled our conversations as I began to plan a trip to see friends living overseas. I looked forward to losing myself in other countries and cultures. After the intensity of the past five years I was ready to stop, to relax and to put a distance between myself and public life. While I had visited many countries and some extraordinary places as part of my public duties, I had done very little personal travel. Now I was free to do as much as I wanted. I planned out four months of travel, during which I would stay with friends in New York and London before continuing to Europe. Greg planned to meet me at the end of my London sojourn, and we would head first to Paris, followed by time in Istanbul and Barcelona. Within nine weeks of the election I was on a plane to New York, the great city of dreams and possibilities. The wheels left the hot tarmac of Sydney airport and the great whoosh of a plane taking flight swept through me. My new life had begun.

*

Tom Wolfe said of New York that 'One belongs to New York instantly, one belongs to it as much in five minutes as in five years.' It's a city that greets the newcomer with arms wide open. Every visitor is a potential convert, yet another to be seduced and won over. As I settled into the SoHo loft apartment of my friend Lily Brett, I felt an instant ease. There seemed few better places to abandon myself to the liberation of 'lostness' and the pleasure of reinvention. I looked forward to the anonymity of the teeming, pulsing life of its streets and its ready acceptance of all comers. Here is a whole world of people come to build a new life, a city where everything seems possible. Beneath New York's vaulting skyline I felt free of my history and the expectations of me that it carried.

So it came as a stark reminder of our shrinking global community when I jumped into a carriage on my first subway ride and ran straight into two young girls from Brisbane. Laden with backpacks and wide-eyed with adventure, they were as surprised to find their former premier in their subway carriage as I was to hear their distinctive accents. I laughed out loud to hear they were fresh off the plane from a Brisbane suburb close to my home, and we chatted happily for several stations. In this new world every thronging crowd holds a familiar face, and

I would have to search for my new self with an ever-present reminder of my old one. I would have to find a way to fold the memories of the public me into my new narrative.

At a table with friends in SoHo's Balthazar restaurant, I heard Lily tell another lunch guest that she thought I was doing fine, given that I was heartbroken. The description took me by surprise, but I felt my throat swell with thick tears and I knew she was right. The past five years had held all the emotional intensity of a love affair. And now it was over.

Travel is a great salve for a tender heart, and I found a growing solace in my absence from Queensland. When Greg joined me in London we were both happy to have this time away. We took the Eurostar to Paris and restarted our conversations about building our new lives. He had resigned as a senior public servant in the Queensland government, feeling unable to serve the agenda of the new regime. He had spent the past few weeks writing job applications and now had several irons in the fire for new positions, all in other parts of Australia. We put aside our worries about jobs and financial security and let ourselves enjoy this rare time together.

In Paris we felt an easy freedom. We felt unfettered and invigorated as we combed its ancient streets and discovered its secret places, continually awed by its glittering monuments. Our days assumed an untroubled pace. We spent hours idling, visiting and revisiting the places of Parisanna, stopping for ice-cold beers on the green chairs of the Luxembourg Gardens and for lemon sorbet at Berthillon on the Île Saint-Louis.

Moving south, we fell comfortably into the heat and amiable lassitude of Istanbul and Barcelona, taking afternoon siestas and eating out late in the soft warm evenings. The undemanding weeks in these lovely old cities were a balm, mending the last scars of the political battlefield, restoring to us a sense of almost youthful hope. As we prepared to return to Brisbane, Greg got word that he had been shortlisted for a position with the New South Wales government and was scheduled for an interview the day we arrived home. He quickly changed his flight to land in Sydney.

Greg must interview well when jet-lagged, because within two weeks he was offered the new job, a senior executive position in Arts New South Wales. His dream of returning to the city of his boyhood became a reality. For all of us, this was a huge change. For me, it brought a wrench from everything familiar and known, and the place that would forever define me. For our boys, it brought decisions about where to live, whether to stay with their friends or move interstate with their parents. For Greg, it brought the challenge of a new job in an entirely new field. Greg has a keen public policy mind and had worked at a senior executive level in Queensland's public sector for more than two decades, making an impact in areas such as economic, transport and environment policy and program development. This would be a new intellectual challenge for him. The job offer also affirmed his talent and capability. Queensland's new LNP government had tried to diminish his achievements with accusations that I had somehow given him his job. In truth, he had won every position through a full and open merit selection process and had worked for both sides of politics during his long career. His appointment by a Liberal government in New South Wales vindicated his ability.

Our relocation meant leaving our family home of almost twenty years, and the weeks ahead were busy with the task of sifting and sorting as we began to pack up and move out. It was a huge but healthy upheaval. The job of packing was full of sentimental rediscoveries of childhood things as long-stored boxes were opened and emptied. It was full too of the pleasure of spring cleaning, a task that the busy responsibilities of the premiership had taken from my life some years ago. We cheerily tossed the flotsam and jetsam of two decades into a mini-skip and cleaned away the detritus of years in one place. We felt the freedom of light travellers as we filled the removal truck with only the necessary and the precious. We were Sydney-bound and life felt full of promise.

My plans were simple. I looked forward to playing the domestic role for a while, to establishing a home for us in a new city and putting roots down in a new life. I was busy enough with regular speaking engagements and was pleased to accept appointments to the boards of Bangarra Dance Company and Medibank. But the pace of my early months in Sydney was one that left plenty of space for pleasure. I rediscovered the delight of gardening, the small miraculous wonder of a new flower emerging from a planted seed and the exquisite satisfaction of eating home-grown tomatoes. I joined a book club and marvelled that my life now had room in it to share my love of reading with likeminded others. I walked for hours through Centennial Park and around the cliffs of Bronte and Clovelly, my feet finding a new and easier rhythm, unhurried by deadlines. I luxuriated in a newfound freedom, enjoyed all the more because it was an interregnum, a planned lull between my old life and my as-yet-undiscovered future. It was a time of introspection and re-acquaintance with a familiar but long-unvisited part of myself.

A person used to the constant gaze of the public eye has to relearn how to live a private life. For me, it was a joy to find my private self there under all the layers of protection that had barnacled themselves to my skin over years. As that life-changing year drew to a close, I could feel myself begin to look outwards again. I could feel a welcome new momentum gathering, and I began to think of the year ahead.

TWELVE

Wild, Wild Life

As the sun sets on 2012, the new year seems full of promise. Sydney has readied herself for her annual New Year's Eve fireworks spectacular. A pageant of light and optimism, it will bring people flocking to the edges of her glittering, matchless harbour. But Greg and I head away from the crowds to celebrate the first new year in our new home city at Bronte Beach, one of our favourite places, on the other side of the great headlands that frame the harbour. For Greg, Bronte is a place of childhood memories, of sunburnt days, melting ice-creams and toy train rides with older cousins. For us both, it's a place that evokes the echoes of family holidays, of surfing with our boys, of long cliff-top walks, the salty tang of fried fish and chips and slow times with friends and their children. We join old friends and new friends for a beachside picnic against the soft pink of a late evening sky.

It is the best of midsummer Sydney, an easy, warm, washed-out evening that draws us to the water and makes us sentimental. Cold beer and crisp wine bring laughter and reminiscence as we peel prawns and share picnic food. The smoky meat smells of barbecues drift across the park while families gather with cricket sets and joggers make one last effort for the year. As night sets in the pull of the fireworks proves too much for some of us and we drive over the headland at Dover Heights to the vantage point of Rose Bay Convent perched high on New South Head Road.

New Year's Eve is an end and a beginning. A moment when we quickly look back then turn with anticipation to firmly look ahead, when we make plans and resolutions and think about what comes next. We dream in that moment of being our better selves, our thinner, healthier, kinder, gentler, better read, harder working and more daring or balanced selves. Contemplating the year ahead under that vivid, blazing sky, it seems full of hopeful brightness. I am settling in to one of the most exciting cities in the world, I am beginning my first full year out of the public limelight in almost twenty years, and I can feel the stirrings of a whole new chapter starting to write itself. As the old year leaves us, I sit high on a brick wall, arms wrapped around my knees, and see a world of possibilities with every shower of light that falls from the midnight sky.

*

For more than a year I had experienced pain in my right foot whenever I ran for more than twenty minutes. It had forced me to abandon running and take up cycling, but otherwise was no inconvenience. I thought it best to have my foot checked in case there was a long-term problem I needed to address. Even having the time to schedule an appointment with a local GP about my foot was indicative of my new life. My foot had been a problem for my last six months as premier, but I was always too busy to pay it any attention. I was now living a life where I could look after myself better and not let little things like this drift. While my new local doctor examined my foot, I mentioned something else I'd noticed recently that perhaps she should look at. During an early-morning shower I'd felt a small lump on the side of my face, near my right ear. I thought little of it, but I had begun to poke and prod it in daily curiosity. It was painless, it didn't seem to grow, but neither did it disappear. I mentioned it almost as an afterthought. The doctor thought it curious but not alarming, and suggested I have it X-rayed at the same time as my foot.

Feeling no rush to resolve minor ailments, I arrived at St Vincent's Clinic in Darlinghurst on a Friday morning for my X-rays some six weeks after that GP visit. By this time, the lump on my face had grown from the size of a pea to that of a large marble, like the tombolas my brothers coveted as little boys. Although it was now visible in the mirror if you knew where to look, I had become quite used to it. I was curious but unconcerned.

After the tests, while I waited in the clinic for the X-rays, a nurse said that the radiologist would like to conduct an ultrasound of the lump on my face. During the ultrasound I learned about the parotid gland for the first time. The parotid is the largest of our saliva glands and wraps around the junction of our jawbones. 'Parotid' means near the ear, and apparently I had something strange in mine. Waiting again for results, I was told they would like to do another test, an MRI with contrast dye. By now it was early afternoon, and I was beginning to understand that my foot was not the problem. By the end of the day, a day that had started out like any other, I knew I had a tumour in my parotid gland. I knew it could be benign or malignant. I also had an appointment to see a head and neck surgeon the following week.

I spent that weekend researching parotid gland tumours. I learned that more than eighty per cent of these tumours are benign, and that they affect more women than men. I learned that the proximity of these glands to the facial nerve can make surgery complicated, but if left unchecked a growing tumour can also put pressure on this nerve and cause some disfigurement. Knowing all the caveats that the medical profession puts on internet medical research, I tried to seek out reputable sites, but of course one site led to another and several times I found myself staring at graphic and gruesome patient photos of facial surgery gone horribly wrong. My research did mean, however, that I was not surprised when the surgeon told me he wanted to remove my lump as soon as possible. He was reassuring and confirmed that these tumours were overwhelmingly benign, reminding me that the word tumour is just a fancy term for a swelling. Surgery was scheduled for a fortnight's time.

Like most people, I hate hospitals. I've had a few minor procedures and know that I hate anaesthetics. This trip to hospital was no better or worse than any other. However, when I finally came to and felt what had been done to the side of my head, I was pleased that I had stumbled upon those gruesome medical websites. Part of my head had been shaved and I had a line of staples down my scalp, leading to stitches behind and in front of my ear. Thankfully, nerves in the area had been temporarily knocked about, causing numbness, so I was foggy but not in pain when I woke to find Greg, Joe and Oliver and his girlfriend waiting for me in my hospital room. After an hour or so, the boys' minds turned inevitably to food and they headed off to the nearby and exceptionally good Messina ice-cream shop, returning with buckets of extraordinary flavours. The atmosphere in my hospital room was almost festive as we ate ice-cream and laughed, relieved that the tumour had been cut out. In a bizarre twist of modern medicine, my surgeon showed me a photo of my tumour on his mobile phone. It was both repulsive and fascinating, red and swollen and larger than I expected. I was very glad that I no longer had it growing in me. Now we just had to wait for the results of the pathology tests, but the worst seemed to be over.

*

Four days later, I sat in a waiting room with other patients, waiting to see my surgeon for a post-operative check-up. The original biopsy had been inconclusive and further pathology tests had been required to discover whether it was benign or malignant. Knowing that the world of science and medicine can be slow, I was unworried by this uncertainty. Nevertheless, I rang my doctor earlier in the day seeking some news, only to be told that he was in surgery and I would have to wait until my appointment later that evening to discuss results with him. It occurred to me that if the results were clear, his assistant would likely have been authorised to advise me, but I brushed this suspicion aside. Greg had a longstanding commitment to join one of his oldest friends at the Sydney Film Festival, but he wanted to cancel and come to my appointment with me. But opportunities like this were among the reasons we'd returned to live in Sydney, so I insisted he go to the film. I had no concerns about going on my own.

But as others were called ahead of me, and I realised I would be the last patient my doctor saw that evening, I started to worry. When he came into the waiting room to call me, he looked around and asked, 'Where's Greg?' I knew this meant he was concerned that I was on my own, and I felt the cold itch of fear.

In his surgery, he first examined my wound. If he had good news he would have rushed to deliver it, I thought. I looked straight at him and asked about the tests.

He looked away briefly and drew a breath. 'I'm very sorry, Anna, but the tumour is malignant,' he said.

This doctor removes growths and tumours for a living, he must have said these words a thousand times – and yet he was uncomfortable, even distressed, to deliver them. These words clearly don't come any easier with the telling. He was professional and didn't sugar-coat anything as he explained what would come next. I knew I was staring at him and worried briefly that my mouth was gaping open. For a while I couldn't even hear him. My ears had snapped shut with the shock of it. When I could hear him again, I couldn't understand him. I heard a litany of words that sounded like death: bone marrow biopsy, PET scan, ECG, chemotherapy, radiation, haematologist.

Death, death, death and death.

Not me, not now, I am not ready.

The news should not have shocked me as it did. I had just had a tumorous growth removed from the side of my face by a head and neck surgeon. I had known for a couple of weeks that the original biopsy had been inconclusive and that there was some possibility that it may be malignant. But I was incredulous to hear it confirmed.

Not me, not now, I am not ready.

I felt numb with disbelief. Recovering enough to know that I didn't understand what I'd just been told, I asked my doctor to say it all again, from the beginning. What we'd thought was a lump in my parotid saliva gland was actually a tumour in a nearby lymph node. I had non-Hodgkin lymphoma and it was going to change everything about this year and much more. Just when I thought all my walls were behind me, when I had done all the hard things my life would demand of me, the universe had served me up another. This time I would not be the first one through it, though. I would be the beneficiary of all the knowledge and research and treatment pioneered by those who had gone before me. To them, I felt the warmest gratitude. I needed further tests to determine how advanced the disease was, I needed to see a haematologist to consider treatment. The doctor had already scheduled these appointments for me over the next six days.

I walked out of the building into the cool darkness of an early winter's night. Greg had left me a text message asking about the results, but I couldn't tell him this in a message. I felt a superstitious fear that it wouldn't be true until I said it, that telling Greg would make it real. I couldn't think of the words for this. I did not want to say the word 'cancer' out loud. It was too big for me and too big for him. I sat, dazed, on a low brick wall in Victoria Street, watching patients shuffle back in through hospital doors and homeless people gather on the corner of the nearby park as a mobile food and coffee van pulled up. I texted Greg to call me during the interval, buying time to collect my thoughts.

I was alone on the footpath, walking back to the car, when Greg called. Seeing my text, he'd known immediately the news wasn't good and left the theatre to call me. As I heard his voice, a hot rush of tears choked me. Gone was my numb calm and my brave face. I gave in to the terror and sorrow of it, gulping back tears, my throat full and unable to talk as Greg tried to find out where I was. He told me to breathe and talked quietly to calm me until I could say, 'It's not okay, it's cancer. I've got lymphoma.' Through the phone I felt it hit him, as it had hit me, like a body-wasting punch. I steadied myself against the car and reassured him that I could drive home and would meet him there.

At home, there was another phone call to make. I needed to call Mum. I craved her comfort like a child just fallen off her bicycle, but I dreaded telling her the news, fearing what it would feel like for her to hear this about a daughter. How could I break this sorry news? This call was even harder than the call to Greg. I didn't want to frighten her. She wanted to be strong and comfort me. We both lost our resolve and cried together. Living with my sister in Grafton, she felt so far away. Having worked in hospitals for much of her life, she knew more than I did about tests and treatment and what came next, but for now she talked tenderly of love and strength and her faith in me. Greg walked through the door as I finished the call and I felt the warmth and comfort of him, like a treasured blanket, as he folded me in his arms. We still had the awful task ahead of telling our boys and we talked at length about the language we would use – honest and accurate but optimistic and hopeful. The conversations with Joe and Oliver were tough. The terrible power of the word 'cancer' frightened them, too, but they were quickly fortified by their need to be strong for me.

*

I suspect that you, like me, expect something as striking as cancer to announce itself with some dramatic fanfare. In truth, I hadn't given it much thought but had some vague notions that it must come accompanied by sudden blinding pain, that it would grip the sufferer in the same way women in the movies are suddenly gripped by the first pangs of childbirth. But cancer comes stealthily. By the time I felt that small lump in the shower, my cells had already started multiplying faster than they should and, critically, they had forgotten how to die. Cancer is not an infection; it is not the invasion of a healthy body by a foreign, toxic organism. There are no bacteria or viral enemies to blame and conquer. A cancer cell is one of my own, mutated by my body. It is my own body, malfunctioning in the most serious way possible, nurturing cells that are multiplying at a deadly rate.

As I embarked on a series of tests to find out how far the lymphoma had advanced, I felt the boundaries of my life contract. Board meetings, lunch dates, arrangements with friends and scheduled plans, all were cancelled and abandoned as medical appointments filled my diary. My life shrank as I danced to the tune of this tumour. In a matter of days, cancer filled my life. It clogged my waking thoughts and night-time fears. It saturated my conversations, my reading list, my inbox and my outbox. I was astonished by its rapacious speed as all my loud and quiet corners and every nook and cranny of my life were suddenly flooded with it.

Lymphoma is a blood cancer, affecting the lymph, or immune, system. I needed a bone marrow biopsy to determine how deep into this system my cancer had stretched. Bone marrow is where our blood cells begin, but it is locked inside our bones and extracting a sample is no easy task. I readily agreed with Greg that I would not do this on my own.

We walked through the doors of the Kinghorn Cancer Centre on Victoria Street for the first of many visits. I had felt ready for this and was keen to know the results, but getting to the biopsy clinic required walking through the chemotherapy ward. On all sides, people were hooked up to bags of chemotherapy drugs, and most were bald. Some were very old and frail, others heartbreakingly young. They were all pale, tired and sick. Soon I would be one of them. My confident pace slowed. I felt my throat thicken with more tears, and I gripped Greg's hand.

The insertion of a large biopsy needle into my pelvic bone at the hip, our largest reservoir of bone marrow, to draw the soft marrow out of my bone, was a painful process. Bones, not containing nerves, cannot be anaesthetised. It has become increasingly common, though, to give patients what is gently called 'twilight sedation' through a self-administered infuser, known as the green whistle. This is a large green whistle-shaped container that I was encouraged to place in my mouth and breathe from deeply as I felt pain. As I lay on my side facing Greg, and the biopsy needle did its job, I needed no encouragement. Using the green whistle had immediate and disconcerting results. I got instant pain relief, but my consciousness was quickly altered. Decorum fell away as I began to sob and tell Greg and the nurses that I was in the wrong place, that I wasn't like the other people in the ward, that I wasn't a sick person and that I did not belong there. I begged Greg to get me out of there, to tell them that I wasn't sick. I begged him to save me. Thanks to the green whistle, I was uncomfortable but not in pain. But its fumes unloosened me, and in my uninhibited delirium all the truth of my fear and denial flowed out of me. Greg was frightened and deeply upset. But the weakness of the body can also be hilarious. After a while I stopped crying and started telling the nurses that they were the best in the world and should be up on a stage getting an award. Apparently I had the whole room laughing. Thankfully, I don't remember any of it.

Next was a PET scan. PET in this context is not a small cuddly animal or a term of endearment. PET is positron emission tomography. This scan was to be accompanied by a CT (computed tomography) scan, and together with the bone marrow biopsy would tell us how far into my lymph system the cancer had penetrated. Despite my fear, I found myself fascinated by the science of these tests. In a PET scan, radioactive sugar is injected into a body that has been fasting and has a very low sugar count. Cancer cells, growing and multiplying so much more quickly than normal cells, are hungry for the sugar and are the first to take up the radioactive substance as it courses through the body. The scanner then photographs these uptake sites as they light up like a Christmas tree.

For patients with lymphoma, a machine that combines a PET scan with a CT scan is used for these tests. This allows a comparison of areas of sugar-filled, higher radioactivity on the PET scan with the more detailed appearance of that area on the CT scan. CT is a technology that uses computer-processed X-rays to produce images that are virtual 'slices' of specific areas of the scanned object, allowing the user to see what is inside it without cutting it open. As I lay on the bed of the scanner and waited for it to move me into the body of the machine for the CT scan, I was injected with a contrast agent that would assist the test. I was told that this would create the sensation that I had wet myself, but not to worry because it was just an illusion. This was one of the strangest things anyone has ever said to me, and I couldn't believe I'd heard correctly. However, it turned out to be exactly and perfectly true, and the sensation so accurately mimics the real thing that I was seized by the humiliating certainty that I was one of the rare few for whom this was not an illusion, but the real thing. Blessedly, this was not the case, and I was struck again by the strange humour of the human body. Here, inside this scary machine, I couldn't believe that my body could deceive me with such precision. I laughed when I reflected that it was this woman's job every day to reassure people that they had not lost control of their bladder, they were simply hallucinating that they'd wet their pants.

As the idea of this deadly imposter quietly eating away at me began to settle in my mind, I felt an intense need for privacy. I wanted only the comfort of very close friends and family. But as I returned over and over again to the different wards and clinics of St Vincent's Hospital, visitors and staff regularly recognised me and stopped to talk, most of them not knowing I was sick. With every hello, I became more fearful that my illness would be exposed.

This anxious fear reached new heights on the morning I arrived early for my next test, an ECG, or electrocardiograph. The ECG measures the electrical impulses of the heart to ensure it is functioning well. Apparently, part of my proposed chemotherapy could affect my heart function, so before I began treatment it was necessary to see how healthy my heart was.

Walking towards the lift, facing another morning of fear and worry, I jumped when I heard my name called. The elderly couple were friendly Labor supporters who recognised me and asked to have a photo taken with me. Happy to oblige, I stood with them and chatted, but they took some time to find their camera, then to seek out a hospital volunteer to take the photo and to fuss about getting the pose right. Their simple request drew attention to me and soon the hospital volunteer also knew who I was. These were all good people, with no wish to do me any harm, but I began to feel anxious about where this photo would end up and who they would talk with about seeing me here. The episode was a sharp reminder of the ubiquity of smartphone cameras. The hope that my increasingly regular attendance at cancer clinics would go unnoticed was rapidly fading. I worried about being too sick to manage the sudden exposure if it came, and about this being added to Greg's growing list of responsibilities.

As I lost control of every small part of my life, I knew I could still control this one decision and its timing. Greg and I wrote a short public statement that one of my former staff, Lorann Downer, kindly agreed to distribute to media. She also agreed to field calls on my behalf. She spoke personally with the senior Queensland political journalists before my statement hit the wires, and took calls well into the evening. It was the first of many generous acts of love and kindness that would come our way as news of my cancer became public knowledge.

My last test was on the Friday morning before the Queen's Birthday long weekend in June 2012. We were scheduled to spend the weekend with two other couples at a friend's farm in

Mittagong, in the highlands south-west of Sydney. We decided to stick with this plan. It would be our last weekend before getting the test results and starting treatment, and we yearned for the solace of close friends. As my media statement began to reach news desks, we also felt the attraction of escaping to the protection and anonymity of a distant farm where we couldn't be found or contacted. As we crawled our way south, hedged in by the Friday evening throng of others also heading away for a country weekend, we unexpectedly got some welcome, early news. My tests showed my lymphoma was restricted to my neck and throat, that it had not yet migrated to other parts of my body. We were glad of the slow traffic as we felt the tears come, this time tears of relief and gratitude. Perversely, we now had something small to celebrate with friends when we arrived at the farm.

Our friend's farm is built along a high ridge overlooking a vast mist-filled valley of state forest. With a large fireplace, big warm kitchen and endless walking tracks, it is a perfect place to cuddle into winter. It was a weekend of slow-cooked meals and long lazy lunches, of crackling roaring fires, full-bodied red wine and hot caramel bread-and-butter pudding, of talking late into the night and sleeping late into the morning, of long walks and the sweet steaming breath of horses. We are all old friends and the paths of our lives had crossed and criss-crossed through the ups and downs of relationships, children, work, travel and holidays and everything in between. Greg Combet was there with his new partner, Juanita, and her young children, and the house expanded with their laughter and games. The leadership of the federal Labor Party was once again brewing to a challenge, and Combet was grappling with big decisions of his own as he weighed up the option of throwing his hat into the leadership ring. Our talks were filled with the gravitas of life-changing questions for us all. Nevertheless, these few days were a happy respite, a pause that gave me just a moment in all the urgent chaos of that week to catch my breath. It was a weekend full of the simple, warm, happy pleasures of life and I clung to them like a board in an ocean rip.

As the news about my illness began to fill the news bulletins, those early days in June began to fill with another kind of warmth. I had made the decision to go public in much the same way I had made other decisions in that week full of medical procedures, as another chore to tick off the list of things that needed doing before my treatment started. I made it because I wanted it dealt with and out of the way. Caught up in the gravity of what was happening to me, I had not contemplated the reaction my announcement would generate or how that might affect us. Within minutes of the first news bulletin, Greg and I began to receive messages from friends and work colleagues, from people we knew well and people we hadn't heard from in years. Every message was full of love. Our phones filled with words like 'heart' and 'prayer' and 'thoughts' and 'care'. The news had come as a shock, and the messages were emotional and immediate, unfiltered by caution or politeness. We began to feel as if people were wrapping their arms around us. We suddenly understood how weary and anxious we had been after just four days of bearing the news together, and how much we needed the love and care of others to hold us up.

*

As I began my treatment, cards and letters full of similar sentiments joined the messages that had filled my phone. Almost without exception, these messages spoke of my strength and the writer's conviction that this would get me through. Like the letter from one of my favourite western Queensland mayors, a politically conservative but very decent man, who wrote: 'I have witnessed your steely resolve and your strength and trust that these qualities will guide you through this, your greatest challenge.' Or the card from Billie, one of my oldest local branch members in Brisbane, who herself had seen plenty of hard knocks. She told me: 'Hey, drought, cyclone and flood could not beat you and cancer won't either.' The card from friends in the Blue Mountains exclaimed, 'Any woman who can win years of ALP backroom brawls can beat a tiny tumour!' Other writers told me their own stories of defeating cancer and exhorted me to be positive. Some messages came with flowers or small gifts like a knitted beanie or a bright purple wig. Many were genuinely heartfelt messages of faith, promises to include me in prayers or appeals to certain saints, and sometimes small religious medals or holy cards would be included. I accepted all these with the same affection with which they had been sent. Even the religious medals felt like talismans of love.

When we talk of cancer, we use the language of war. We speak of people winning or losing their battle with cancer. We talk of strength and courage and bravery. Sometimes I found this very helpful. For much of my treatment, I imagined my body as a warzone. I saw the lymphoma as an imperialist invader that had breached my borders and had expansionary motives. Every time I lined up for a chemotherapy session I thought of the chemicals as thermonuclear warheads being dispatched with ruthless military efficiency to push back and defeat this invader. Chemotherapy is a cocktail of potent chemicals and each cocktail has its own acronym depending on its particular components. My chemo cocktail was called R–CHOP, and I loved the sound of it. It had the ring of a deadly karate move, the kind of single, vicious kick that can break an opponent's neck, which is exactly how I wanted my drugs to work. My treatment would involve six rounds of chemotherapy, each a fortnight apart.

My first session extended for almost seven hours. As I walked into the ward, I was again assailed by its clinical miasma of sickness, and again I rebelled against the idea that I had any place here, wanting to flee as soon as I walked in. I felt a great unfairness about this disease, that there was some injustice in its arriving at my doorstep.

Settling into a large chemotherapy chair, I looked across at a young woman opposite me, her mother sitting beside her. As the nurse prepared her drugs, she was asked to state her name and date of birth. As she spoke, I did the calculation and realised that she would turn eighteen in two days' time. A cold reality hit me. If anyone didn't belong in this ward it was this young woman, who should have been out buying a new dress and preparing for her birthday party. My self-pity evaporated as I felt a sudden rush of gratitude for my fifty-three years of healthy life, for my own happy eighteenth birthday party and all the ones after it, for the chances and opportunities, the fun, the anger, the fears, the success, the failures, the sheer remarkable life of it. I gave a quiet thanks that it was me being hooked up to the bag of chemicals and not one of my sons. That I was not, like this mother opposite me, watching with terror and sorrow as one of my children was treated.

Each chemotherapy session was a long and exhausting process of refilling my body with deadly chemicals. I was reminded of just how toxic they were at one session, when one of the intravenous tubes split slightly and the chemotherapy drugs dripped onto the floor. As soon as staff realised the problem, they cordoned off my treatment area with tape marked 'toxic spill' and suited up into full-body moon suits in order to deal with it.

It gets harder and harder to front up for each chemotherapy session. You know with each session how awful you will feel, how the illness and the fatigue will last for days and how it all gets worse every time you do it. As my treatment progressed, I often felt that I just couldn't face one more session. As each treatment day loomed, I would find myself using the language of war like a mind trick. Telling myself that I was entering the combat zone, that I was deploying weapons of mass destruction against the cancer, that the enemy didn't stand a chance, was a helpful psychological ploy to get me back through the door and back on the drip.

But all this talk of battle and combat was also unhelpful. I was struck by the constant references both friends and strangers made to my strength and resilience and their belief that this would help me conquer the enemy. It is true that I am a strong person, but it is equally true that many very strong, determined people do not survive cancer. It is not because they are weak or lack resolve, or that they do not fight hard enough or are not positive enough. Surviving cancer is about many factors all going your way, like finding it early, like having a cancer that is treatable, like not having other health problems to complicate things, like the drugs working on your particular tumour, like living in a place that has good and affordable cancer care – and there are many, many more factors that affect survival. It's not quite a lottery, but it felt to me that it needed as much luck as it needed strength.

At the end of it all, I can say that the language of love is just as powerful as the language of war. Having spent so much of my life out front, being the one who helps, the one who makes things happen, cancer forced me to stop, to wait and to let others do things for me. At first, this was a hard lesson. I did not want to be weak or needy, and I found it hard to ask for help when I needed it. But help came anyway. It arrived over and over again in many tender ways, and even now, more than a year after my treatment, this feels like the real truth of the experience.

Help came in the ever-comforting form of food. My friend Lily in New York, knowing that I would not be able to eat much, sent her mother's recipe for 'Jewish Mother's Chicken Soup' to our mutual friend Audette in Sydney, along with instructions for making it exactly right. Audette, by her own admission no chef, spent whole weekends making this soup, spooning it into containers and driving it across the city to store in my freezer. Lily's mother's recipe is centuries old. It has survived pogroms, Nazi death camps and international migrations and came to me, via Audette, with generations of maternal solicitude. There were endless days when this soup was all I could eat. I came to think of it as having magical powers.

Our friend John, who understood that even when I could eat I could barely face the smells that came with cooking, offered to cook us meals. On one occasion, a misunderstanding almost derailed this kindness. Greg and I pulled up at his house only to find John and his wife, Sabina, packing up their car with all the food and pans and utensils needed to cook for me at our home. Thankfully, our paths crossed at the right time and we helped them unpack the car and enjoy a meal at their home.

When my mouth filled with ulcers and it hurt to eat almost everything, Greg drove into the cold of Sydney winter nights to find me the city's best vanilla ice-cream.

Help arrived too in a myriad of considerate gifts. When my Brisbane friends understood that great literature was beyond me and bought me subscriptions to glossy magazines instead, making me feel like I was at the hairdresser, even when I was without hair and had no need of one. When they flew to Sydney to be with me on my birthday. When Sabina bought me the box set of *Friday Night Lights* and introduced me to Scandinavian television dramas; when she knitted with me and bought me new wool. When I unwrapped the unexpected parcel from Ros Kelly in London to find a beautiful red cashmere sweater to keep me warm. When friends filled my email inbox with jokes and cartoons and crazy, hilarious things they found on the internet. When my sons, my brave young men, brought card games and a Scrabble set and sat with me through chemotherapy. Help came with the friends who sat beside me in the chemo ward, who talked and didn't talk, who didn't care if I talked, who let me sleep and drove me home. It came in phone calls and cups of tea and knitting patterns. It came when I asked for it and when I didn't, when I knew I needed it and when I didn't. I wondered how anyone did this alone.

And help came when it was time to confront my impending hair loss. My doctor warned me that chemotherapy would make me lose my hair. Chemotherapy works by coursing through the body and killing cells that are reproducing at a faster than normal rate. Like all weapons of mass destruction, it is an indiscriminate killer. As it mowed down my cancer cells, it would take out other rapidly reproducing cells as collateral damage. It would take the follicle cells of my hair and the lining of my stomach and my mouth, among others. I felt deeply, instinctively fearful of being without a head full of hair.

The first images that came to mind were of my boys when they were very little. As yet another round of head lice swept through their childcare centre, their father took them to the barber. They returned sporting number-one crew cuts. It mattered very little to them, and was a matter of practicality for Greg, but the sight filled me with horror. I was stunned by how different they looked and how the sudden removal of their hair had stripped away something unique and precious about them. Gone, the gorgeous red locks of my eldest. Gone, the spiky brown mop of my youngest. For me, the sudden exposure of their pale scalps made them look sick, raw and dehumanised like new army recruits or Holocaust survivors. I was not happy that day, and I was now fearful in remembering it.

The best advice was that a combination of good hats and beanies, along with a wig for more formal occasions, would get me through my baldness. I'd also been advised to visit a wig shop before treatment started, so the wig experts could see my hairstyle and colour before any damage was done.

With some trepidation, I'd headed off to The Individual Wig on Oxford Street with my friend Dee Madigan, whom I could trust to be brutally honest. At The Individual Wig, assistants Cheryl and Bridgette brought out a series of options, everything from long, wavy black hair to a short spiky blonde look. Dee pursed her lips and vetoed every one of them until we settled on something almost identical to my existing hair. As I sat there, listening to these women advise me and joke around, I was struck by the fact that they did this every day. Cheryl and Bridgette, and others in shops just like theirs, held the hands of cancer patients as they confronted yet another scary moment, easing the fear as best they could. Their easy charm washed over me like a tonic. I had walked in full of worry and walked out smiling, as so many others must have done.

*

In the week after my second round of chemotherapy, great chunks of my hair began to fall out. It fell into my food, it fell into my mouth as I talked. It left large bald patches as it fell. It was time. My hairdresser, Bruce, generously offered to keep his salon open after closing time so that I could have the remaining strands shaved in private. Deciding that private was good, but lonely was bad, our friends John and Sabina joined me, Greg, Oliver and his girlfriend at Bruce's salon for the unusual social event of champagne and a shave.

No woman gives up her hair and all that goes with it – the styling, the colouring, the dos – with ease or nonchalance. But my fear was more visceral. I remembered again those images of death camp survivors, new army recruits and prisoners and knew that our hair and what we do with it is a big part of defining our individuality; it distinguishes us from each other in a unique way. To shave someone's head is so often the fastest way to strip them of their distinctive individuality and humanity, to diminish, shame and humiliate them. It was this that had made me recoil when I saw my young sons all those years ago, and it was this that I feared now. That in shaving my head, I would lose something much more precious than my hair, that somehow I would lose some essential part of me.

But the jokes of my husband and our friends made for a very different event from the one I had feared. Having your head shorn as an aggressive act of dehumanisation is vastly different from what surrounded me that night. I left looking like an egghead but feeling cared for, protected and loved. I had hoped for a result close to Sinead O'Connor or Sigourney Weaver's Ripley in *Alien 3*, both of whom made bald look sexy. Regrettably, I looked eerily like my younger brother and my husband, both of whom have number-one cuts to manage creeping natural baldness. Nevertheless, it was not as bad as I had feared.

Months later, as my treatment came to an end, I was invited by the *Australian Women's Weekly* to join a number of other Australian women for a story in their eightieth-anniversary edition. I was pleased to be included and went along to the photo shoot with my scarf and wig, hoping for the best. After almost two hours in the studio, the photographer asked me if he could shoot me with my head uncovered. I was very reluctant, but the *Weekly* promised not to use any photo without my permission, and I thought, if nothing else, it would be good to have a photo of this big event in my life.

After the shoot, the *Weekly*'s editor, Helen McCabe, called to tell me that she was looking at the proofs and the bald photo was the standout. Again she promised not to use it unless I agreed and invited me in to view the proofs myself.

I went along to view the photos with a lot of scepticism. Of course, I understood why the *Weekly* would want to use this photo – it would make headlines, there were no other photos of me bald and it had shock value. However, when I looked at the proof sheet I could see what Helen had seen. It was a shock to see, but this photo was the honest photo. The wig looked fake, the scarf covered me up, but this photo said loud and clear 'This is what cancer looks like.' We all know what bald men look like – we see them every day in our families, in our workplaces, our pubs and our streets. Yet there are thousands of women, of all ages, every day, grappling with their scarves and their wigs as they deal with their treatment and their baldness, and they are all hidden.

Helen and I talked it through from every angle. I worried that the *Weekly*'s talented make-up artists had made me look more glamorous bald than I was ever likely to look when my hair came back. We both worried that we might offend some patients whose treatment was not as effective as mine. In the end, Helen showed the photo to her mother, who was about to undergo surgery for breast cancer and had months of treatment ahead of her. Her response was overwhelmingly positive and she told Helen that the image made her feel stronger about what she had ahead of her. I took a deep breath and gave my consent to the *Weekly* to use the photo.

As predicted, the photo received a lot of news and media attention. I kept a low profile and gave no interviews about it. I thought the photo and the article, which was written by the talented Caroline Overington, said all that needed to be said. More surprising was the public reaction. Once again I received cards and letters, particularly from women, but also from their husbands, boyfriends and fathers, all grateful that I had lifted the veil of secrecy on this issue. Despite my reluctance, this photo had a powerful effect, especially on the many out there who have experienced chemotherapy themselves or supported a loved one through it. It continues to draw comment from time to time and I'm very glad I overcame my own vanity and shyness to go public with it.

*

Chemotherapy slows your life down to a glacial pace. At first, I saw the months of treatment stretching out in front of me not quite as a holiday, but as a kind of time off work. I had imagined reading, knitting and gardening. I could never have imagined the days and days that felt like walking through treacle, the dreadful, slow-moving, do-nothing days when even holding a book was beyond me. Once again, I found myself thinking about strength. Without doubt, a course of chemotherapy is a test of physical strength, but my experience of it didn't match the language that people were using about being strong. I knew they meant something more than physical fitness; they were urging me to reach for some inner resilience, a combination of courage and grit and a steely emotional determination not to

318

fail. I know what it feels like to summon that kind of strength and resolve, and this was not like that.

For me, the experience was closer to that of childbirth in the sense that, despite the pain and the exhaustion and the hugeness of it, it's not optional. I know I'm not the only mother in the world to have contemplated leaving the delivery room and giving up on the whole event halfway through. But we all know that our baby and our body and the whole messy birthing business can't be left behind in the birthing suite, so we grit our teeth and keep going until it's over. This demands a physical strength and endurance that most of us don't know we have until we experience it. I certainly felt the need for physical strength as I endured my cancer treatment, but I also knew that I was not in an optional situation. Of course, it is possible to opt out of cancer treatment, unlike childbirth, once it has begun, but the alternative is just as unthinkable as walking out of the birthing suite.

The times when I've had to dig down and call on my reserves of that different kind of strength are the times when I've faced tough and difficult things that were optional, when I consciously decided to take on something that I didn't need to, when I could have taken an easier path but chose not to. When I decided to run for parliament, when I took on the churches and established a royal commission into institutional child abuse, when I walked onto the stage to face the angry mob in Gympie, when I put my hand up to be premier, when I took on the leadership of our floods and disasters, I had to consciously reach for courage. Every time I've reached for this, I've felt the weight of it and felt myself grapple to balance the load of it.

In choosing chemotherapy treatment, I was choosing to live. That was the easiest of choices. It didn't require strength or courage; it barely required any thought. In my head, I'm about twenty-eight, maybe thirty, years old. I'm much older, of course, and the mirror regularly confirms it, but I don't feel it. When you think you're twenty-eight, choosing life feels like the easy path. I think this is why my diagnosis shook me so much. I felt healthy, I felt young and I was ready for a lot more life. Enduring chemotherapy, losing my hair, and coping with the many side effects were all a cheap ticket price for another shot at life, and I was happy to pay it. It's a cliché to say that facing death makes you see life differently, but it's a cliché because it's true.

I have heard of some cancer patients saying their cancer was a gift. They say this as a way of capturing the difference their cancer made to their life, how facing death made them grab life in a new and more deliberate and meaningful way. I do not think of my cancer as a gift. I wanted to be rid of it every day of my treatment and hope to live the rest of my life and never see it again. But it is true that being sick did make me stop for longer than I'm used to, and in so doing to see the value in being still and in taking time. After years of living life at an overwhelming pace, this was a lesson worth learning and maybe a lesson that I had to learn the hard way. As four months of treatment came to an end, I started climbing the long hill of recovery. I had another PET scan a month later, and this time I was given the all clear. I will have to return for regular blood tests for five years, but I have emerged healthy. Healthy, new and changed again.

Epilogue

I climbed my way out of cancer and chemotherapy with a hungry longing for life. Casting off the inertia of illness, I was filled with the need to immerse myself in every possible activity. My mind refocused on my central project – building a life after politics – and I returned to the busy business of living with renewed enthusiasm.

First, back to exercise with an appetite that hasn't left me. Now a regular at my local gym, I feel a constant gratitude that my body can once again enjoy the pleasure of physical exertion. In the long, light evenings of Sydney in summer, my husband and I seek out the pools of the eastern beaches, where my limbs pull me through the cool salt water.

Frustrated by the never-ending challenge of parking in this teeming city, I got my motorcycle licence and now ride a Vespa scooter with all the exhilaration of a middle-aged man on a Harley-Davidson Fat Boy. Serendipitously, one of Australia's oldest charities, YWCA NSW, began to search for a new CEO just as I was ready to re-enter the world of work. The more I looked at the opportunity, the more it seemed a perfect fit. As I began 2014 at the CEO's desk of this remarkable organisation, I felt my life turn full circle, back to the passions of my youth, working with women, children, young people and families to change lives, create new opportunities and overcome disadvantage and vulnerability. I now lead a team of passionate people committed to making a difference every day.

There are still times when homesickness cuts me like a keen blade. There is something about the tropical heat of Queensland, its lush, wet humidity, that gets into your blood. Like all places, it has a smell and feel that defines it. The backyard of our old Queensland home was a riotous jungle of trees that had a thick, overgrown abundance to it. I always felt that if I stood still too long amongst it I would soon feel a thick green vine make its way up my leg. Now I feel that way whenever I return to Queensland, whether it's Brisbane, the Gold Coast or Cairns – it's the thick, green lushness that tells me I'm home. But as my Vespa and I zip through the rushing streets of Sydney, it too is starting to feel known and familiar. I am making a new home and thriving on discovering it.

So what about that wall? As I've reflected on that time in my life while writing this book, I have come to understand more fully how bloodied I was pushing my way through it. But I was not critically injured, just bruised and scratched as I carved that path. And, in any case, it's not my bruises and scratches that I want others to see. I want them to see the hole in the wall – all eyes should be on it. There is only one thing that will diminish and eliminate all the constituent parts of the wall and that's a constant stream of other women pushing through it until it crumbles altogether. As we work for a more balanced sharing of power, in our parliaments, in our workplaces and in our lives, we are busting up the status quo. It won't always be easy. But as women shift into leadership roles in all spheres of life, the novelty will begin to wear off, the isolating sense of difference will dissipate, the experience will be normalised and opponents will be silenced.

Now, on the other side of the wall, I have the scar tissue that comes with forcing a hole in a fortress. But I have, too, a list of opportunities, experiences and achievements that makes every bruise worth it. Holding the reins of power is a big life experience like no other and there will always be a price to pay for the privilege. Right now, the ticket price for women is more expensive than the one paid by their male counterparts, but it is a price worth paying.

There are more battles to be had and there will be more bruises and scar tissue earned by more women as they too carve out new paths in their own unchartered territories. The challenge for us all is to confront and change the social, institutional and psychological barriers that get in their way.

*

As these pages went to print, Queensland voters returned to the ballot box and a tidal wave of electoral discontent swept Campbell Newman and his LNP government out of office. In just three short years he lost all the goodwill and hope that had carried him into the premier's office in 2012. Newman also lost his own seat of Ashgrove, defeated after just one term by the talented and energetic Kate Jones, the former Environment Minister in my government. Annastacia Palaszczuk, my former Minister for Transport, looks set to become Queensland's second female premier and the first Australian woman to lead her party from opposition to government. And Leeanne Enoch has become the first Aboriginal woman to be elected to the Queensland parliament. Along with other strong, capable women such as Jackie Trad, who won my own seat of South Brisbane after I retired and worked tirelessly to help secure this astonishing victory, they have all jumped through the wall. It fills me with renewed hope and joy that the wall is tumbling down at last.

Acknowledgements

I would like to thank the superlative editorial talent of Virginia Lloyd, who worked alongside me as each chapter of this book took shape. I acknowledge also Catherine Milne, Jude McGee and all the terrific team at HarperCollins for seeing the possibility of this book and helping me to realise it.

My grateful thanks to the generous Suzy Wilson, who first seriously suggested a book to me and took the time, on the sunny deck of her wonderful bookshop in Brisbane, Riverbend Books, to talk about getting it started. To the incomparable writing women in my life, Lily Brett and Kaz Cooke, who took the baton and spent two years urging and cajoling me to put pen to paper, quelling my fears as they arose. My thanks also to my friend Ros Kelly, who helped me believe my story should be told. To Glyn Davis, who added regular encouragement as the book took shape. To Sabina Wynn and the 'bookies' of our book club, who have returned to me the joy of the written word and helped me put my mind to filling pages with it. To Kathryn Anderson, in whose Melbourne apartment Greg and I spent ten days over Easter 2014, during which the first four chapters of this book came to life. To Audette Exel, who warned me that writing a book requires a special kind of madness and Dee Madigan who proved the madness can be survived.

I acknowledge also my staff, without whose loyalty, hard work and camaraderie there would be no story to tell. In particular, I thank Bronwen Griffiths, Murray Watt, Mike Kaiser and Nicole Scurrah, who took on the challenge of being my chief of staff. To my longest-serving member of staff, my driver Peter Lloyd, who delivered me safe and on time, rain, hail and shine to all the places where this story unfolded. To Caroline Fisher, Shari Armistead, Steve Keating, Don Wilson, Cynthia Kennedy, Belinda Taylor, Chris Taylor, Stephen Beckett, Tina Langford and the many other others who served with me in the trenches, and encouraged me to aim higher.

To friends of a lifetime, Anne Warner, Di Fingleton, Jackie Trad, Jo Clifford, Fiona McKenna, Tanya Ritchie and Greg Combet, who urged me on at every turn. To my mother, Frances Tancred, who hates the glare of the limelight and conquered much to allow me to share some of her in these pages.

Acknowledgement also goes to the great ship of the Australian Labor Party and all who sail in her for giving me a political home, for giving me every chance to succeed, for backing me against the odds. My thanks goes to my parliamentary colleagues, my caucus and to all who served in Cabinet with me, whose strength and commitment fuelled our collective achievements. Warmest thanks to Paul Lucas and Andrew Fraser, both of whom served as my Deputy, whose loyalty and comradeship I will always cherish. My special thanks to the true believers of the South Brisbane Labor Party branches who raised funds, stuffed envelopes, debated ideas, argued politics with endless passion and always kept the faith.

My most loving thanks go to my family, Greg, Joe and Oliver, whose belief in me has fuelled my every step. Without their love, these pages would have remained forever empty.